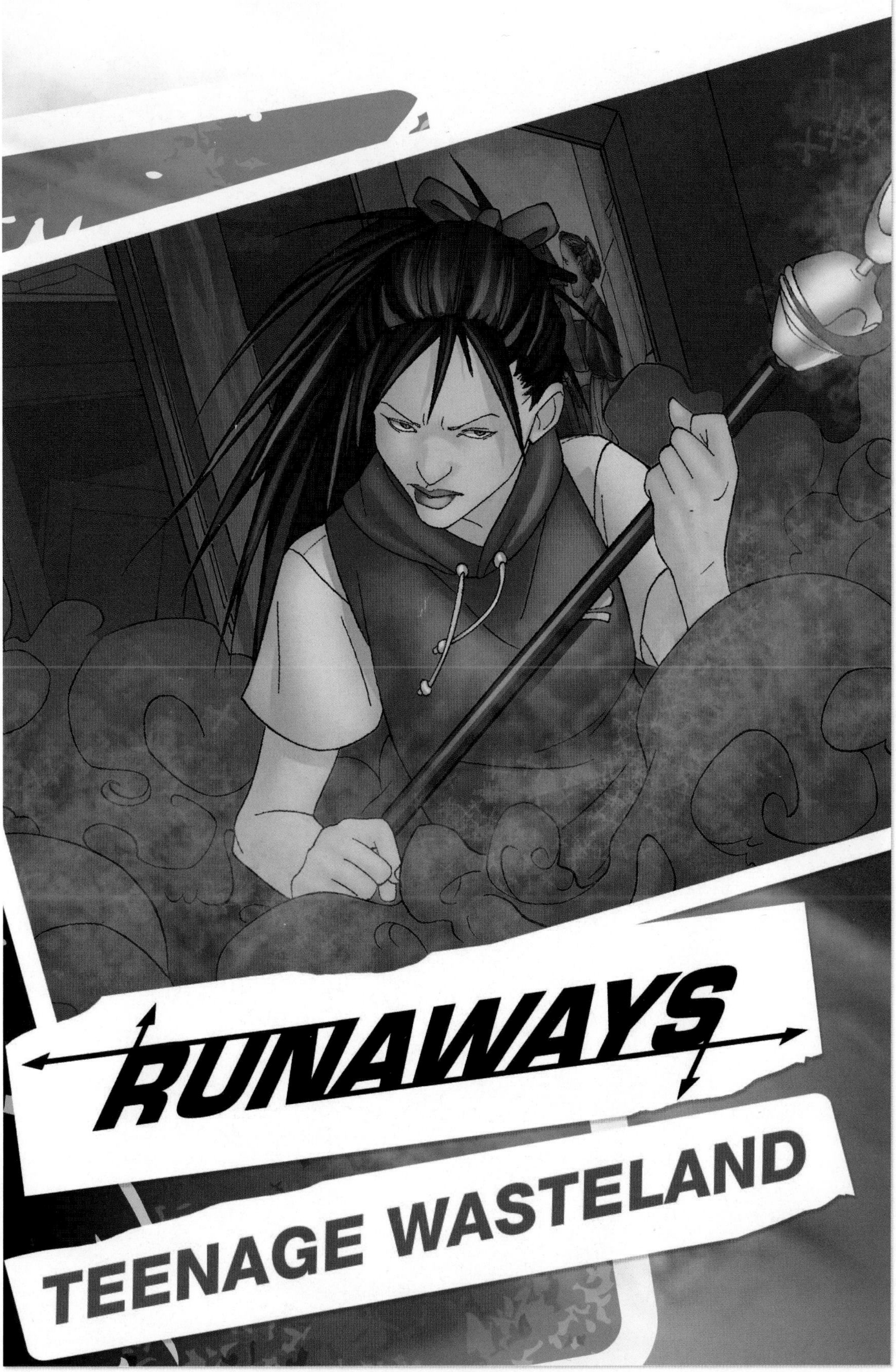
RUNAWAYS
TEENAGE WASTELAND

RUNAWAYS

TEENAGE WASTELAND

WRITER: **BRIAN K. VAUGHAN**

"TEENAGE WASTELAND"
PENCILER: **ADRIAN ALPHONA**
INKER: **CRAIG YEUNG**

"LOST AND FOUND"
PENCILER: **TAKESHI MIYAZAWA**
INKER: **DAVID NEWBOLD**

COLORIST: **UDON'S CHRISTINA STRAIN**
WITH **BRIAN REBER**
LETTERER: **VC'S RANDY GENTILE**
COVER ART: **JO CHEN**
WITH **JOSH MIDDLETON** (ISSUES #11-12)
ASSISTANT EDITOR: **MACKENZIE CADENHEAD**
EDITOR: **C.B. CEBULSKI**
RUNAWAYS CREATED BY **BRIAN K. VAUGHAN** & **ADRIAN ALPHONA**

COLLECTION EDITOR: **JENNIFER GRÜNWALD**
EDITORIAL ASSISTANT: **ALEX STARBUCK**
ASSISTANT EDITORS: **CORY LEVINE** & **JOHN DENNING**
EDITOR, SPECIAL PROJECTS: **MARK D. BEAZLEY**
SENIOR EDITOR, SPECIAL PROJECTS: **JEFF YOUNGQUIST**
SENIOR VICE PRESIDENT OF SALES: **DAVID GABRIEL**

EDITOR IN CHIEF: **JOE QUESADA**
PUBLISHER: **DAN BUCKLEY**
EXECUTIVE PRODUCER: **ALAN FINE**

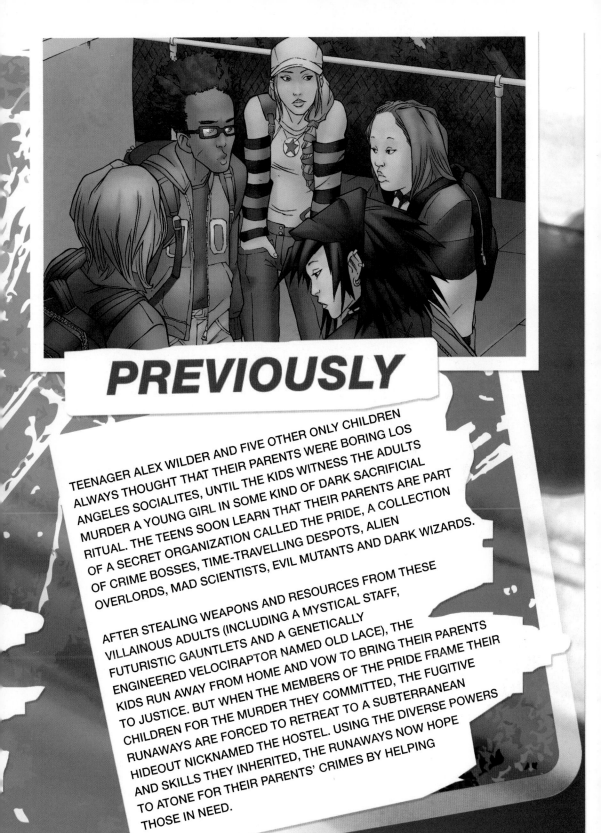

PREVIOUSLY

TEENAGER ALEX WILDER AND FIVE OTHER ONLY CHILDREN ALWAYS THOUGHT THAT THEIR PARENTS WERE BORING LOS ANGELES SOCIALITES, UNTIL THE KIDS WITNESS THE ADULTS MURDER A YOUNG GIRL IN SOME KIND OF DARK SACRIFICIAL RITUAL. THE TEENS SOON LEARN THAT THEIR PARENTS ARE PART OF A SECRET ORGANIZATION CALLED THE PRIDE, A COLLECTION OF CRIME BOSSES, TIME-TRAVELLING DESPOTS, ALIEN OVERLORDS, MAD SCIENTISTS, EVIL MUTANTS AND DARK WIZARDS.

AFTER STEALING WEAPONS AND RESOURCES FROM THESE VILLAINOUS ADULTS (INCLUDING A MYSTICAL STAFF, FUTURISTIC GAUNTLETS AND A GENETICALLY ENGINEERED VELOCIRAPTOR NAMED OLD LACE), THE KIDS RUN AWAY FROM HOME AND VOW TO BRING THEIR PARENTS TO JUSTICE. BUT WHEN THE MEMBERS OF THE PRIDE FRAME THEIR CHILDREN FOR THE MURDER THEY COMMITTED, THE FUGITIVE RUNAWAYS ARE FORCED TO RETREAT TO A SUBTERRANEAN HIDEOUT NICKNAMED THE HOSTEL. USING THE DIVERSE POWERS AND SKILLS THEY INHERITED, THE RUNAWAYS NOW HOPE TO ATONE FOR THEIR PARENTS' CRIMES BY HELPING THOSE IN NEED.

RUNAWAYS: TEENAGE WASTELAND. Contains material originally published in magazine form as RUNAWAYS #7-12. First printing 2009. Hardcover ISBN# 978-0-7851-3973-7. Softcover ISBN# 978-0-7851-4075-7. Published by MARVEL PUBLISHING, INC., a subsidiary of MARVEL ENTERTAINMENT, INC. OFFICE OF PUBLICATION: 417 5th Avenue, New York, NY 10016. Copyright © 2003, 2004 and 2009 Marvel Characters, Inc. All rights reserved. Hardcover: $19.99 per copy in the U.S. (GST #R127032852). Softcover: $16.99 per copy in the U.S. (GST #R127032852). Canadian Agreement #40668537. All characters featured in this issue and the distinctive names and likenesses thereof, and all related indicia are trademarks of Marvel Characters, Inc. No similarity between any of the names, characters, persons, and/or institutions in this magazine with those of any living or dead person or institution is intended, and any such similarity which may exist is purely coincidental. **Printed in the U.S.A.** ALAN FINE, EVP - Office Of The Chief Executive Marvel Entertainment, Inc. & CMO Marvel Characters B.V.; DAN BUCKLEY, President of Publishing - Print & Digital Media; JIM SOKOLOWSKI, Chief Operating Officer; DAVID GABRIEL, SVP of Publishing Sales & Circulation; DAVID BOGART, SVP of Business Affairs & Talent Management; MICHAEL PASCIULLO, VP Merchandising & Communications; JIM O'KEEFE, VP of Operations & Logistics; DAN CARR, Executive Director of Publishing Technology; JUSTIN F. GABRIE, Director of Publishing & Editorial Operations; SUSAN CRESPI, Editorial Operations Manager; ALEX MORALES, Publishing Operations Manager; STAN LEE, Chairman Emeritus. For information regarding advertising in Marvel Comics or on Marvel.com, please contact Mitch Dane, Advertising Director, at mdane@marvel.com. For Marvel subscription inquiries, please call 800-217-9158.

10 9 8 7 6 5 4 3 2 1

7

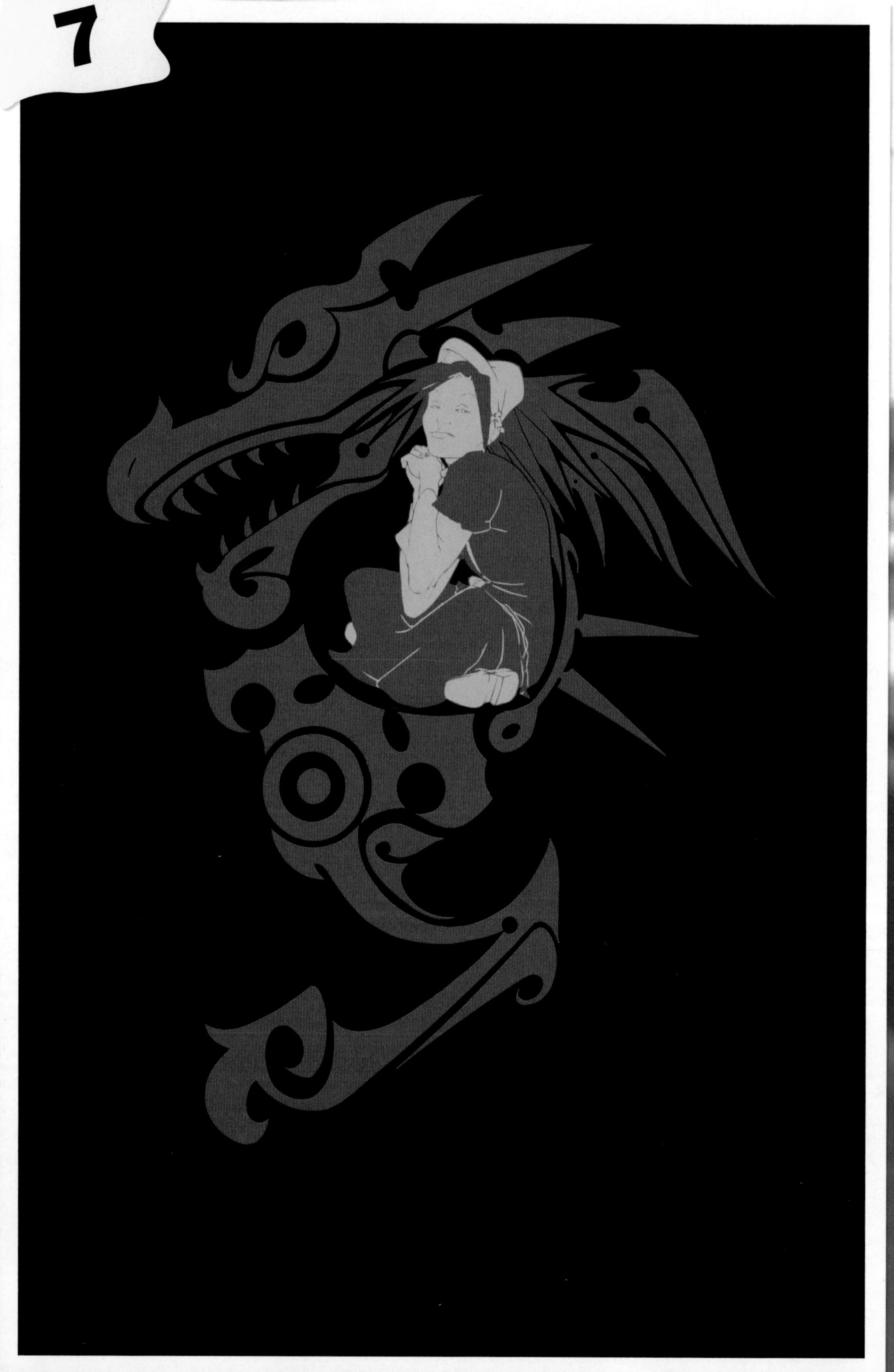

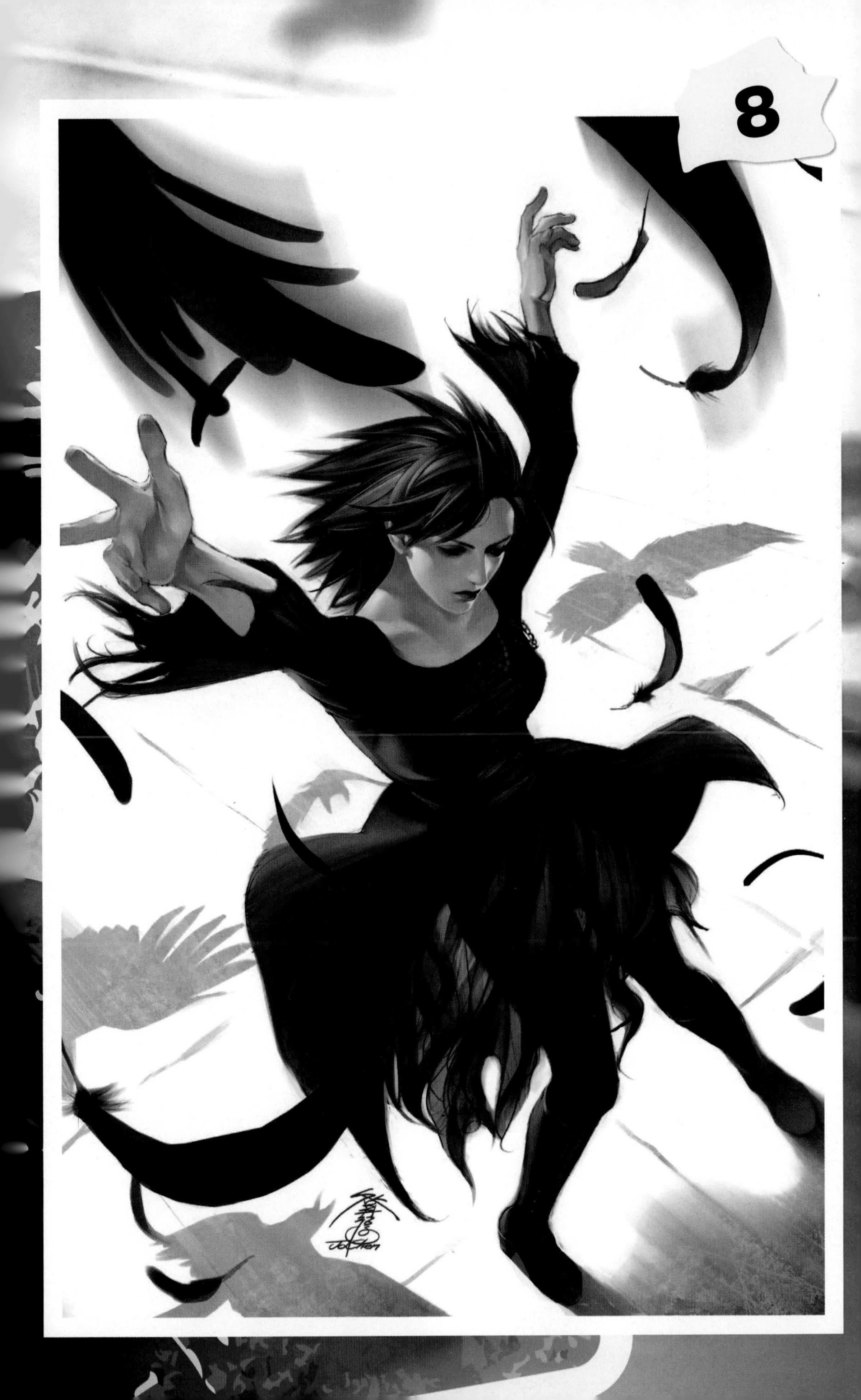
8

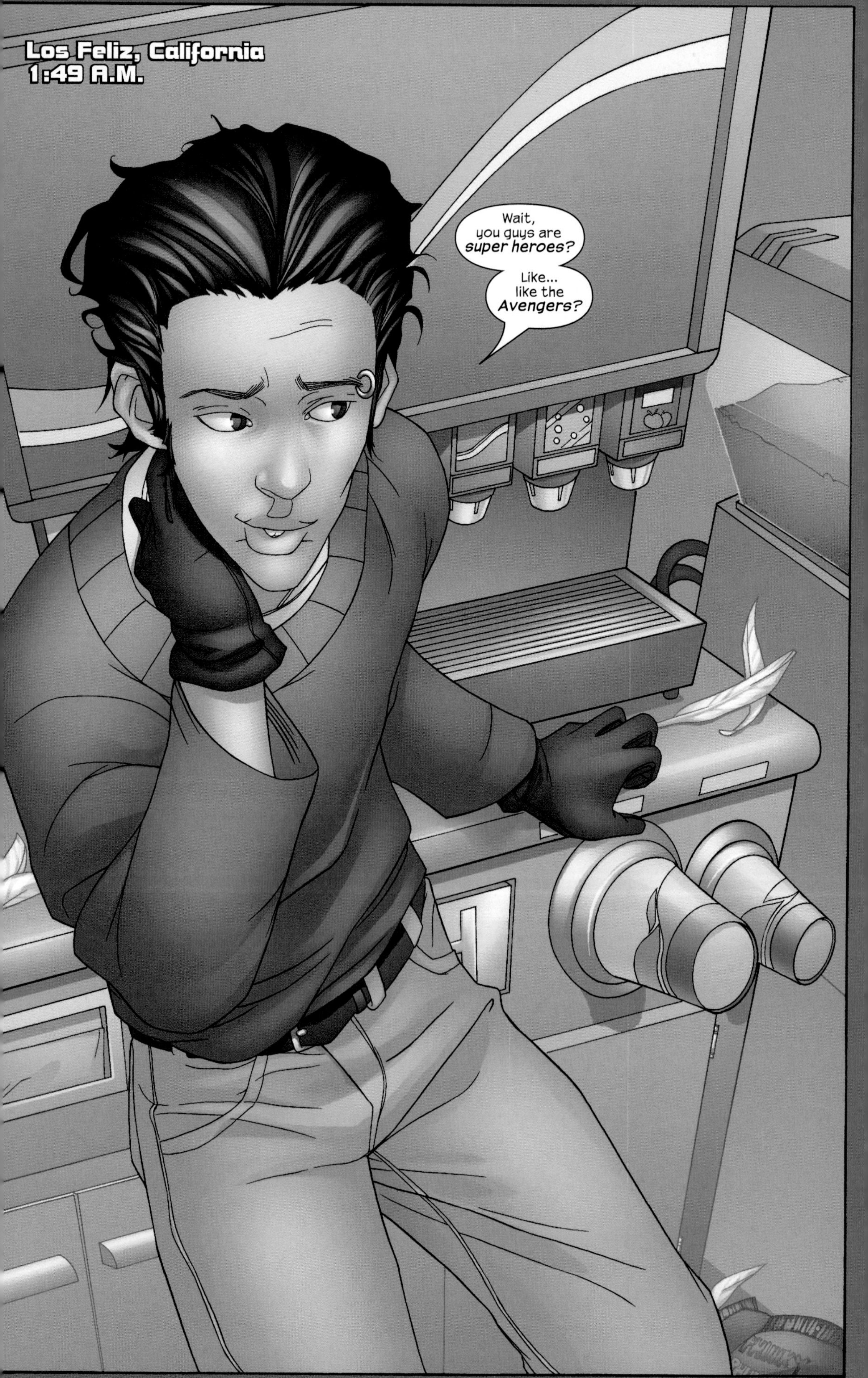
Los Feliz, California
1:49 A.M.
Wait, you guys are *super heroes?*
Like... like the *Avengers?*

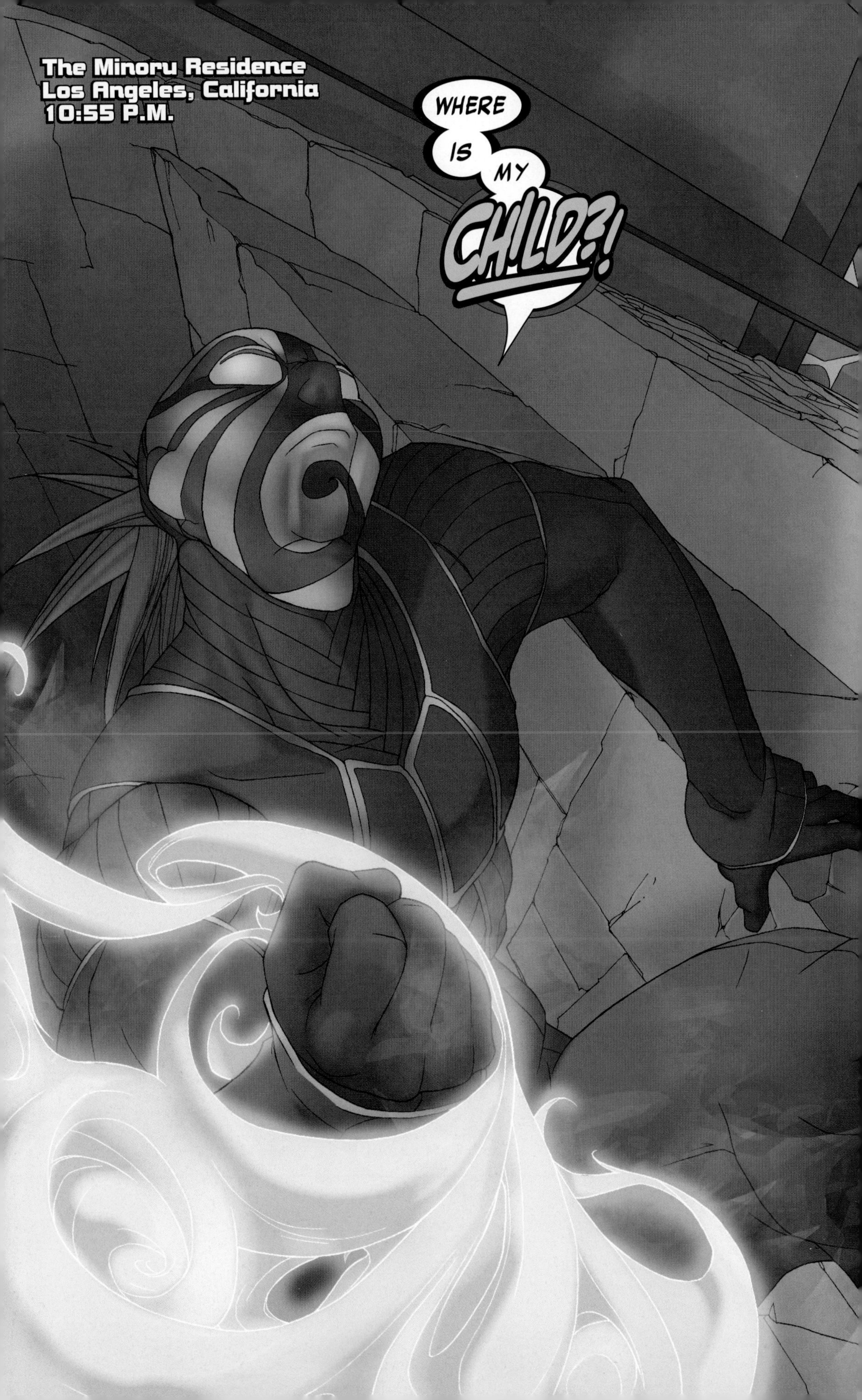
The Minoru Residence
Los Angeles, California
10:55 P.M.
WHERE IS MY CHILD?!

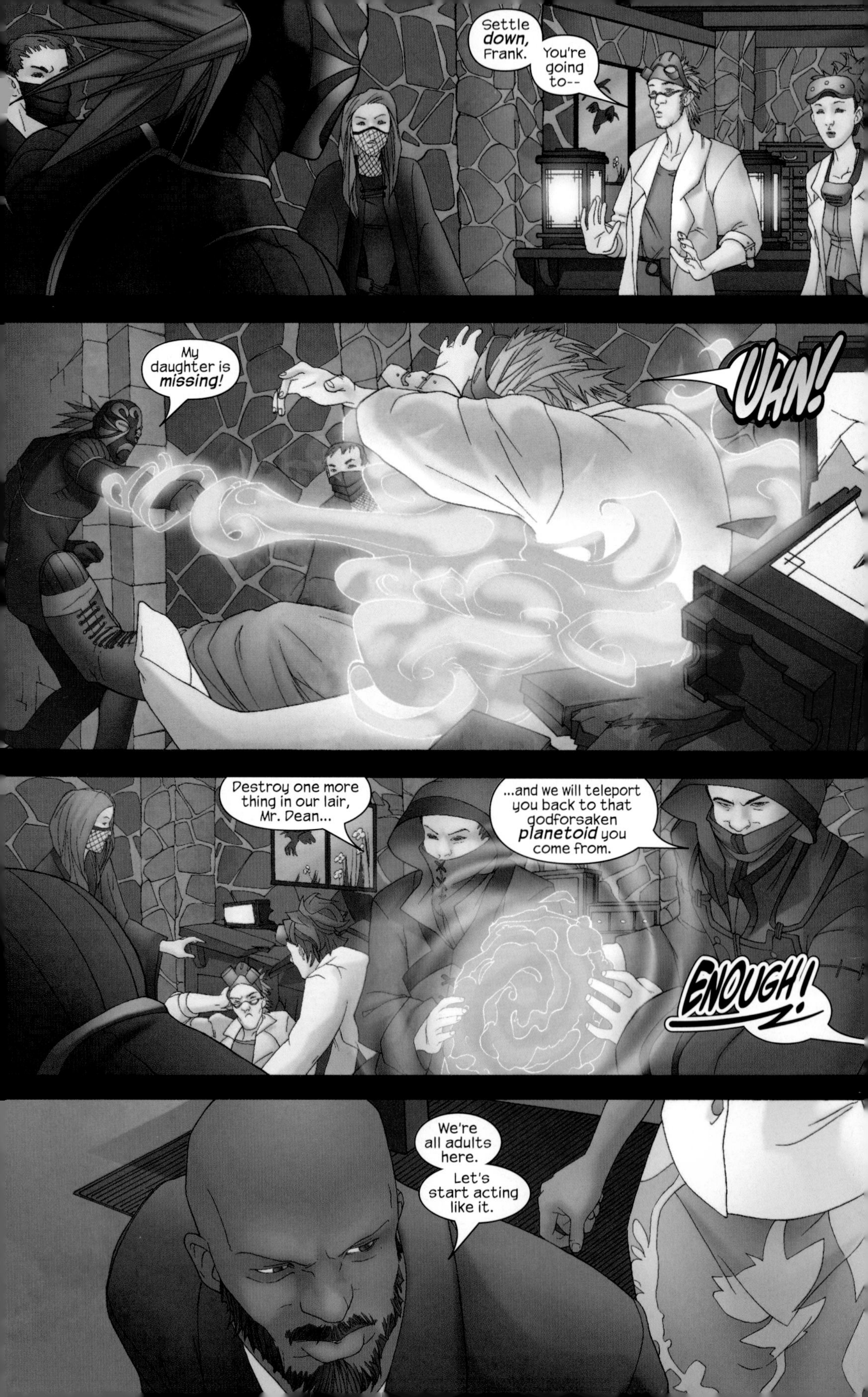
Settle *down,* Frank.
You're going to--
My daughter is *missing!*
UHN!
Destroy one more thing in our lair, Mr. Dean...
...and we will teleport you back to that godforsaken *planetoid* you come from.
ENOUGH!
We're all adults here.
Let's start acting like it.

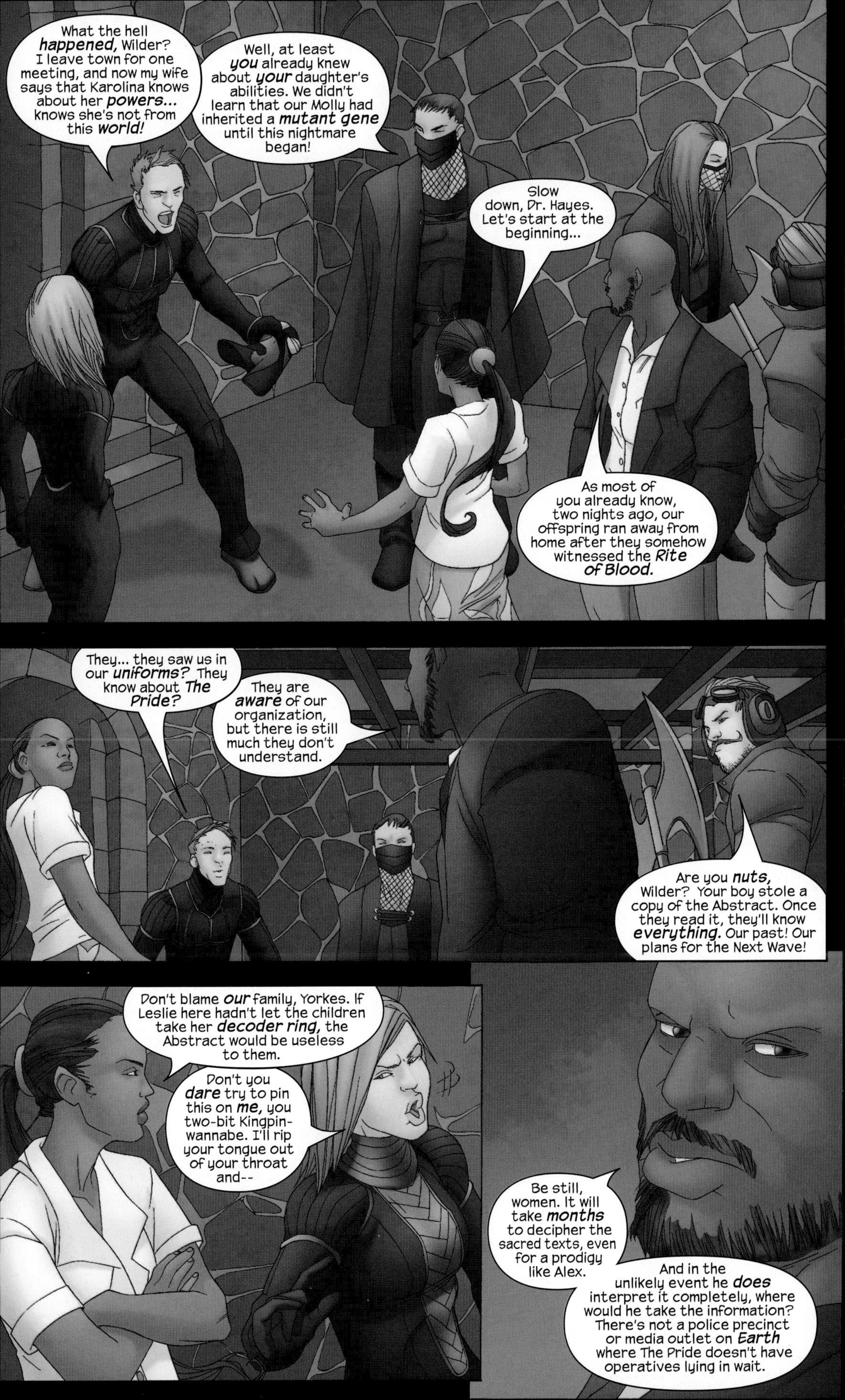
What the hell happened, Wilder? I leave town for one meeting, and now my wife says that Karolina knows about her powers... knows she's not from this world!
Well, at least you already knew about your daughter's abilities. We didn't learn that our Molly had inherited a mutant gene until this nightmare began!
Slow down, Dr. Hayes. Let's start at the beginning...
As most of you already know, two nights ago, our offspring ran away from home after they somehow witnessed the Rite of Blood.
They... they saw us in our uniforms? They know about The Pride?
They are aware of our organization, but there is still much they don't understand.
Are you nuts, Wilder? Your boy stole a copy of the Abstract. Once they read it, they'll know everything. Our past! Our plans for the Next Wave!
Don't blame our family, Yorkes. If Leslie here hadn't let the children take her decoder ring, the Abstract would be useless to them.
Don't you dare try to pin this on me, you two-bit Kingpin-wannabe. I'll rip your tongue out of your throat and--
Be still, women. It will take months to decipher the sacred texts, even for a prodigy like Alex.
And in the unlikely event he does interpret it completely, where would he take the information? There's not a police precinct or media outlet on Earth where The Pride doesn't have operatives lying in wait.

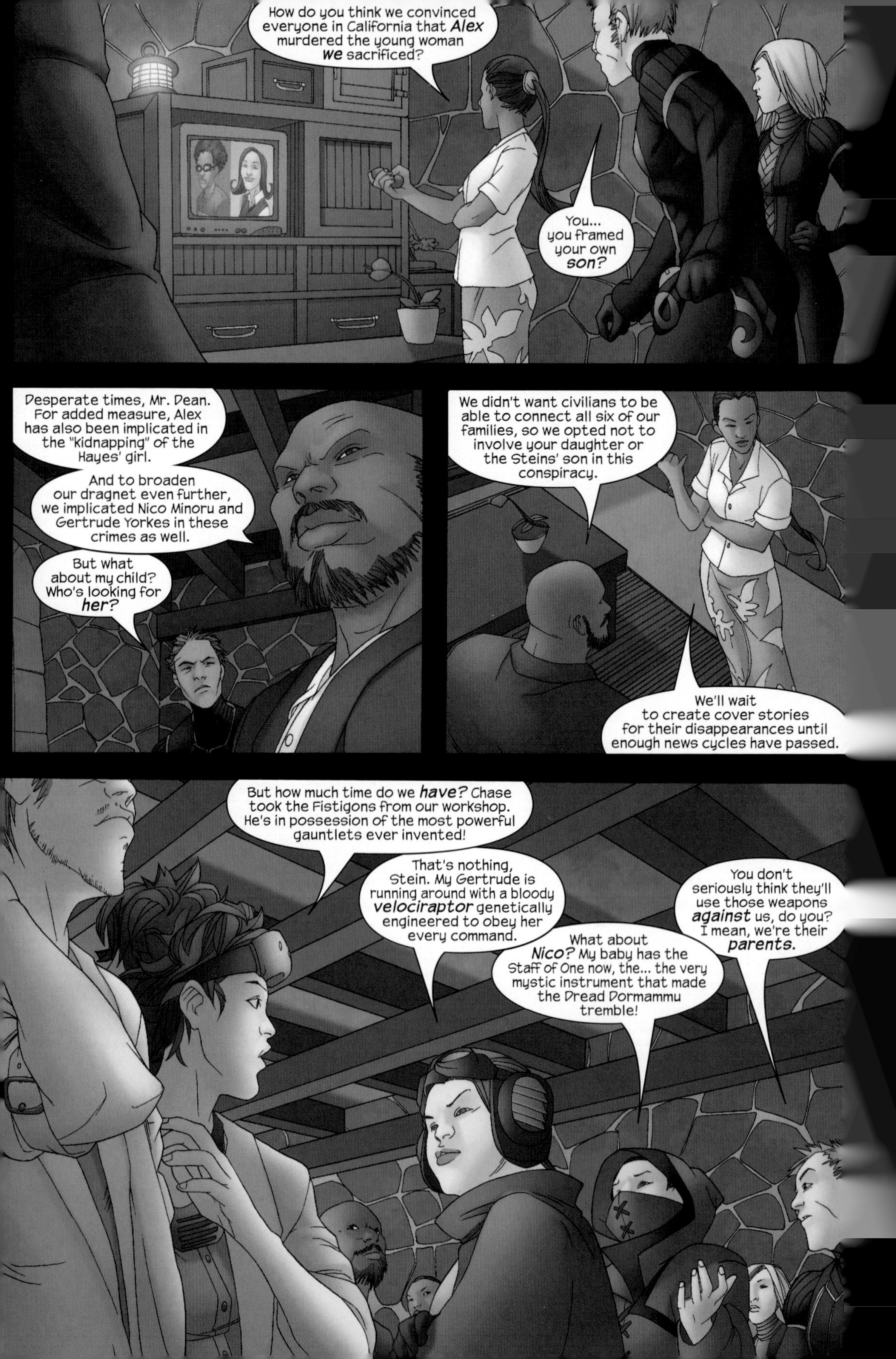
How do you think we convinced everyone in California that *Alex* murdered the young woman **we** sacrificed?
You... you framed your own *son?*
Desperate times, Mr. Dean. For added measure, Alex has also been implicated in the "kidnapping" of the Hayes' girl.
And to broaden our dragnet even further, we implicated Nico Minoru and Gertrude Yorkes in these crimes as well.
But what about my child? Who's looking for *her?*
We didn't want civilians to be able to connect all six of our families, so we opted not to involve your daughter or the Steins' son in this conspiracy.
We'll wait to create cover stories for their disappearances until enough news cycles have passed.
But how much time do we *have?* Chase took the Fistigons from our workshop. He's in possession of the most powerful gauntlets ever invented!
That's nothing, Stein. My Gertrude is running around with a bloody *velociraptor* genetically engineered to obey her every command.
What about *Nico?* My baby has the Staff of One now, the... the very mystic instrument that made the Dread Dormammu tremble!
You don't seriously think they'll use those weapons *against* us, do you? I mean, we're their *parents.*

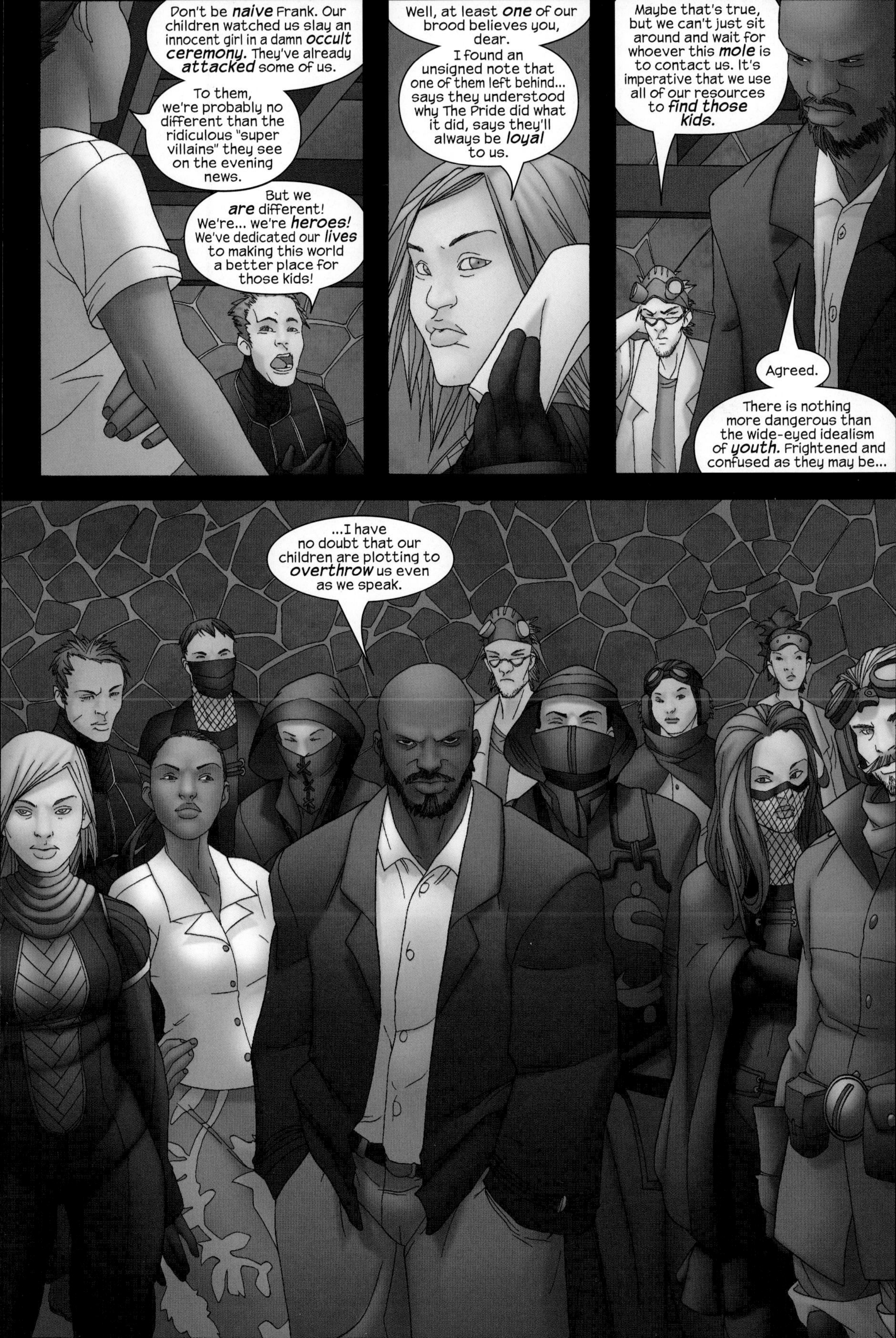
Don't be naive Frank. Our children watched us slay an innocent girl in a damn occult ceremony. They've already attacked some of us.
To them, we're probably no different than the ridiculous "super villains" they see on the evening news.
But we are different! We're... we're heroes! We've dedicated our lives to making this world a better place for those kids!
Well, at least one of our brood believes you, dear.
I found an unsigned note that one of them left behind... says they understood why The Pride did what it did, says they'll always be loyal to us.
Maybe that's true, but we can't just sit around and wait for whoever this mole is to contact us. It's imperative that we use all of our resources to find those kids.
Agreed.
There is nothing more dangerous than the wide-eyed idealism of youth. Frightened and confused as they may be...
...I have no doubt that our children are plotting to overthrow us even as we speak.

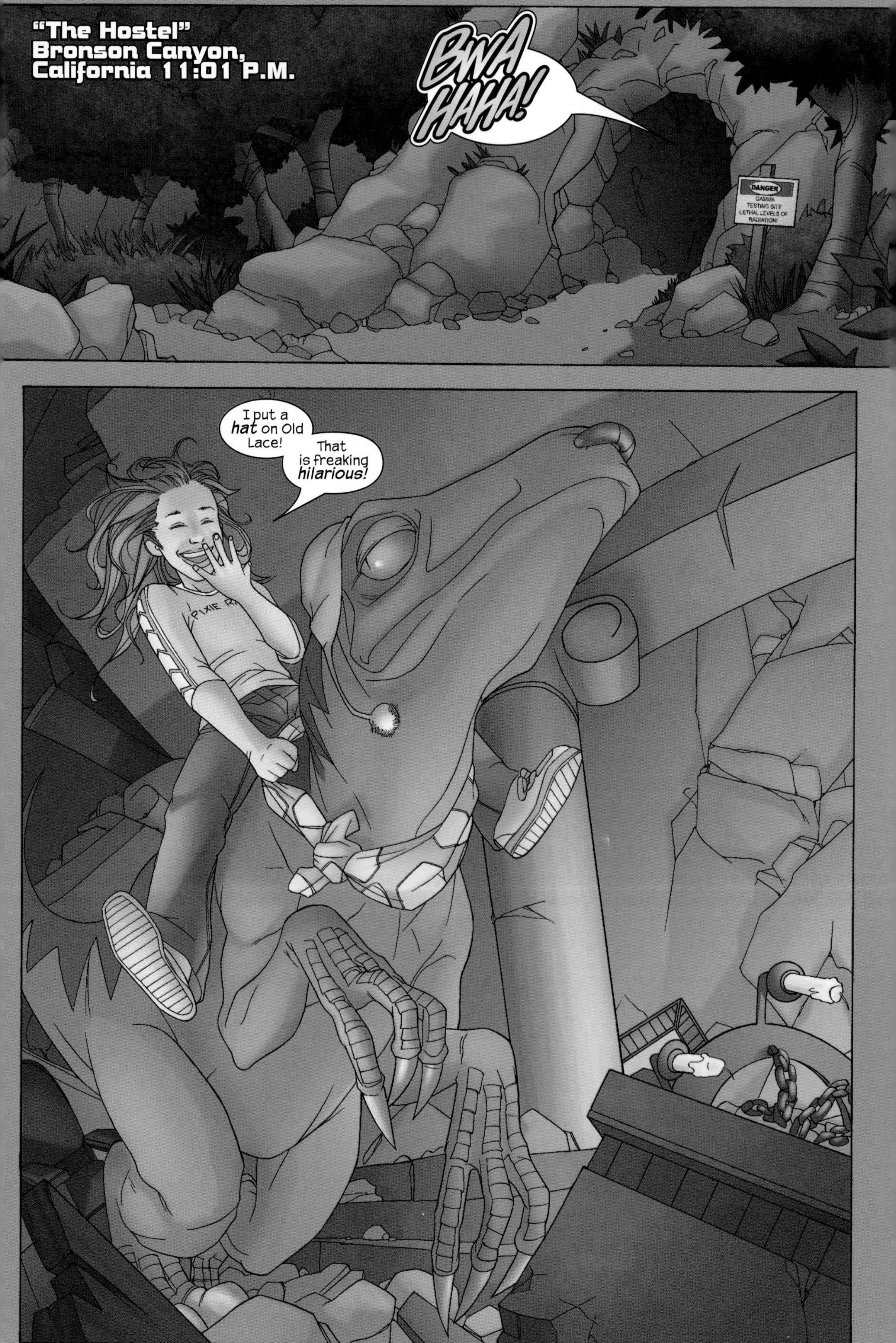
"The Hostel"
Bronson Canyon, California 11:01 P.M.
BWA HAHA!
DANGER
GAMMA TESTING SITE LETHAL LEVELS OF RADIATION!
I put a *hat* on Old Lace!
That is freaking *hilarious!*

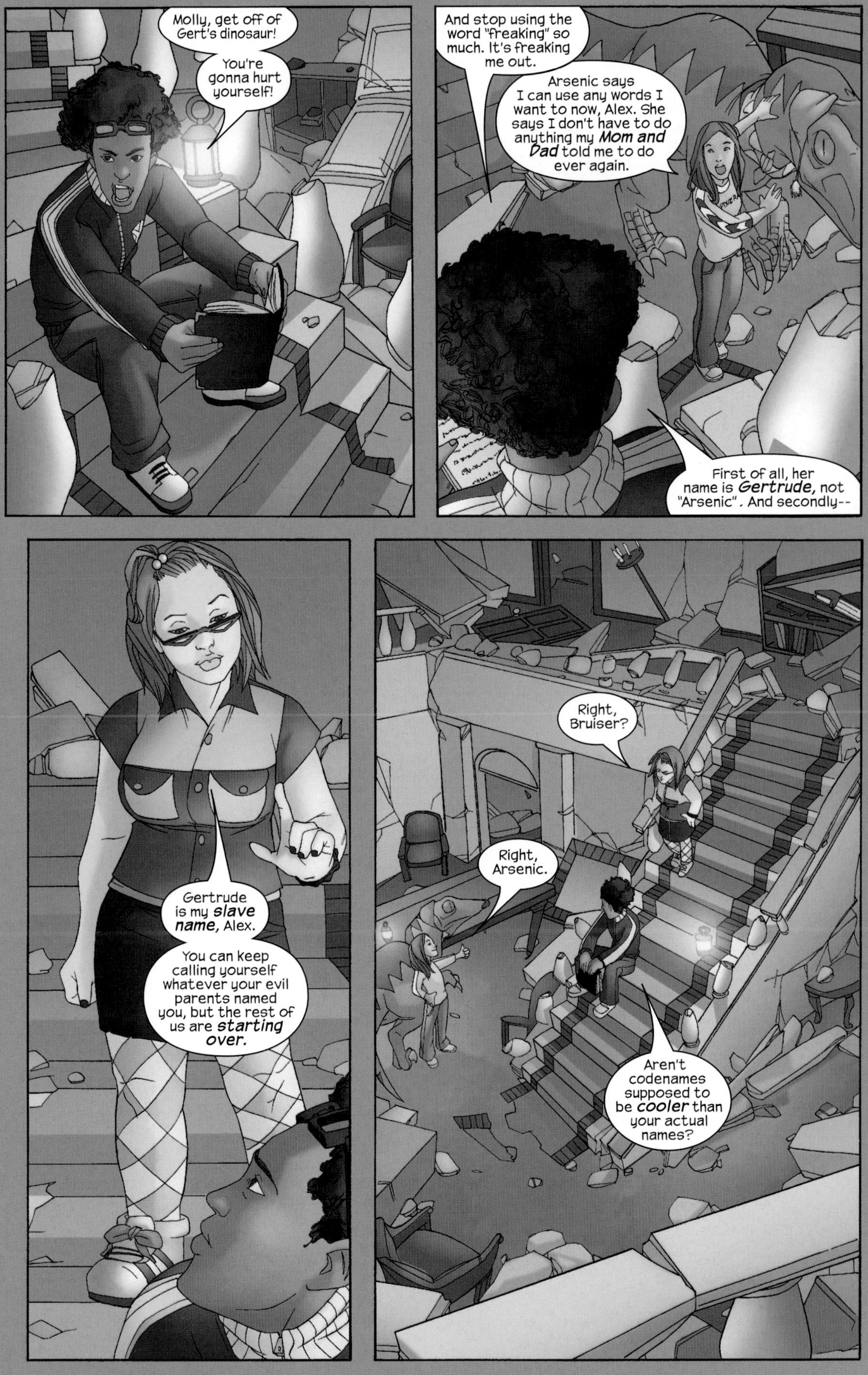

Molly, get off of Gert's dinosaur!
You're gonna hurt yourself!
And stop using the word "freaking" so much. It's freaking me out.
Arsenic says I can use any words I want to now, Alex. She says I don't have to do anything my **Mom and Dad** told me to do ever again.
First of all, her name is **Gertrude,** not "Arsenic". And secondly--
Gertrude is my **slave name,** Alex.
You can keep calling yourself whatever your evil parents named you, but the rest of us are **starting over.**
Right, Bruiser?
Right, Arsenic.
Aren't codenames supposed to be **cooler** than your actual names?

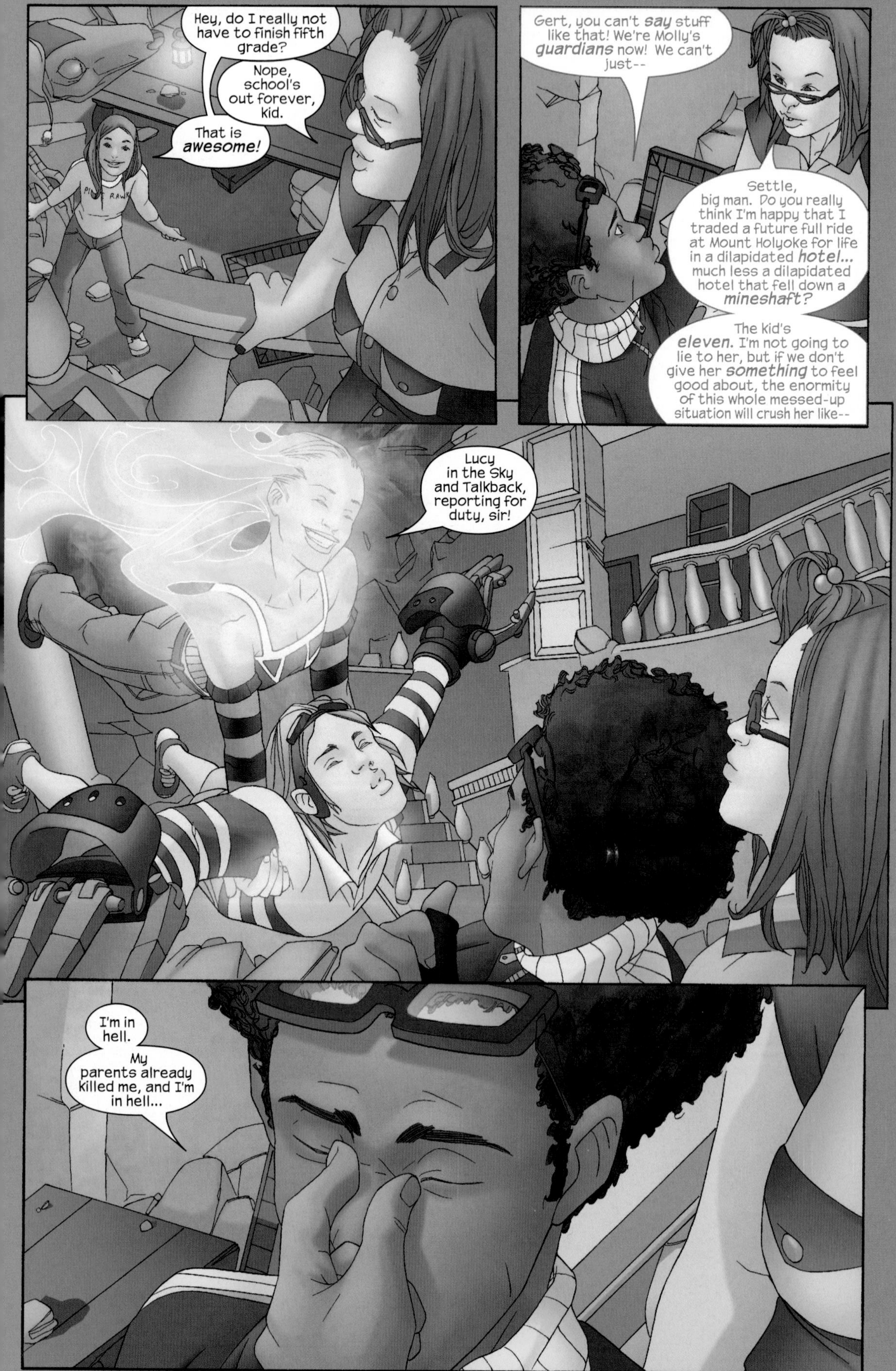
Hey, do I really not have to finish fifth grade?
Nope, school's out forever, kid.
That is *awesome!*
Gert, you can't *say* stuff like that! We're Molly's *guardians* now! We can't just--
Settle, big man. Do you really think I'm happy that I traded a future full ride at Mount Holyoke for life in a dilapidated *hotel...* much less a dilapidated hotel that fell down a *mineshaft?*
The kid's *eleven.* I'm not going to lie to her, but if we don't give her *something* to feel good about, the enormity of this whole messed-up situation will crush her like--
Lucy in the Sky and Talkback, reporting for duty, sir!
I'm in hell.
My parents already killed me, and I'm in hell...

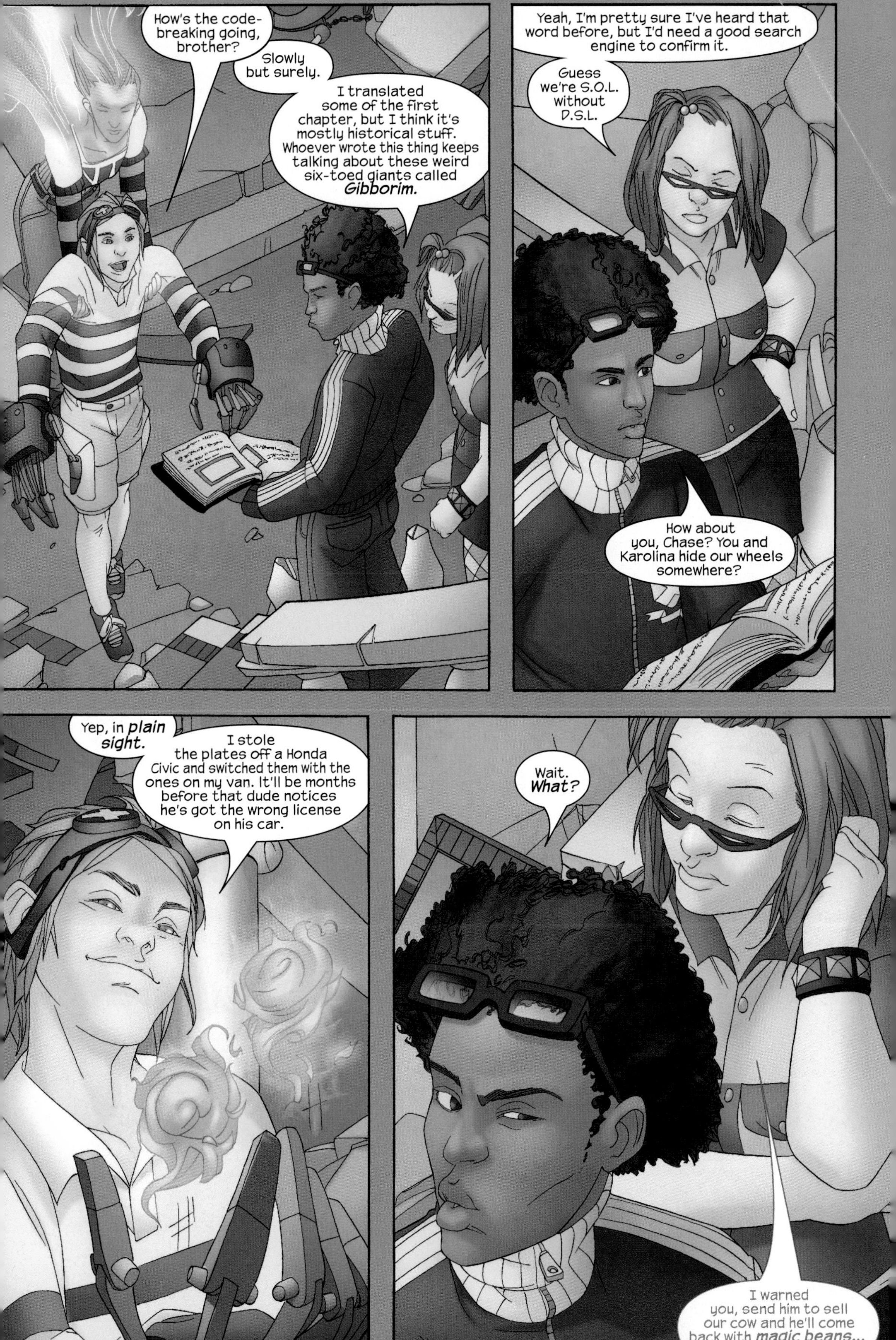

How's the code-breaking going, brother?
Slowly but surely.
I translated some of the first chapter, but I think it's mostly historical stuff. Whoever wrote this thing keeps talking about these weird six-toed giants called *Gibborim.*
Yeah, I'm pretty sure I've heard that word before, but I'd need a good search engine to confirm it.
Guess we're S.O.L. without D.S.L.
How about you, Chase? You and Karolina hide our wheels somewhere?
Yep, in *plain sight.*
I stole the plates off a Honda Civic and switched them with the ones on my van. It'll be months before that dude notices he's got the wrong license on his car.
Wait. *What?*
I warned you, send him to sell our cow and he'll come back with *magic beans...*

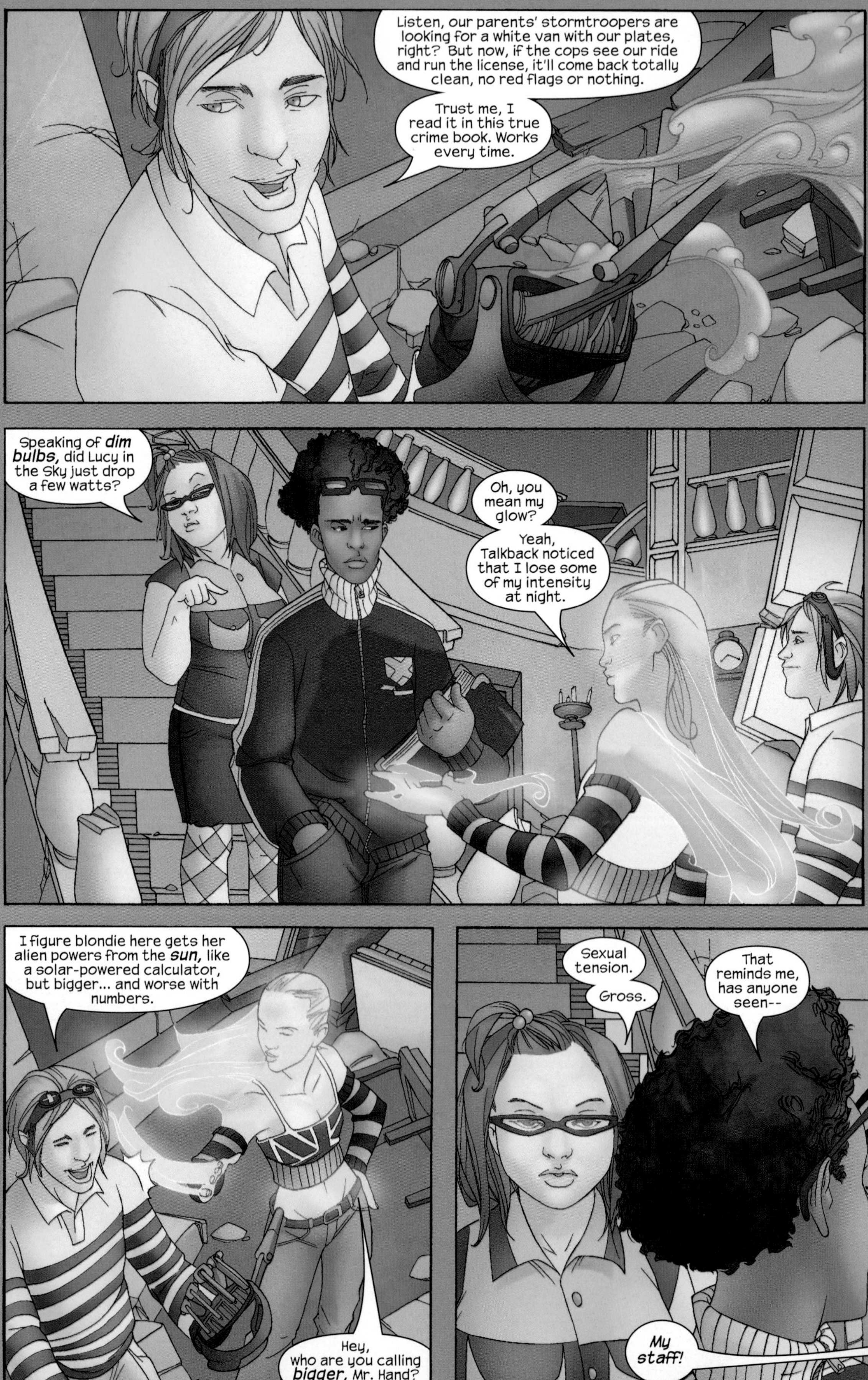

Listen, our parents' stormtroopers are looking for a white van with our plates, right? But now, if the cops see our ride and run the license, it'll come back totally clean, no red flags or nothing.
Trust me, I read it in this true crime book. Works every time.
Speaking of **dim bulbs,** did Lucy in the Sky just drop a few watts?
Oh, you mean my glow?
Yeah, Talkback noticed that I lose some of my intensity at night.
I figure blondie here gets her alien powers from the **sun,** like a solar-powered calculator, but bigger... and worse with numbers.
Hey, who are you calling **bigger,** Mr. Hand?
Sexual tension.
Gross.
That reminds me, has anyone seen--
My staff!

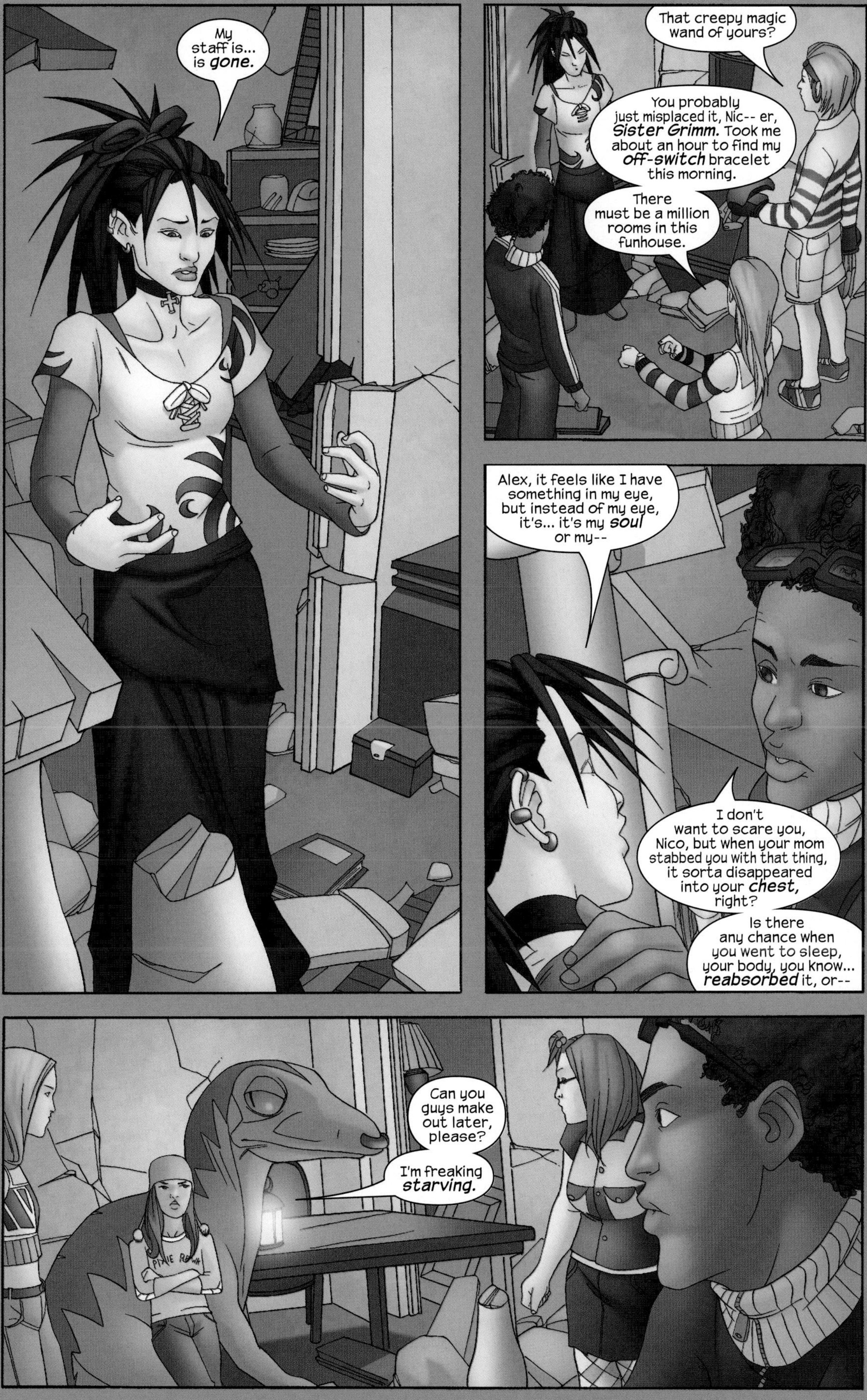
My staff is... is gone.
That creepy magic wand of yours?
You probably just misplaced it, Nic-- er, Sister Grimm. Took me about an hour to find my off-switch bracelet this morning.
There must be a million rooms in this funhouse.
Alex, it feels like I have something in my eye, but instead of my eye, it's... it's my soul or my--
I don't want to scare you, Nico, but when your mom stabbed you with that thing, it sorta disappeared into your chest, right?
Is there any chance when you went to sleep, your body, you know... reabsorbed it, or--
Can you guys make out later, please?
I'm freaking starving.

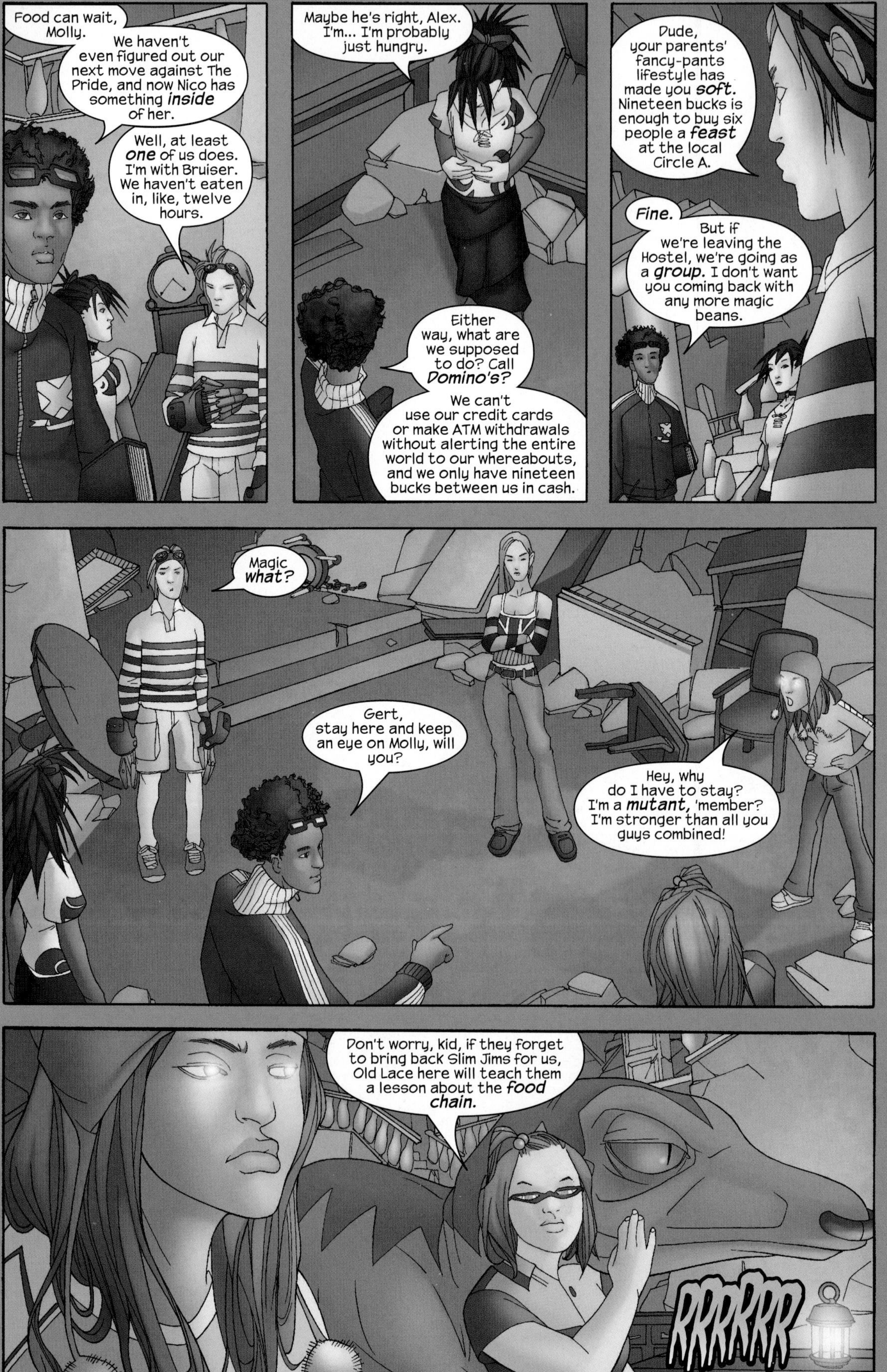
Food can wait, Molly.
We haven't even figured out our next move against The Pride, and now Nico has something inside of her.
Well, at least one of us does. I'm with Bruiser. We haven't eaten in, like, twelve hours.
Maybe he's right, Alex. I'm... I'm probably just hungry.
Either way, what are we supposed to do? Call Domino's?
We can't use our credit cards or make ATM withdrawals without alerting the entire world to our whereabouts, and we only have nineteen bucks between us in cash.
Dude, your parents' fancy-pants lifestyle has made you soft. Nineteen bucks is enough to buy six people a feast at the local Circle A.
Fine.
But if we're leaving the Hostel, we're going as a group. I don't want you coming back with any more magic beans.
Magic what?
Gert, stay here and keep an eye on Molly, will you?
Hey, why do I have to stay? I'm a mutant, 'member? I'm stronger than all you guys combined!
Don't worry, kid, if they forget to bring back Slim Jims for us, Old Lace here will teach them a lesson about the food chain.
RRRRRR

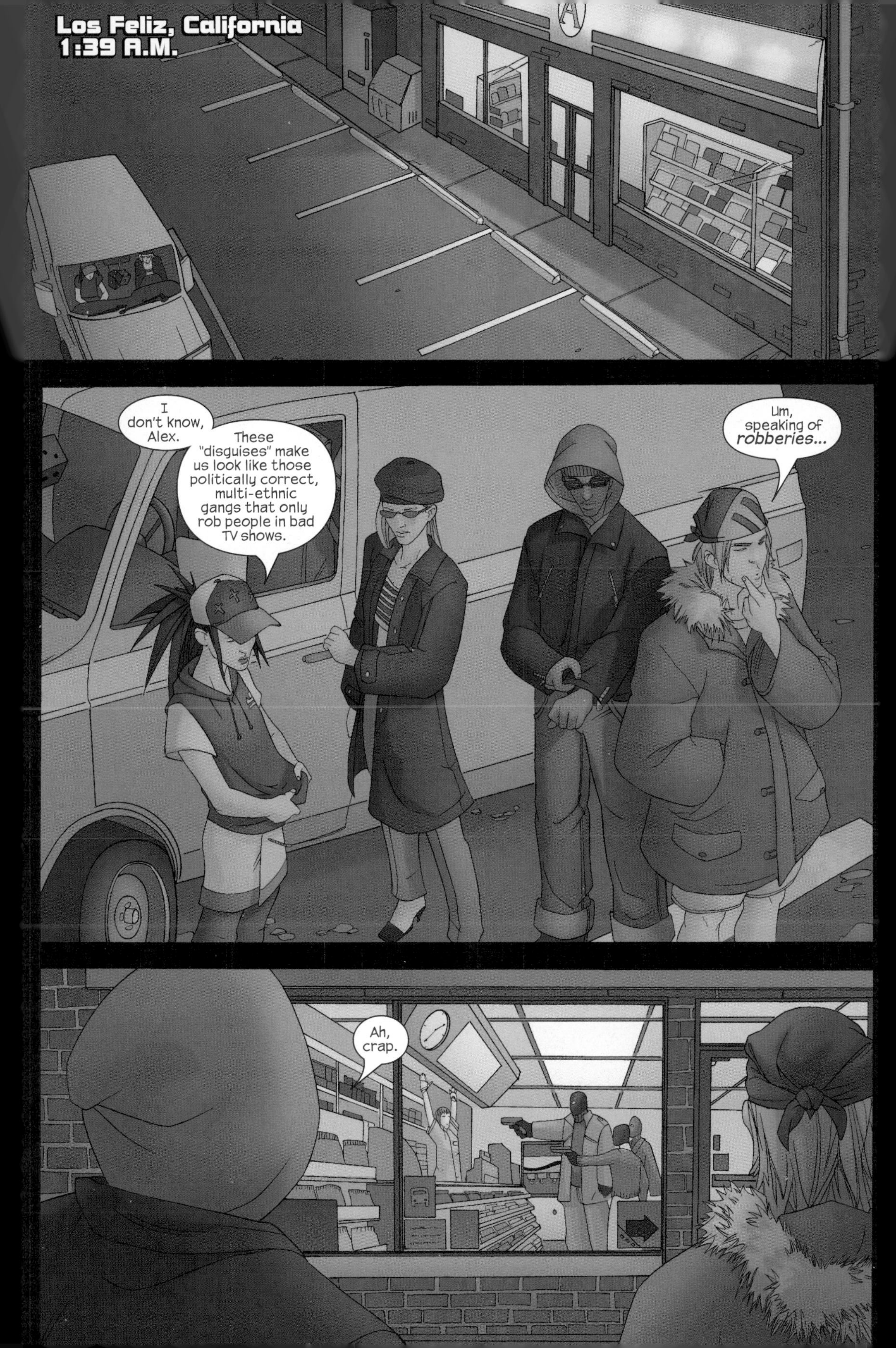
Los Feliz, California
1:39 A.M.
I don't know, Alex.
These "disguises" make us look like those politically correct, multi-ethnic gangs that only rob people in bad TV shows.
Um, speaking of *robberies...*
Ah, crap.

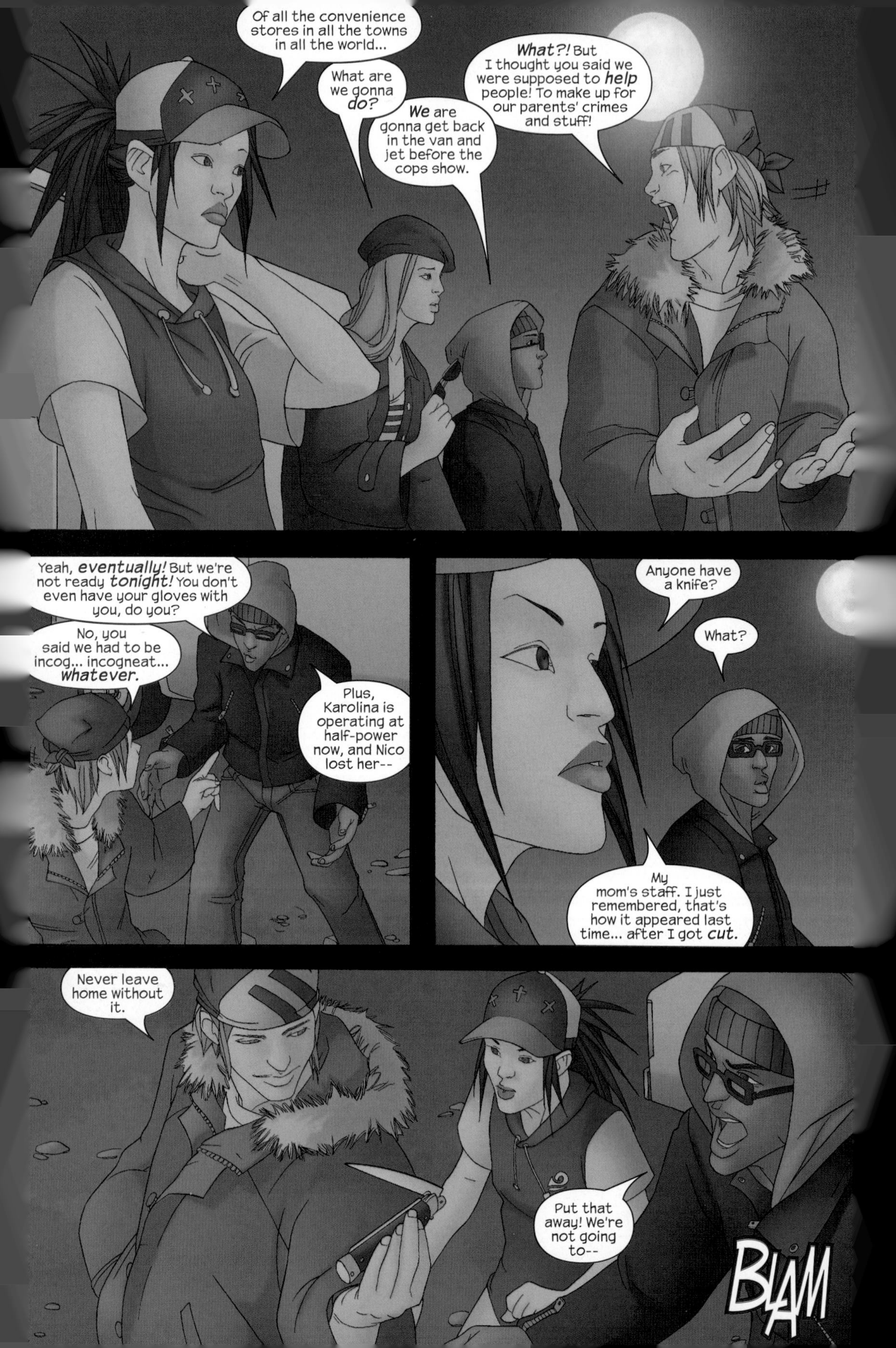
Of all the convenience stores in all the towns in all the world...
What are we gonna do?
We are gonna get back in the van and jet before the cops show.
What?! But I thought you said we were supposed to help people! To make up for our parents' crimes and stuff!
Yeah, eventually! But we're not ready tonight! You don't even have your gloves with you, do you?
No, you said we had to be incog... incogneat... whatever.
Plus, Karolina is operating at half-power now, and Nico lost her--
Anyone have a knife?
What?
My mom's staff. I just remembered, that's how it appeared last time... after I got cut.
Never leave home without it.
Put that away! We're not going to--
BLAM

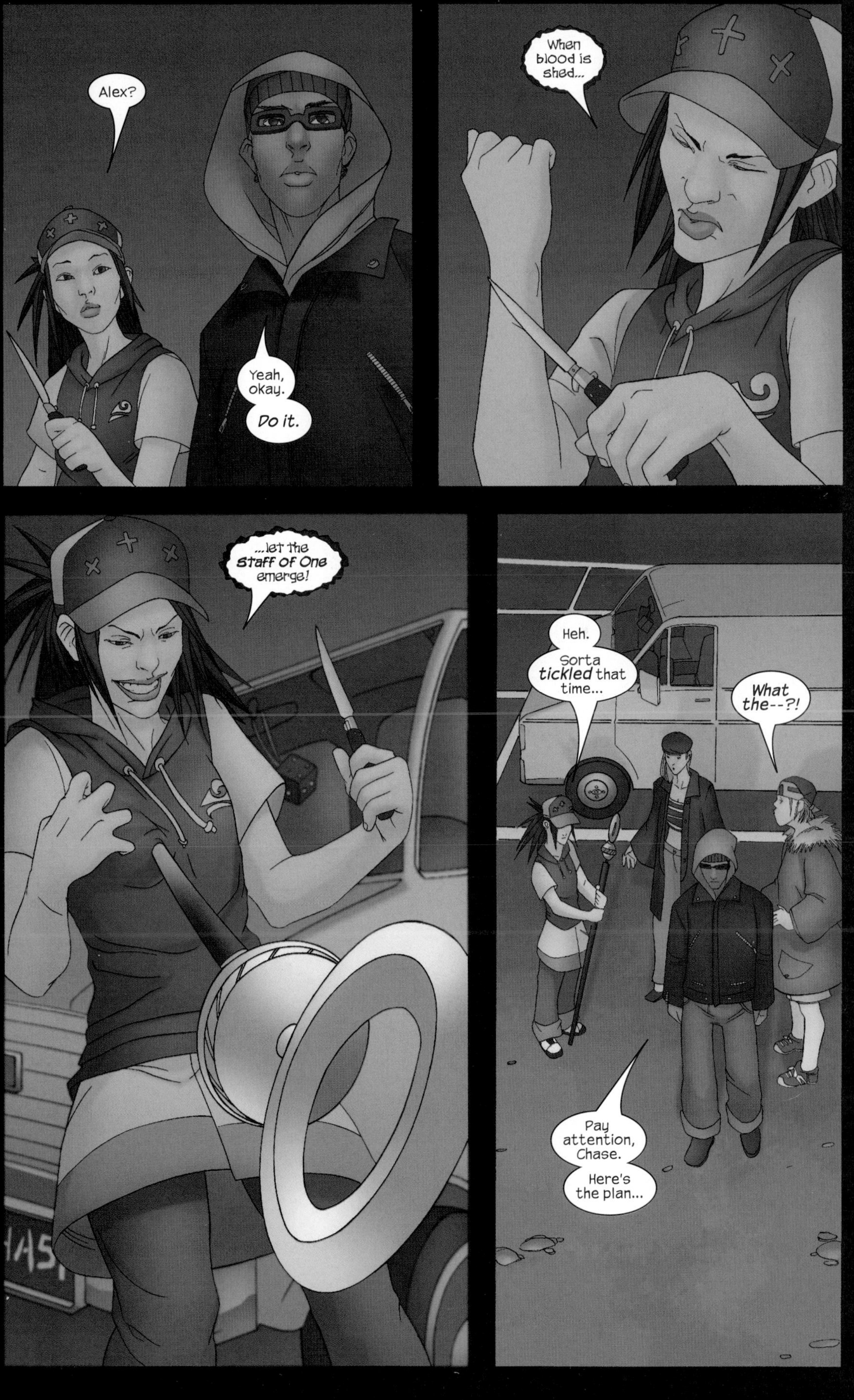
Alex?
Yeah, okay.
Do it.
When blood is shed...
...let the Staff of One emerge!
Heh.
Sorta tickled that time...
What the--?!
Pay attention, Chase.
Here's the plan...

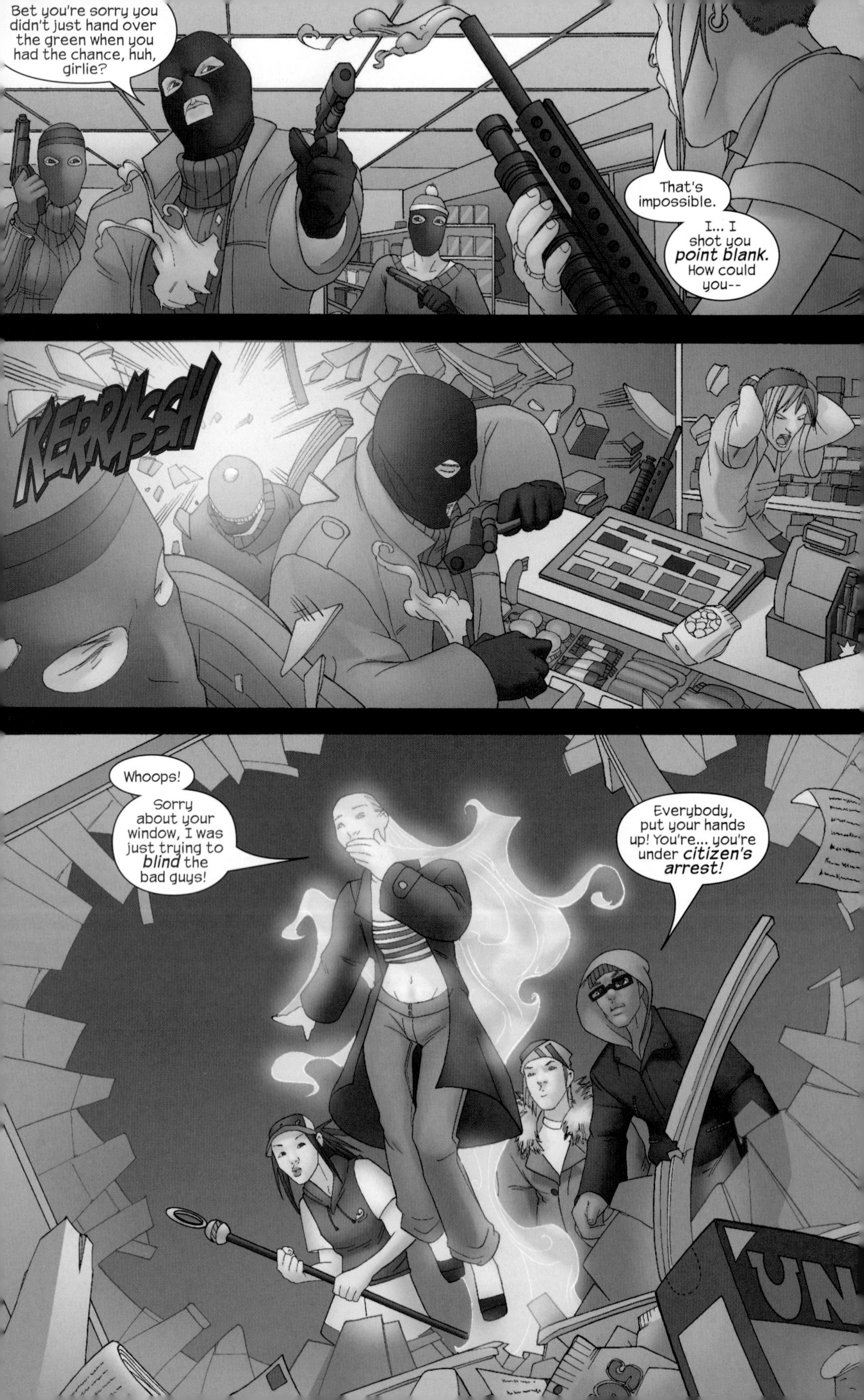
Bet you're sorry you didn't just hand over the green when you had the chance, huh, girlie?
That's impossible.
I... I shot you point blank. How could you--
KERRASSH
Whoops!
Sorry about your window, I was just trying to blind the bad guys!
Everybody, put your hands up! You're... you're under citizen's arrest!

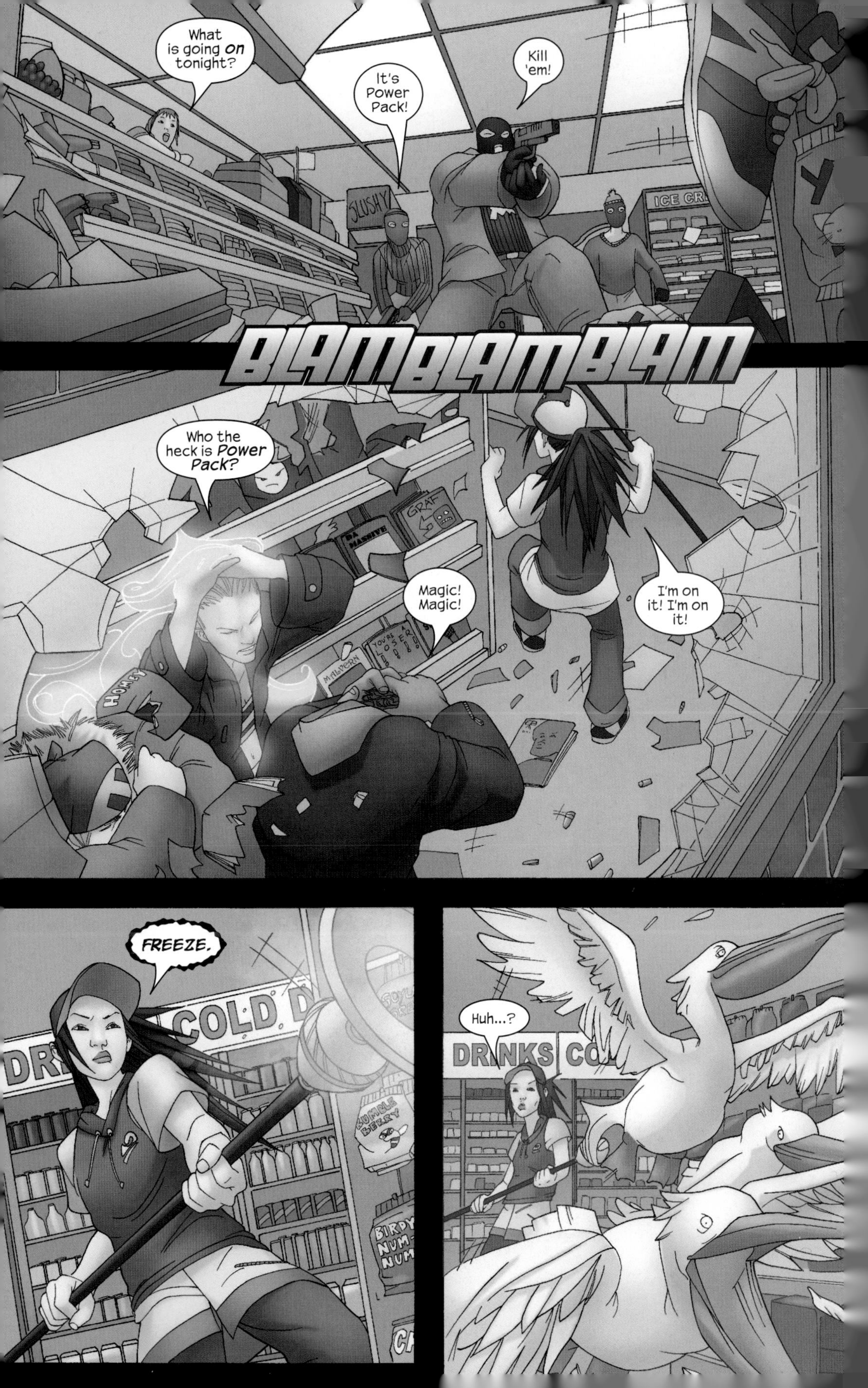

What is going on tonight?
It's Power Pack!
Kill 'em!
SLUSHY
ICE CR
BLAM BLAM BLAM
Who the heck is Power Pack?
DA MASSIVE
GRAF
Magic! Magic!
YOU'RE A LOSER
MALVERN
HOMEY
I'm on it! I'm on it!
FREEZE.
COLD D
DR
BUMBLE BERRY
BIRDY NUM-NUM
Huh...?
DRINKS CO

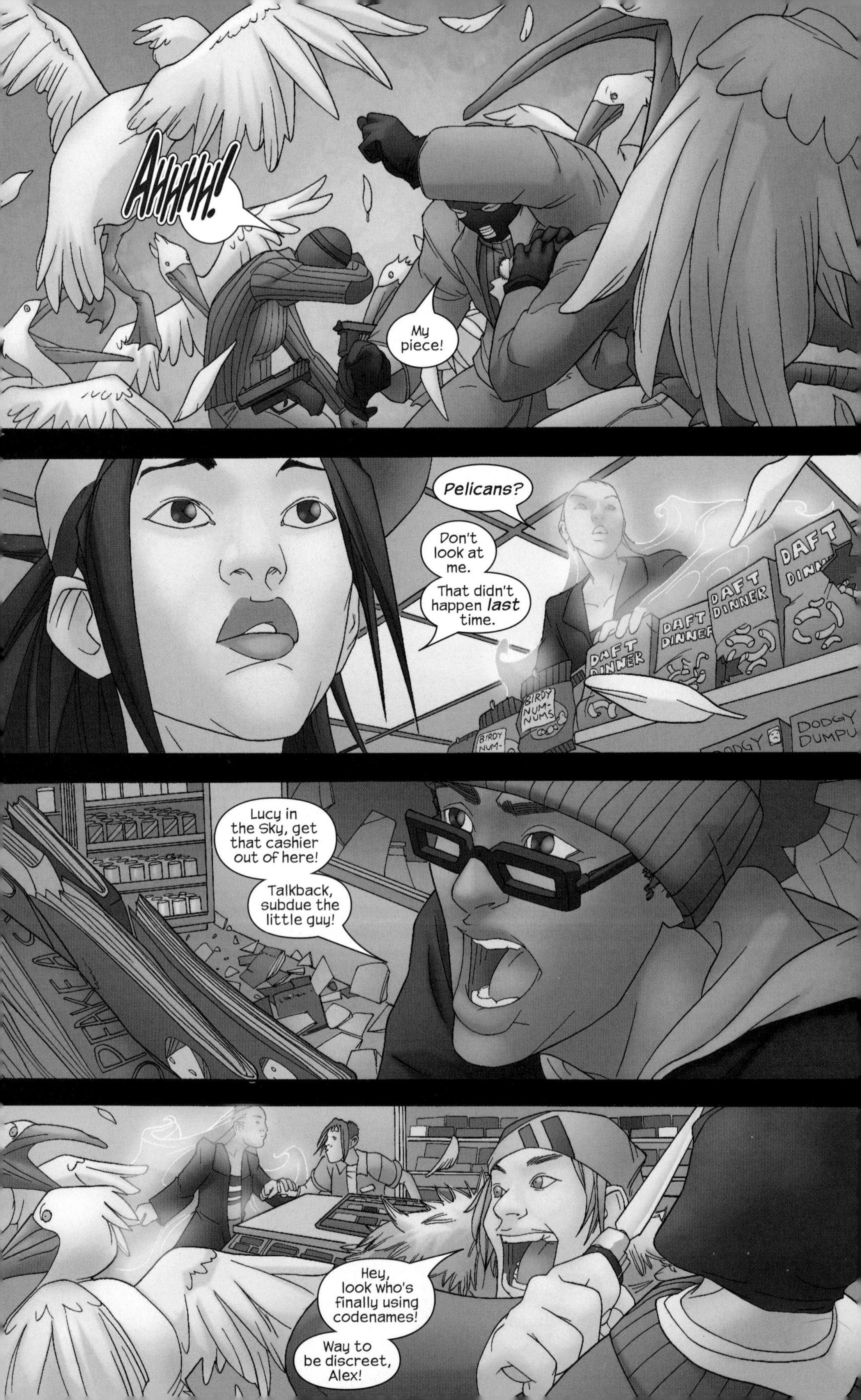
AHHHH!
My piece!
Pelicans?
Don't look at me.
That didn't happen *last* time.
DAFT DINNER
BIRDY NUM-NUMS
DODGY DUMPU
Lucy in the Sky, get that cashier out of here!
Talkback, subdue the little guy!
Hey, look who's finally using codenames!
Way to be discreet, Alex!

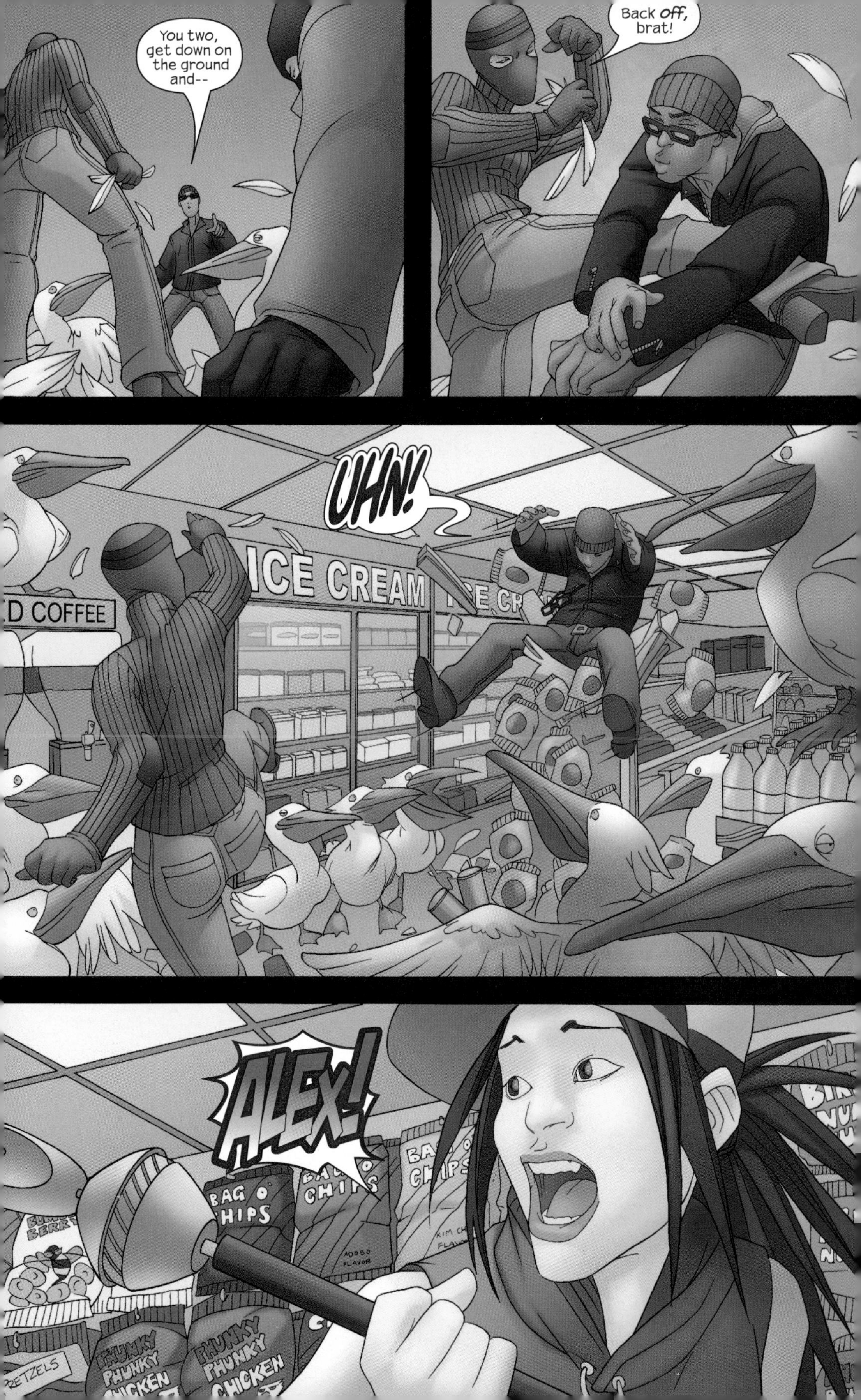
You two, get down on the ground and--
Back off, brat!
UHN!
ICE CREAM
D COFFEE
ALEX!
BAG O' CHIPS
BAG O' CHIPS
BAG O' CHIPS
ADOBO FLAVOR
PHUNKY PHUNKY CHICKEN
PHUNKY PHUNKY CHICKEN
RETZELS

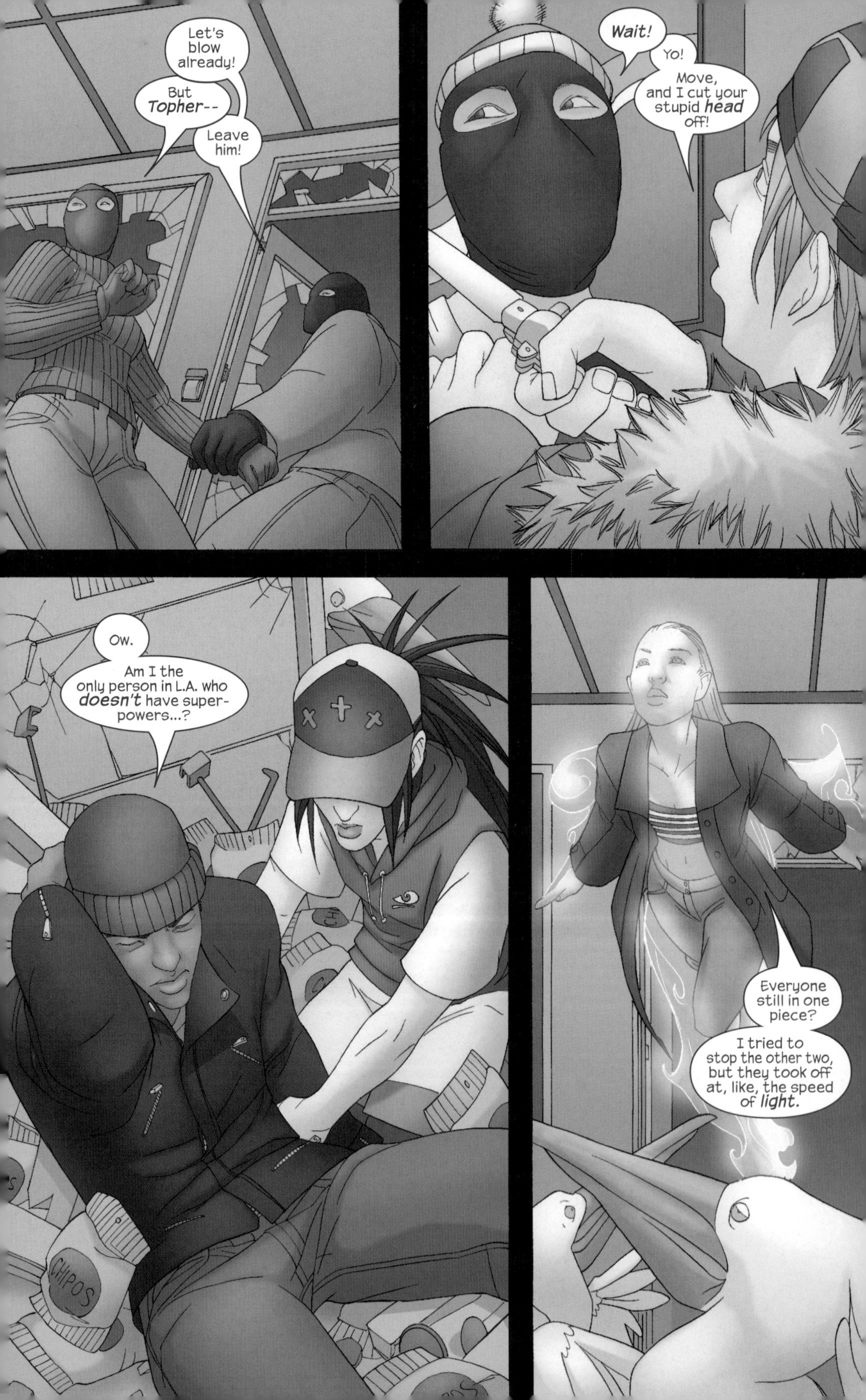
Let's blow already!
But *Topher*--
Leave him!
Wait!
Yo!
Move, and I cut your stupid ***head*** off!
Ow.
Am I the only person in L.A. who ***doesn't*** have super-powers...?
Everyone still in one piece?
I tried to stop the other two, but they took off at, like, the speed of ***light.***
CHIPOS

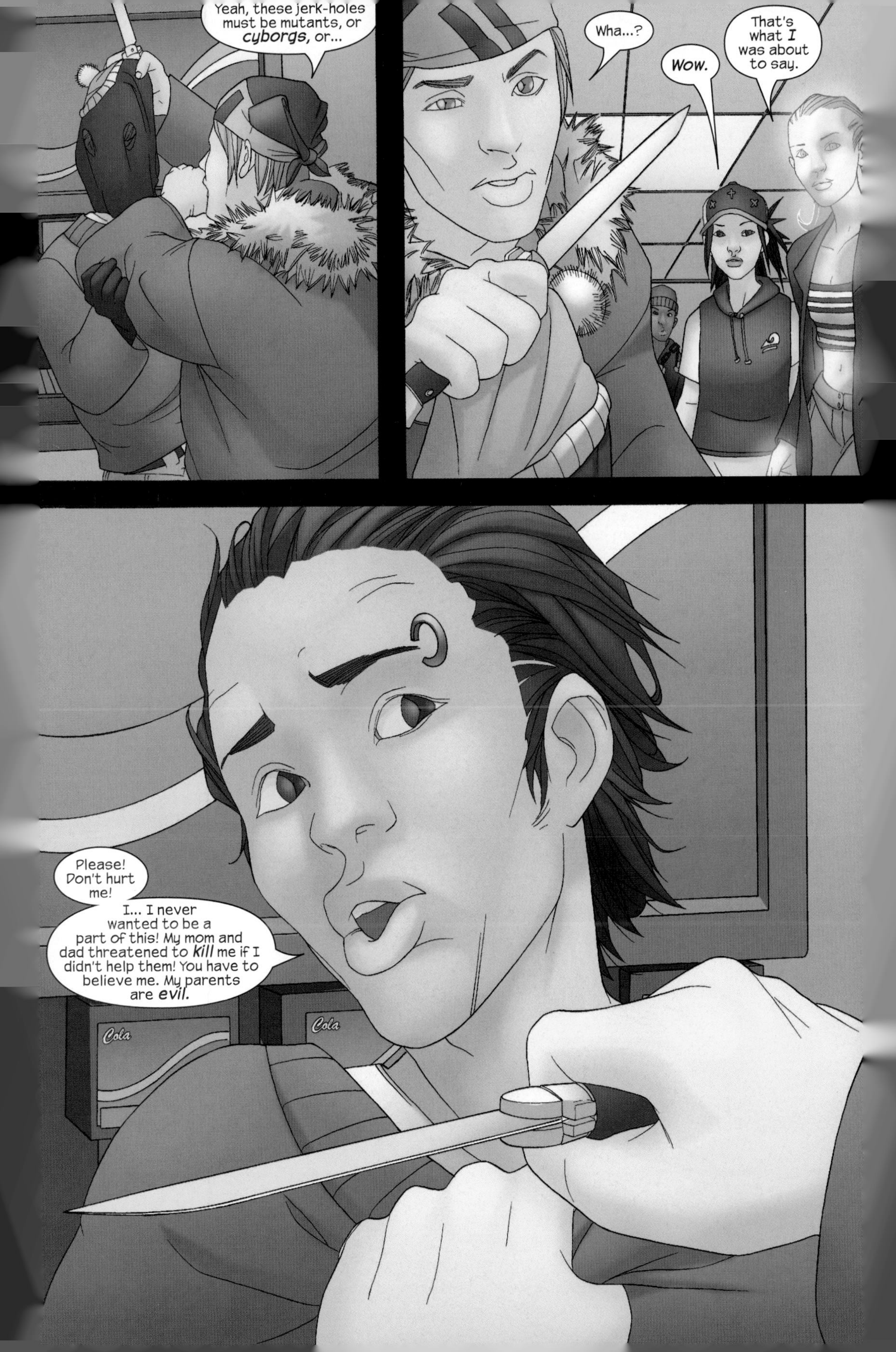
Yeah, these jerk-holes must be mutants, or cyborgs, or...
Wha...?
Wow.
That's what I was about to say.
Please! Don't hurt me!
I... I never wanted to be a part of this! My mom and dad threatened to kill me if I didn't help them! You have to believe me. My parents are evil.
Cola
Cola

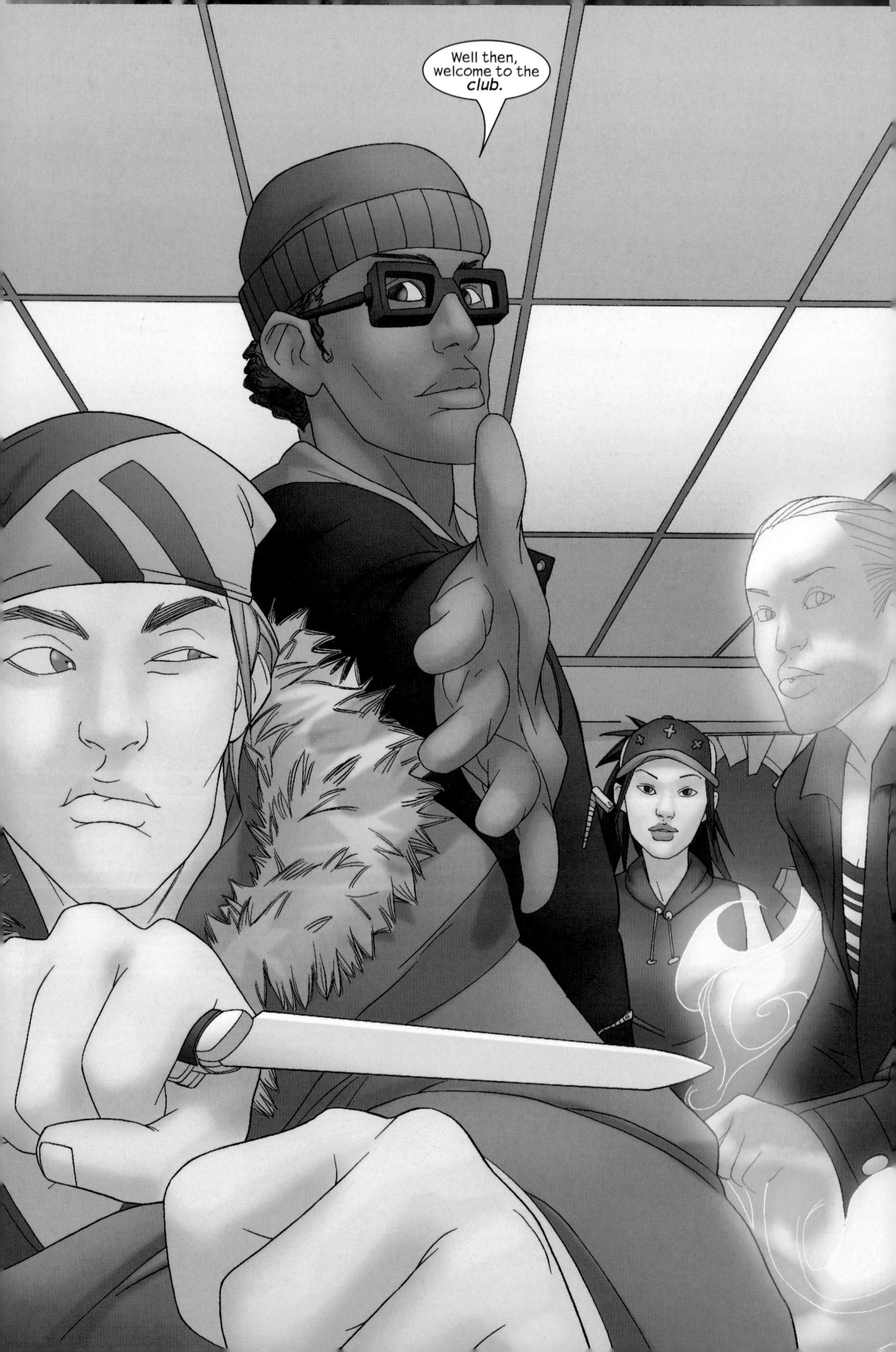
Well then, welcome to the *club.*

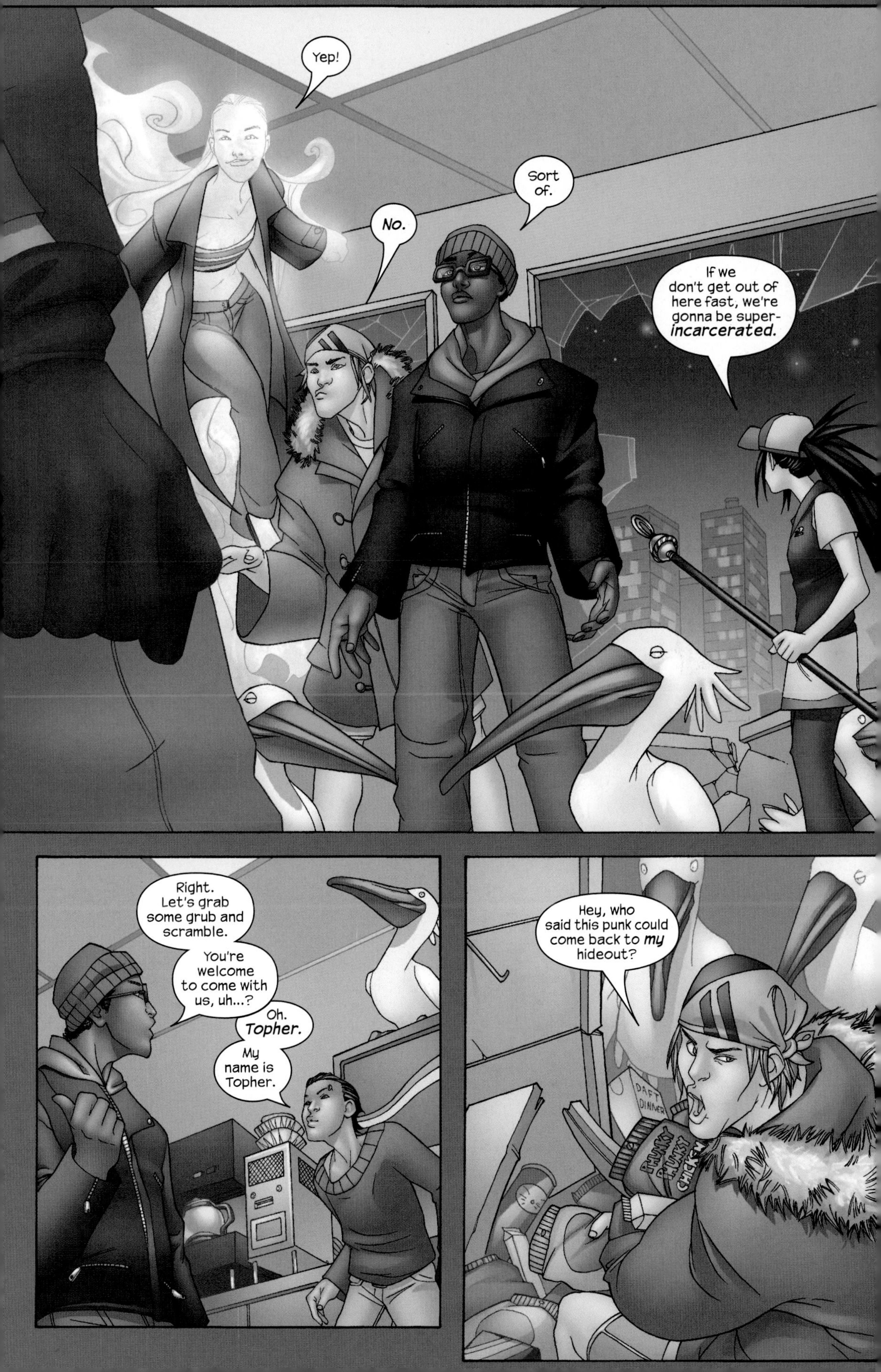
Yep!
No.
Sort of.
If we don't get out of here fast, we're gonna be super-*incarcerated*.
Right. Let's grab some grub and scramble.
You're welcome to come with us, uh...?
Oh. *Topher.*
My name is Topher.
Hey, who said this punk could come back to *my* hideout?
DAFT DINNER
PHUNKY PHUNKY CHICKY

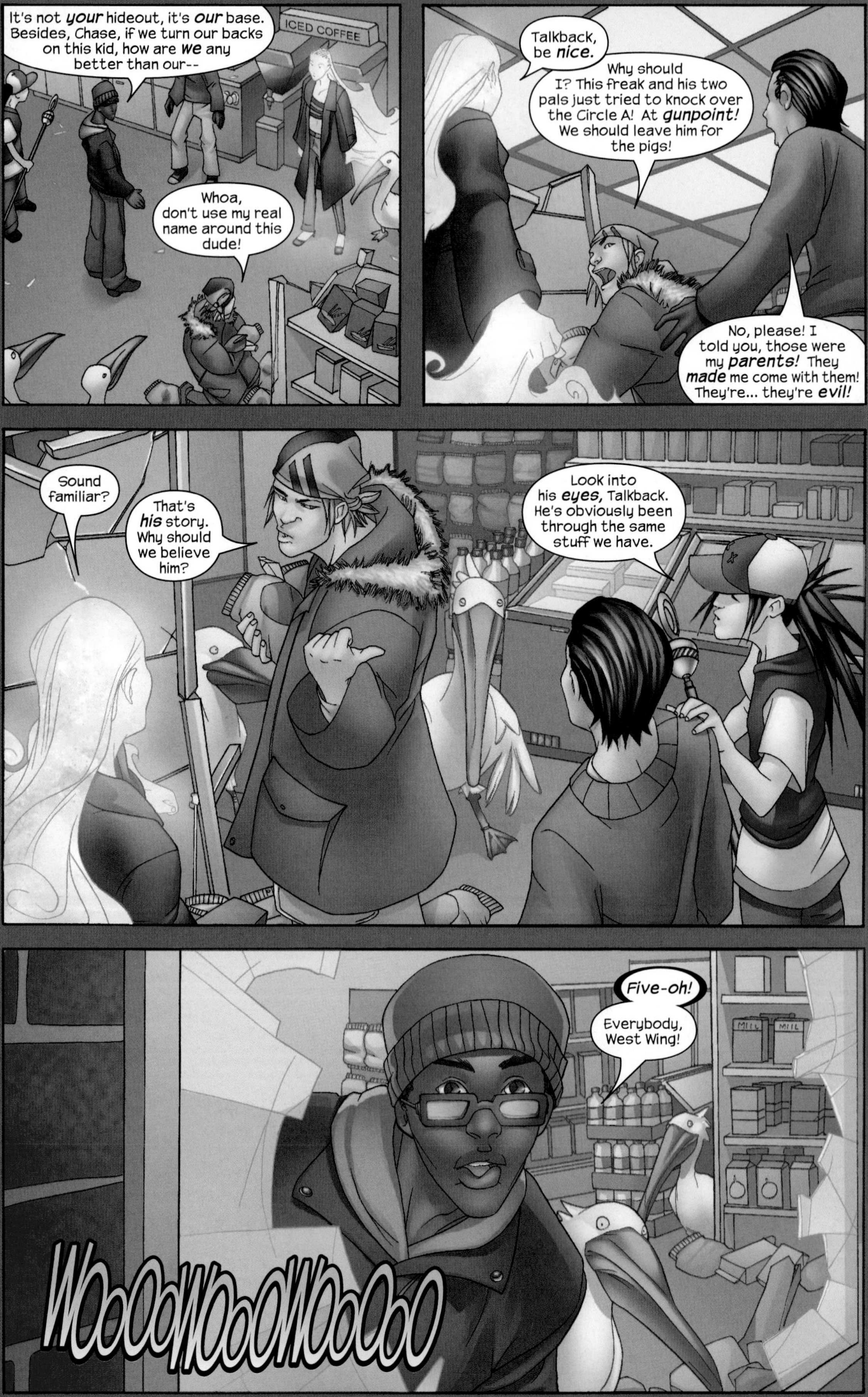
It's not *your* hideout, it's *our* base. Besides, Chase, if we turn our backs on this kid, how are *we* any better than our--
ICED COFFEE
Whoa, don't use my real name around this dude!
Talkback, be *nice.*
Why should I? This freak and his two pals just tried to knock over the Circle A! At *gunpoint!* We should leave him for the pigs!
No, please! I told you, those were my *parents!* They *made* me come with them! They're... they're *evil!*
Sound familiar?
That's *his* story. Why should we believe him?
Look into his *eyes,* Talkback. He's obviously been through the same stuff we have.
Five-oh!
Everybody, West Wing!
WOoOoWOoOWOoOoO

"West Wing?"

Walk fast, talk fast.

You have to learn to speak "Alex" if you're gonna run with the Children of the Damned...

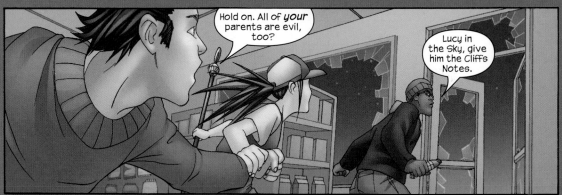

Hold on. All of *your* parents are evil, too?

Lucy in the Sky, give him the Cliffs Notes.

Six of us ran away from home after we found out that our parents are part of this sick secret society called The Pride... and I mean *bad* sick, not cool sick.

They framed us for a murder we didn't commit, but we're using the powers and weapons we took from them to try and *help* people.

Wow, you're... you're like a junior version of the A-Team.

What's an A-Team?

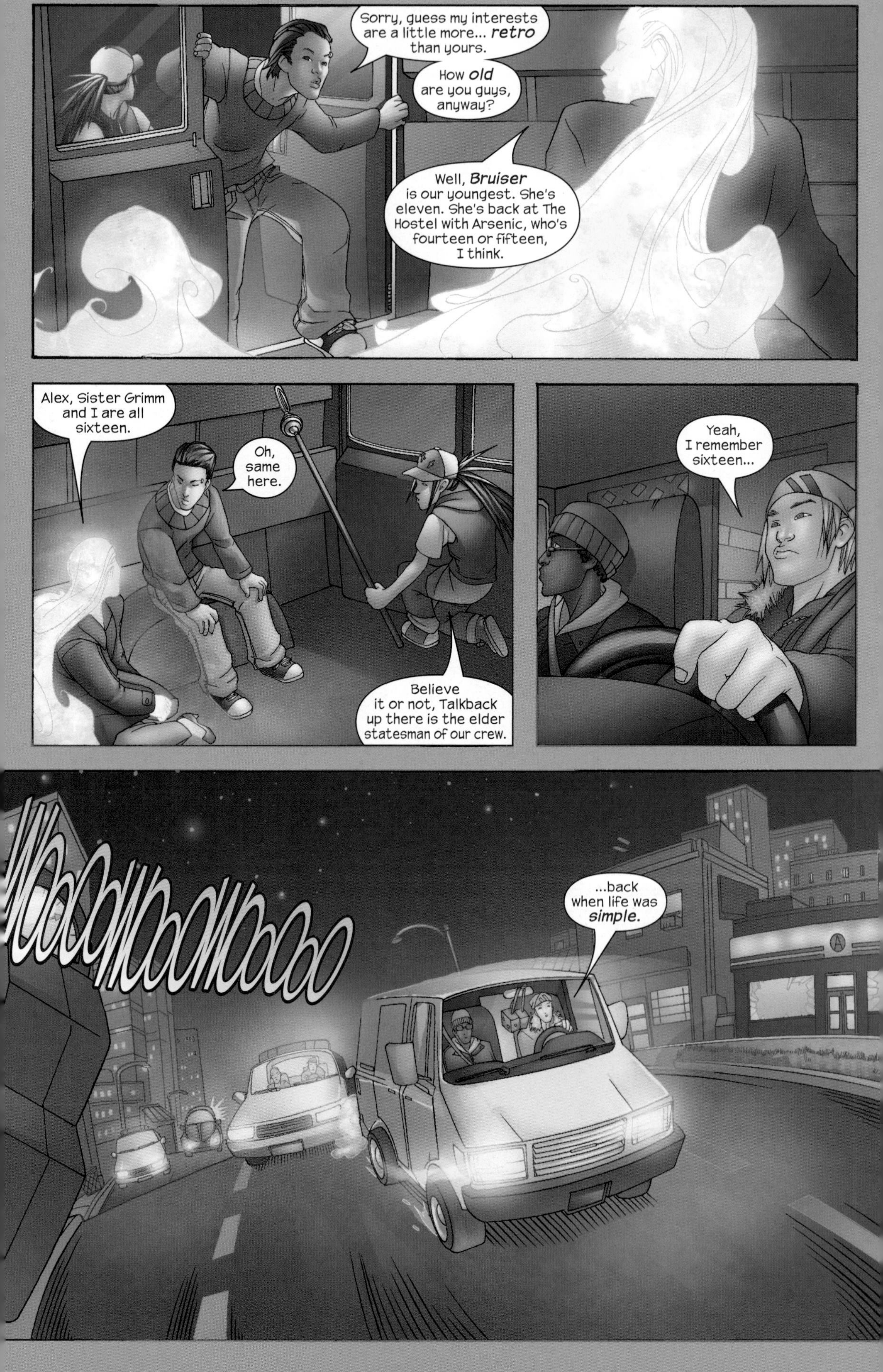
Sorry, guess my interests are a little more... *retro* than yours.
How *old* are you guys, anyway?
Well, *Bruiser* is our youngest. She's eleven. She's back at The Hostel with Arsenic, who's fourteen or fifteen, I think.
Alex, Sister Grimm and I are all sixteen.
Oh, same here.
Believe it or not, Talkback up there is the elder statesman of our crew.
Yeah, I remember sixteen...
WOOOWOOOWOOOOO
...back when life was *simple*.

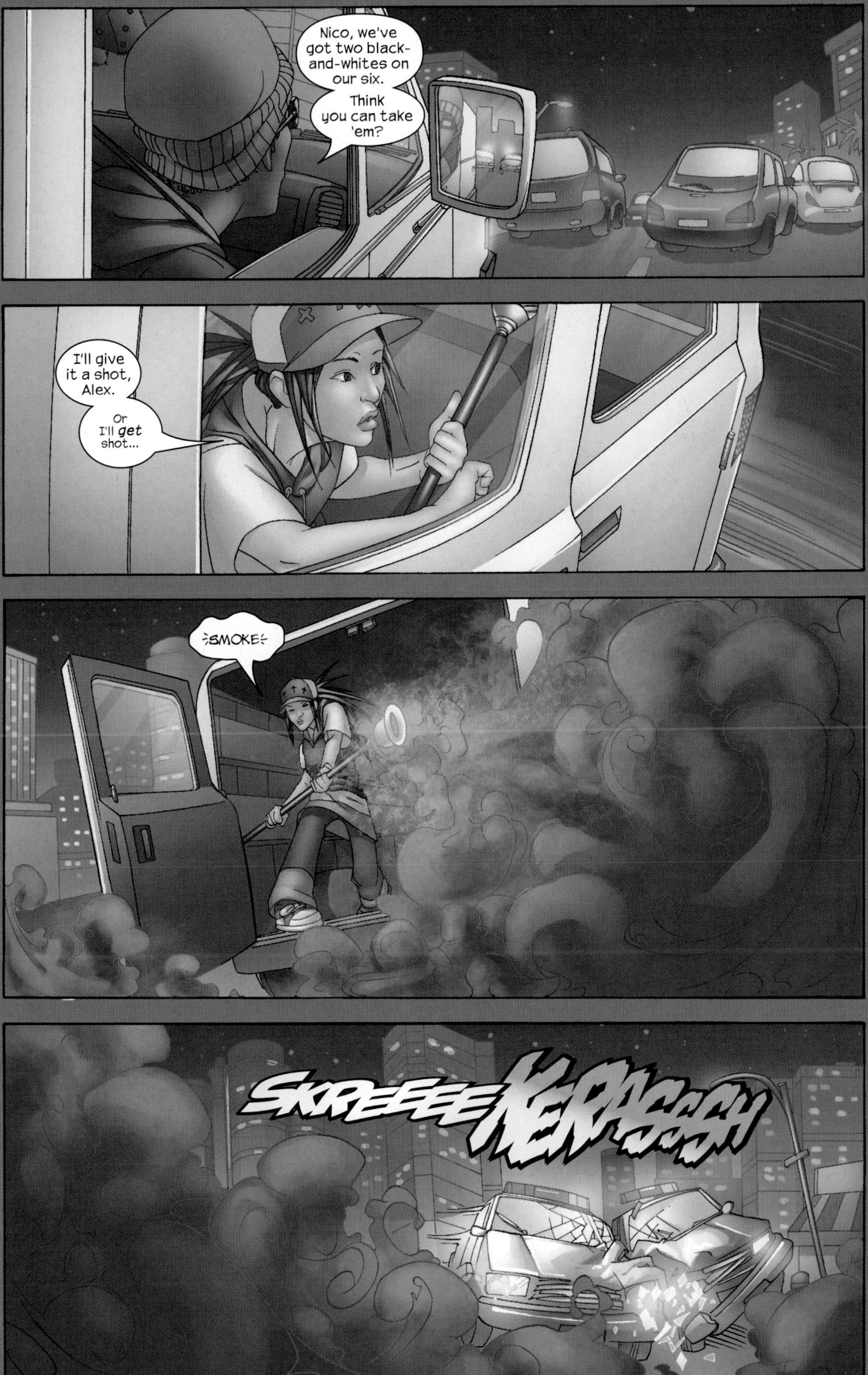
Nico, we've got two black-and-whites on our six.
Think you can take 'em?
I'll give it a shot, Alex.
Or I'll *get* shot...
SMOKE
SKREEEEE KERASSSH

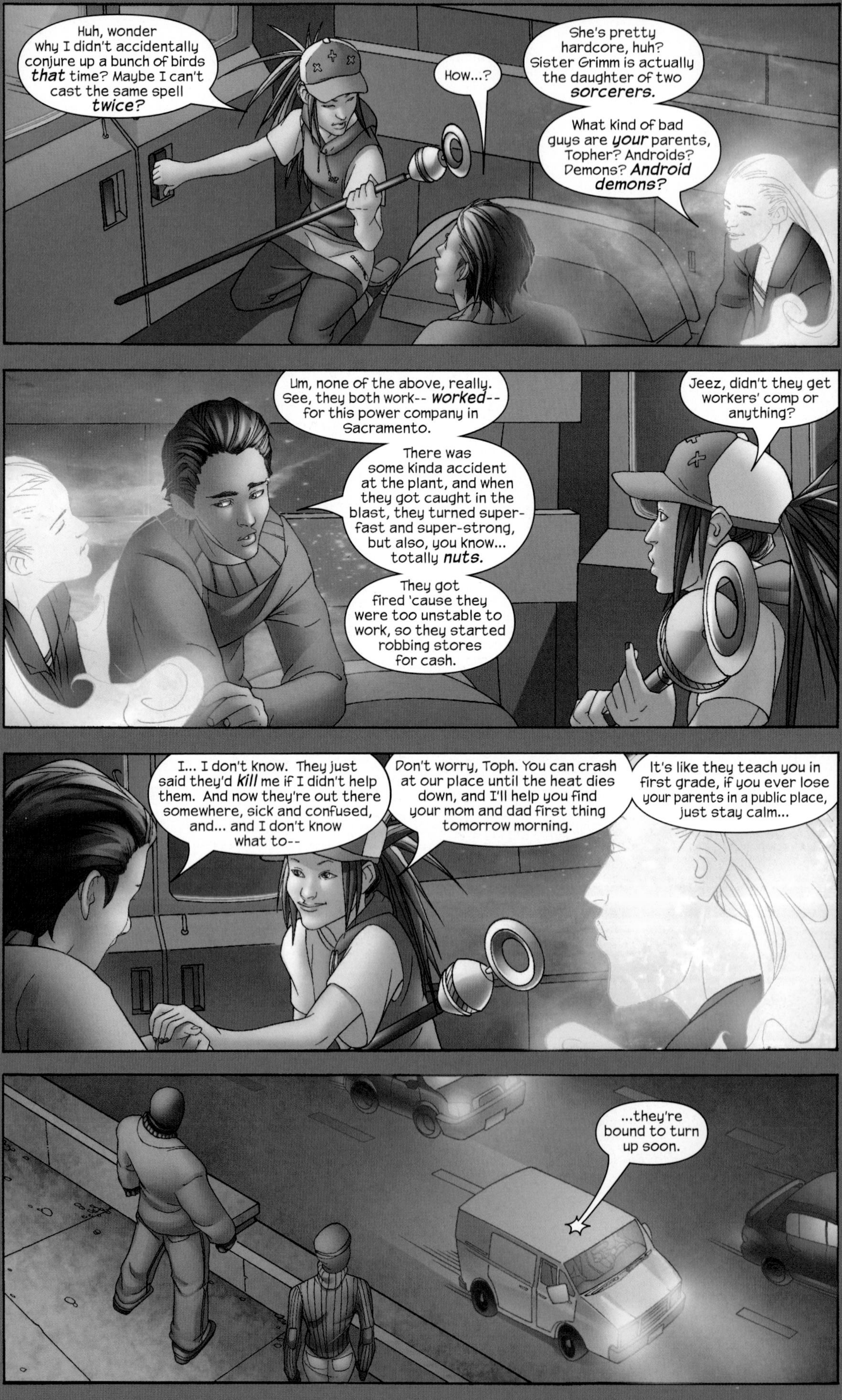
Huh, wonder why I didn't accidentally conjure up a bunch of birds that time? Maybe I can't cast the same spell twice?
How...?
She's pretty hardcore, huh? Sister Grimm is actually the daughter of two sorcerers.
What kind of bad guys are your parents, Topher? Androids? Demons? Android demons?
Um, none of the above, really. See, they both work-- worked-- for this power company in Sacramento.
There was some kinda accident at the plant, and when they got caught in the blast, they turned super-fast and super-strong, but also, you know... totally nuts.
They got fired 'cause they were too unstable to work, so they started robbing stores for cash.
Jeez, didn't they get workers' comp or anything?
I... I don't know. They just said they'd kill me if I didn't help them. And now they're out there somewhere, sick and confused, and... and I don't know what to--
Don't worry, Toph. You can crash at our place until the heat dies down, and I'll help you find your mom and dad first thing tomorrow morning.
It's like they teach you in first grade, if you ever lose your parents in a public place, just stay calm...
...they're bound to turn up soon.

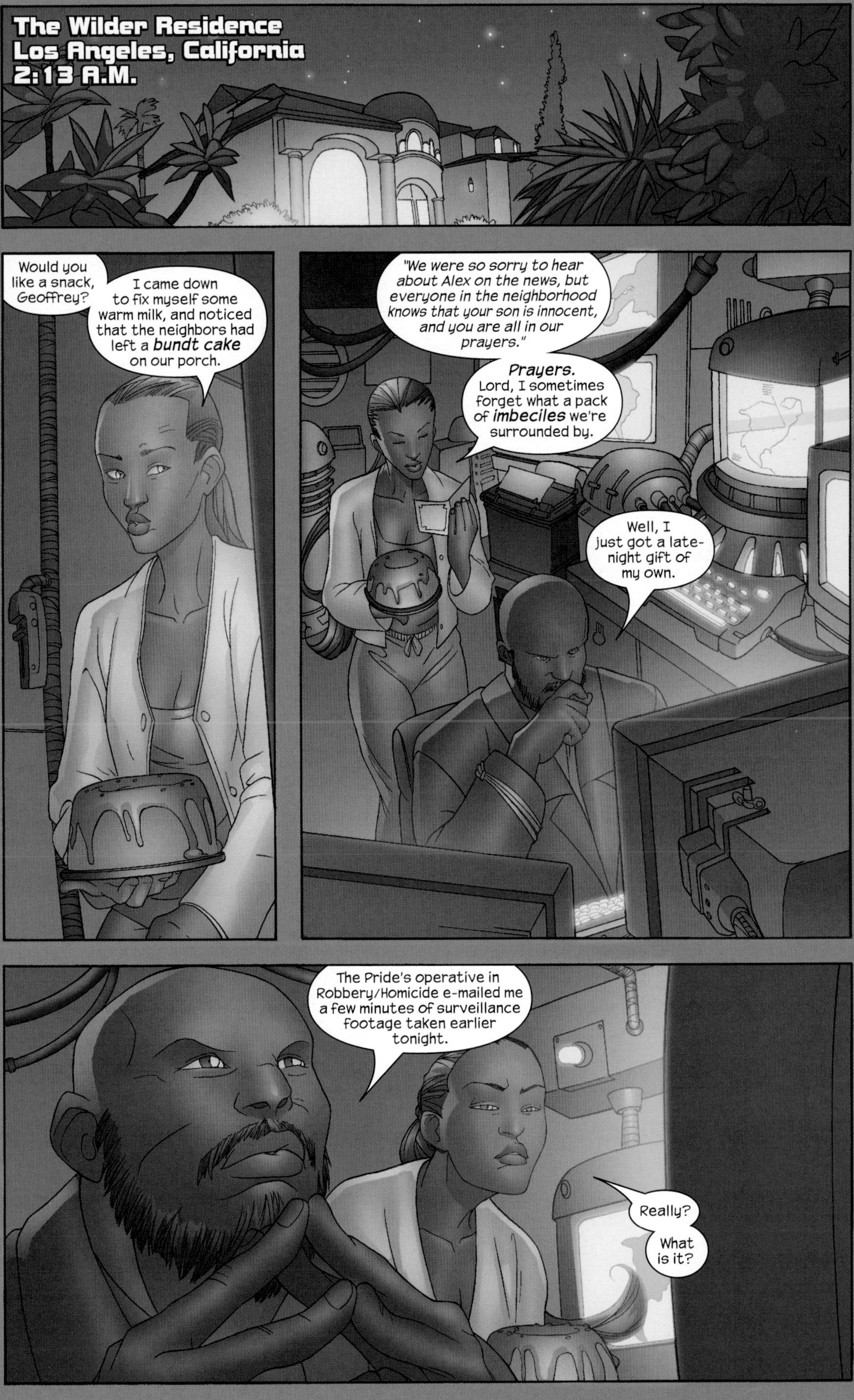
The Wilder Residence
Los Angeles, California
2:13 A.M.
Would you like a snack, Geoffrey?
I came down to fix myself some warm milk, and noticed that the neighbors had left a *bundt cake* on our porch.
"We were so sorry to hear about Alex on the news, but everyone in the neighborhood knows that your son is innocent, and you are all in our prayers."
Prayers. Lord, I sometimes forget what a pack of *imbeciles* we're surrounded by.
Well, I just got a late-night gift of my own.
The Pride's operative in Robbery/Homicide e-mailed me a few minutes of surveillance footage taken earlier tonight.
Really?
What is it?

An answer to our prayers.

That's Alex! Where... where was this taken?

A convenience store in Los Feliz.

The kids are still in *California*? I thought they'd be halfway to *Canada* by now!

Do we know who they're fighting here?

A trio of thieves... new players. Whoever they are, they certainly didn't request a permit from The Pride to rob stores in *our* city.

Regardless, if the children have opted to start playing crimefighter, it's more imperative than ever that we find them quickly...

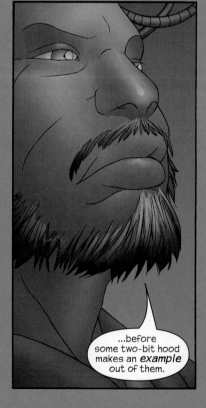

...before some two-bit hood makes an *example* out of them.

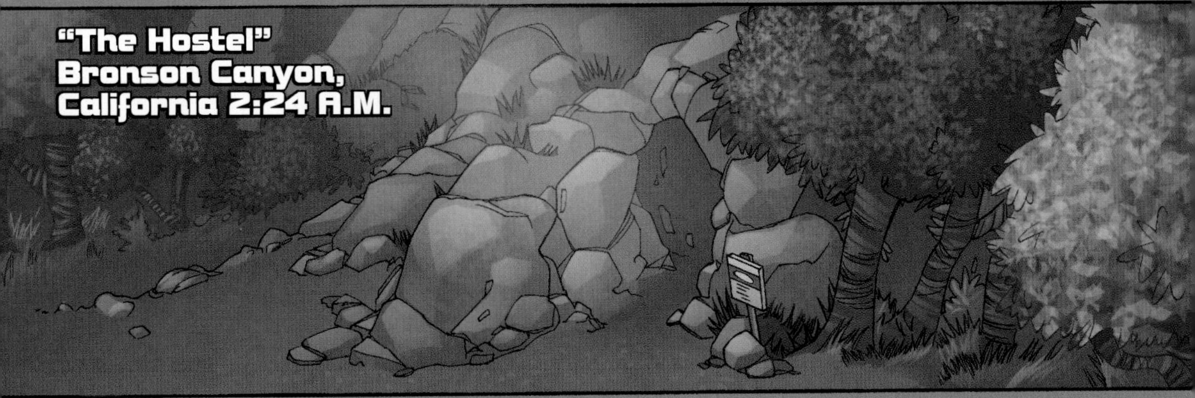
"The Hostel"
Bronson Canyon,
California 2:24 A.M.

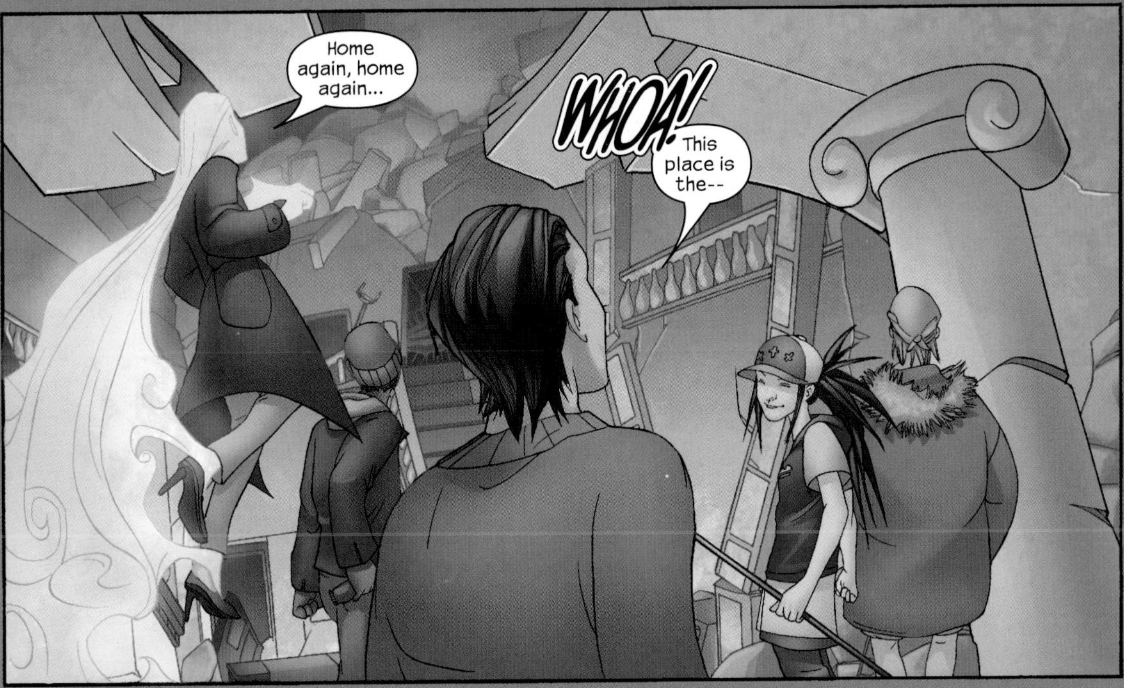
Home again, home again...
WHOA!
This place is the--

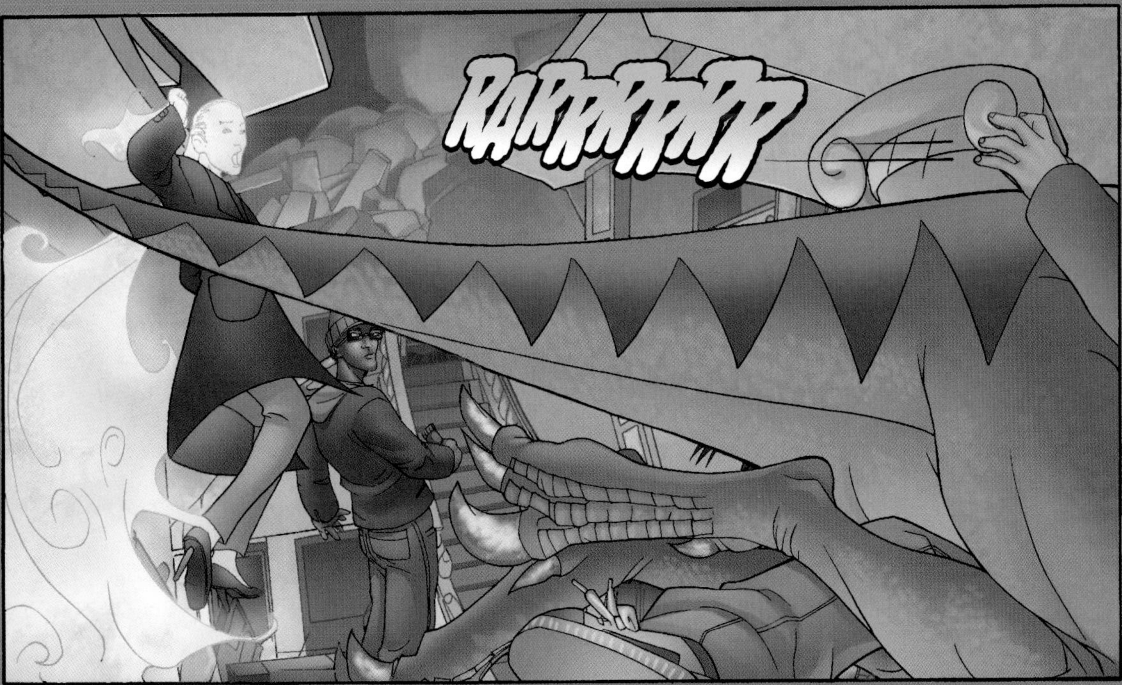
RARRRRRRR

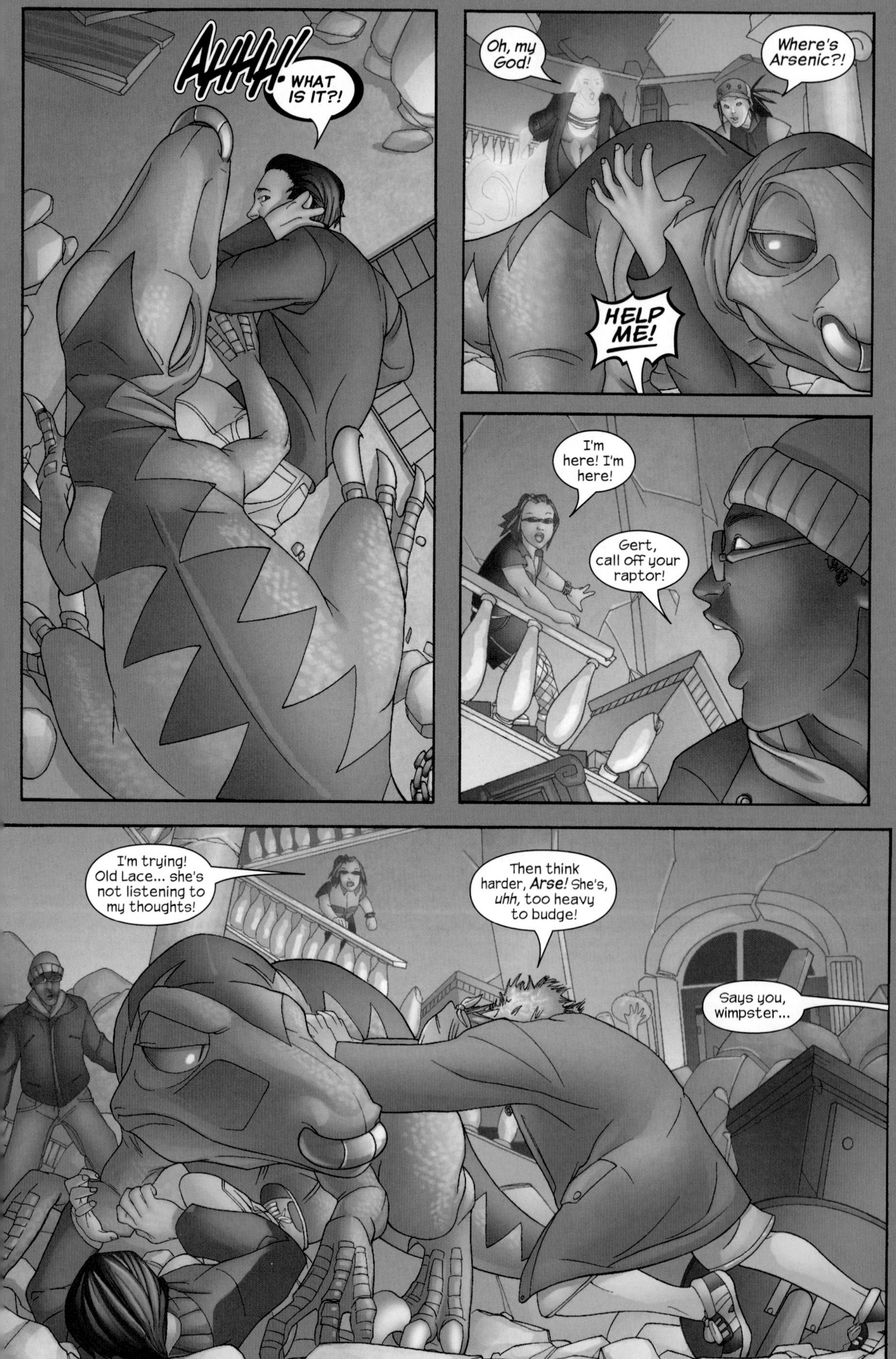
AHHH!
WHAT IS IT?!
Oh, my God!
Where's Arsenic?!
HELP ME!
I'm here! I'm here!
Gert, call off your raptor!
I'm trying! Old Lace... she's not listening to my thoughts!
Then think harder, Arse! She's, uhh, too heavy to budge!
Says you, wimpster...

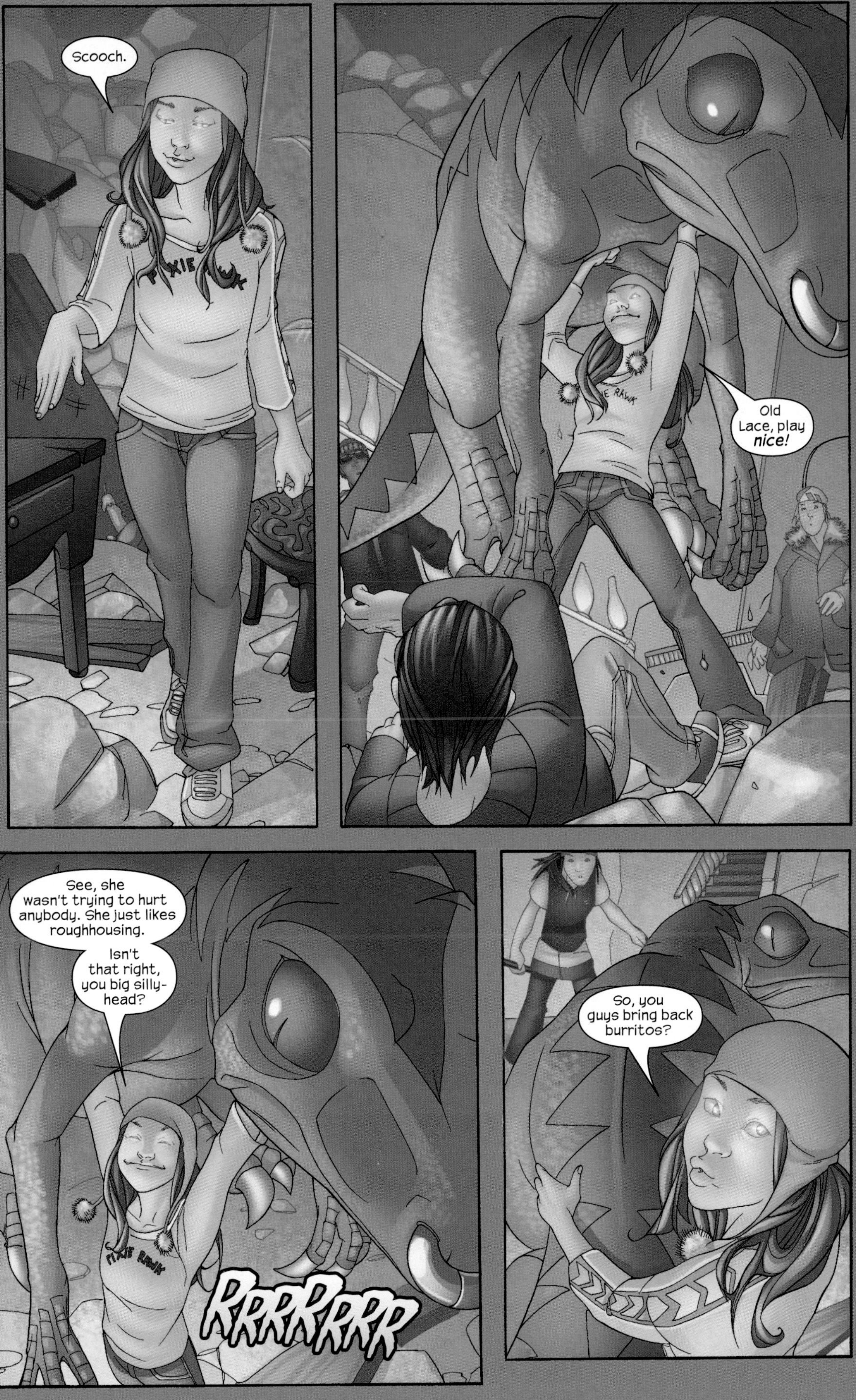
Scooch.
Old Lace, play *nice!*
See, she wasn't trying to hurt anybody. She just likes roughhousing.
Isn't that right, you big silly-head?
RRRRRRR
So, you guys bring back burritos?

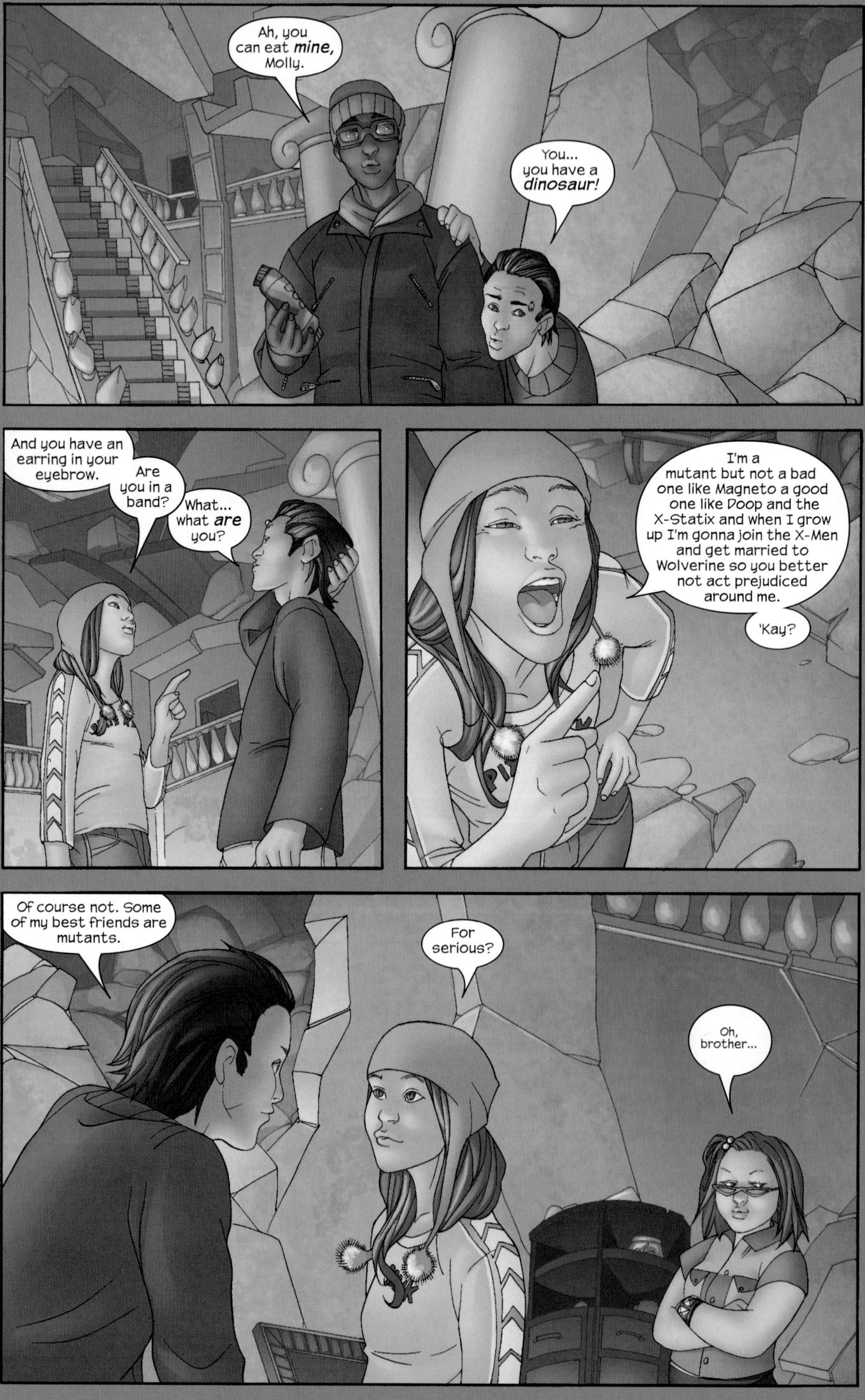
Ah, you can eat *mine,* Molly.
You... you have a *dinosaur!*
And you have an earring in your eyebrow.
Are you in a band?
What... what *are* you?
I'm a mutant but not a bad one like Magneto a good one like Doop and the X-Statix and when I grow up I'm gonna join the X-Men and get married to Wolverine so you better not act prejudiced around me.
'Kay?
Of course not. Some of my best friends are mutants.
For serious?
Oh, brother...

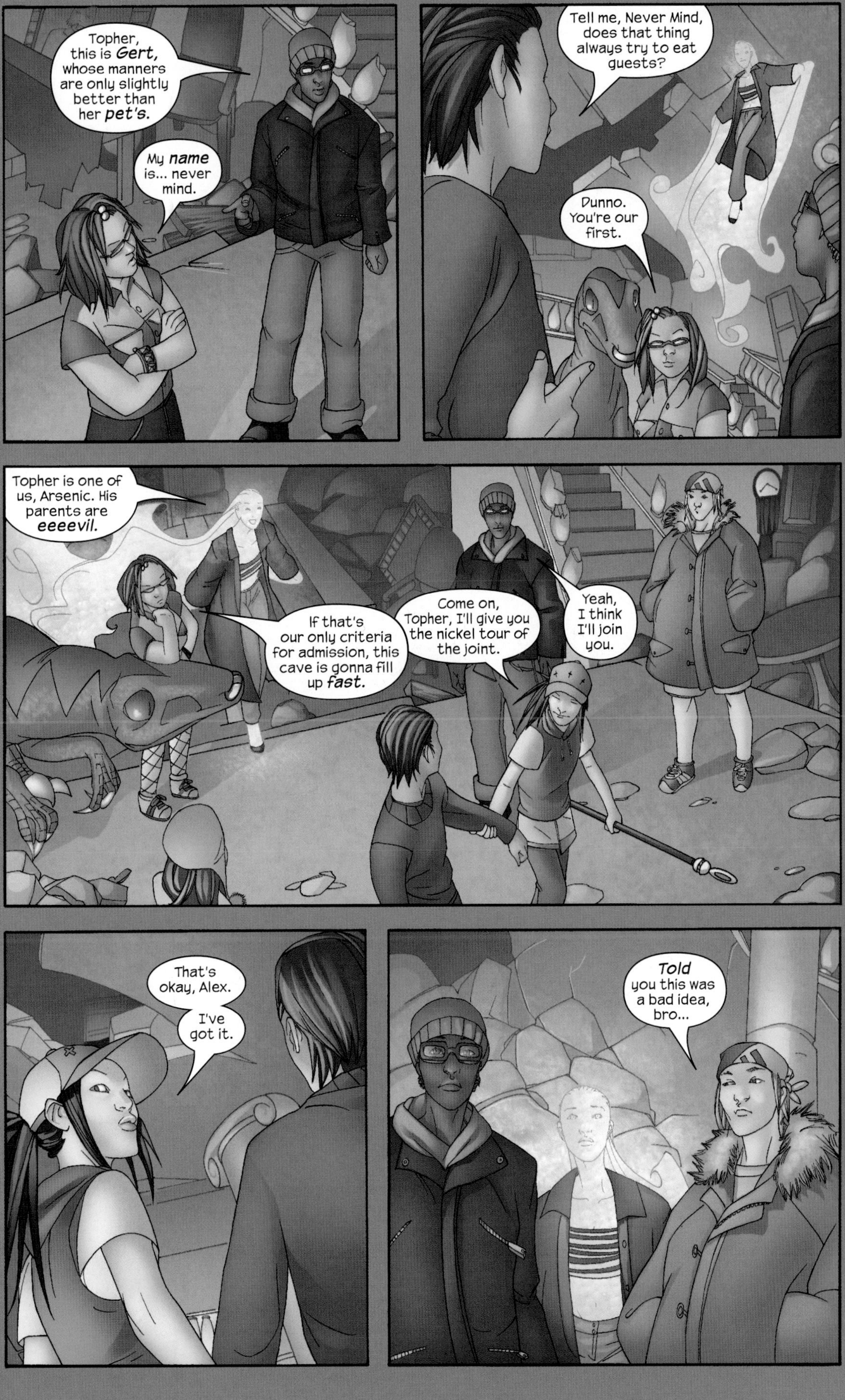

Topher, this is *Gert,* whose manners are only slightly better than her *pet's.*
My *name* is... never mind.
Tell me, Never Mind, does that thing always try to eat guests?
Dunno. You're our first.
Topher is one of us, Arsenic. His parents are *eeeevil.*
If that's our only criteria for admission, this cave is gonna fill up *fast.*
Come on, Topher, I'll give you the nickel tour of the joint.
Yeah, I think I'll join you.
That's okay, Alex.
I've got it.
Told you this was a bad idea, bro...

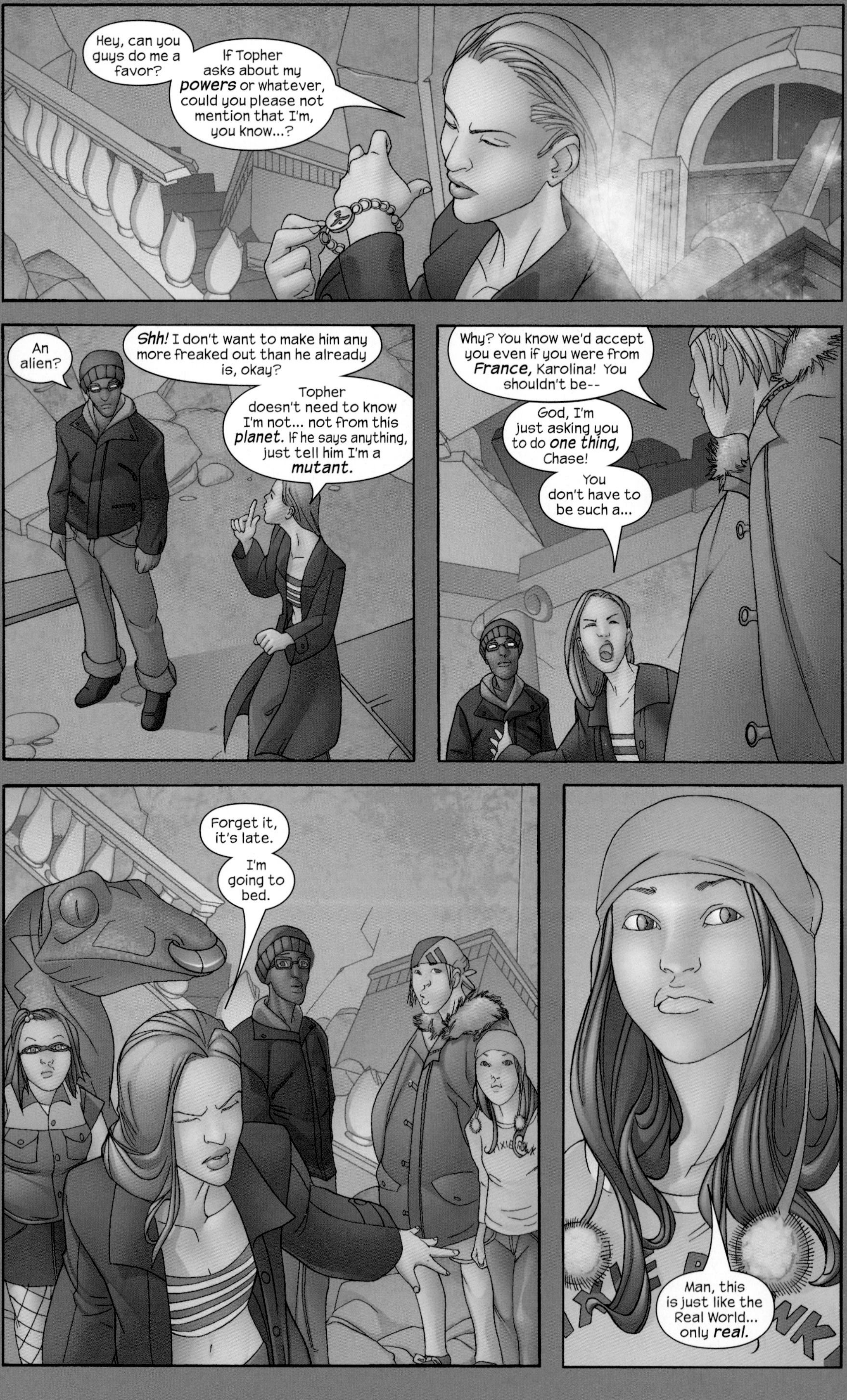
Hey, can you guys do me a favor?
If Topher asks about my powers or whatever, could you please not mention that I'm, you know...?
An alien?
Shh! I don't want to make him any more freaked out than he already is, okay?
Topher doesn't need to know I'm not... not from this planet. If he says anything, just tell him I'm a mutant.
Why? You know we'd accept you even if you were from France, Karolina! You shouldn't be--
God, I'm just asking you to do one thing, Chase!
You don't have to be such a...
Forget it, it's late.
I'm going to bed.
Man, this is just like the Real World... only real.

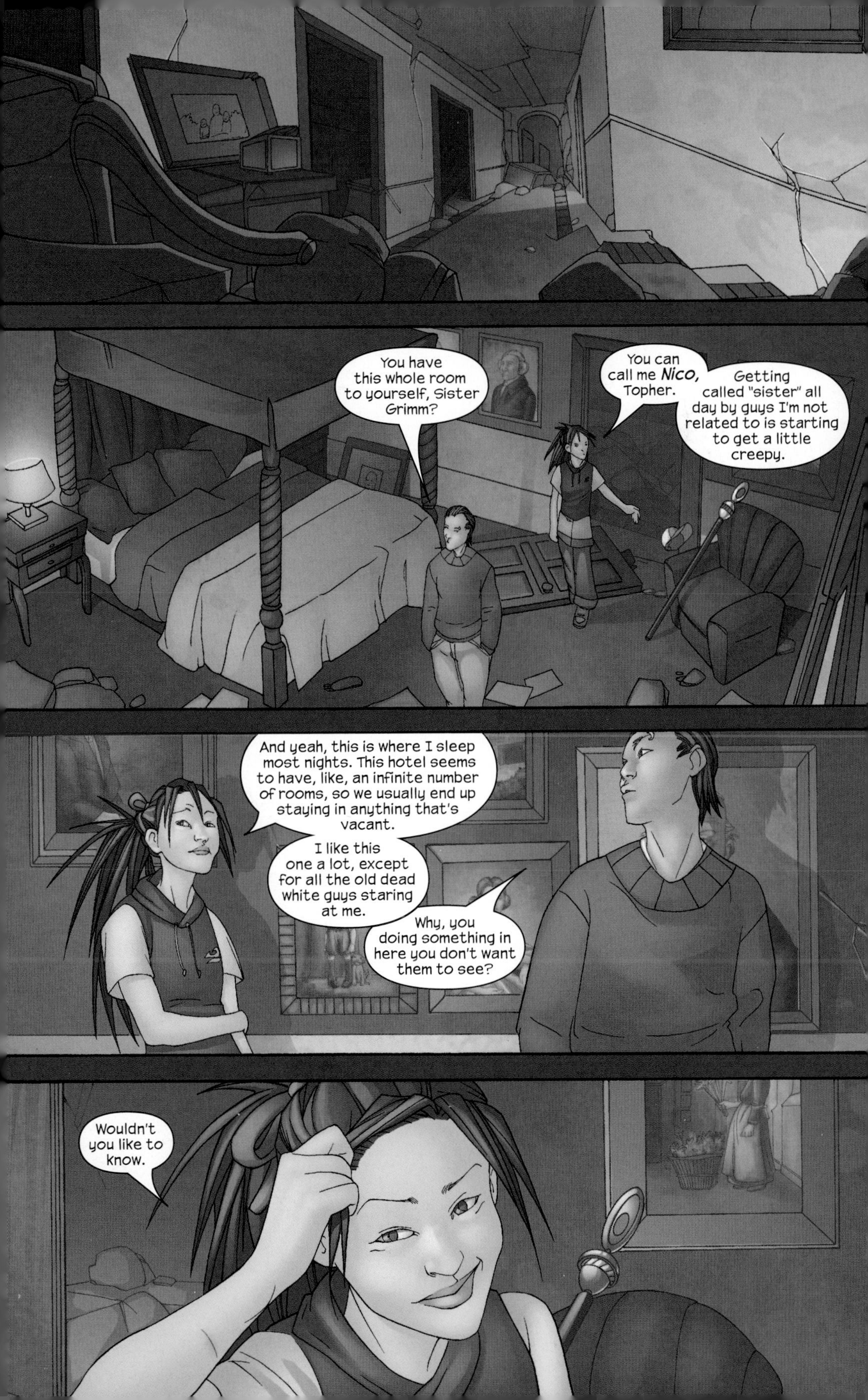
You have this whole room to yourself, Sister Grimm?
You can call me Nico, Topher.
Getting called "sister" all day by guys I'm not related to is starting to get a little creepy.
And yeah, this is where I sleep most nights. This hotel seems to have, like, an infinite number of rooms, so we usually end up staying in anything that's vacant.
I like this one a lot, except for all the old dead white guys staring at me.
Why, you doing something in here you don't want them to see?
Wouldn't you like to know.

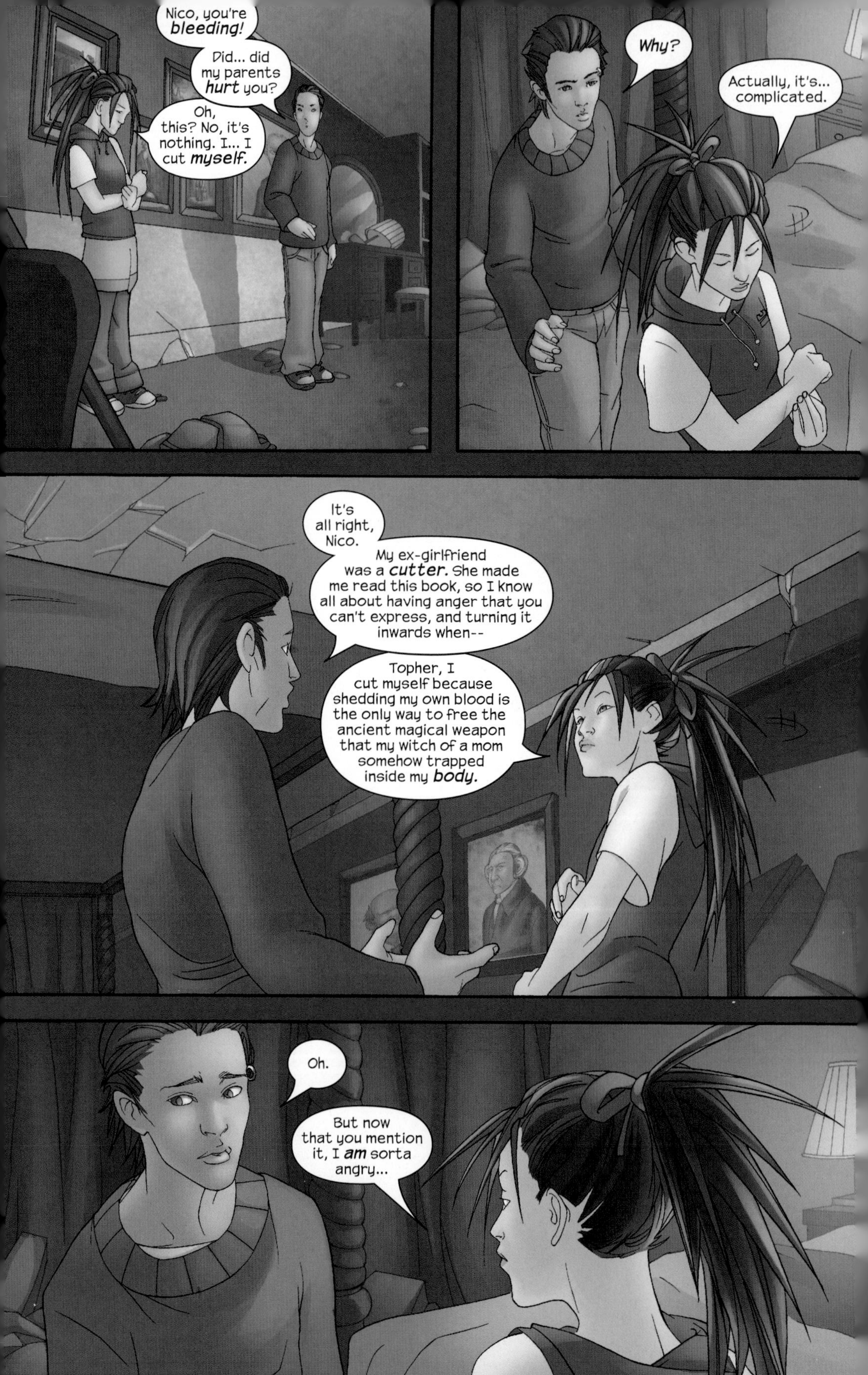

Nico, you're bleeding!
Did... did my parents hurt you?
Oh, this? No, it's nothing. I... I cut myself.
Why?
Actually, it's... complicated.
It's all right, Nico.
My ex-girlfriend was a cutter. She made me read this book, so I know all about having anger that you can't express, and turning it inwards when--
Topher, I cut myself because shedding my own blood is the only way to free the ancient magical weapon that my witch of a mom somehow trapped inside my body.
Oh.
But now that you mention it, I am sorta angry...

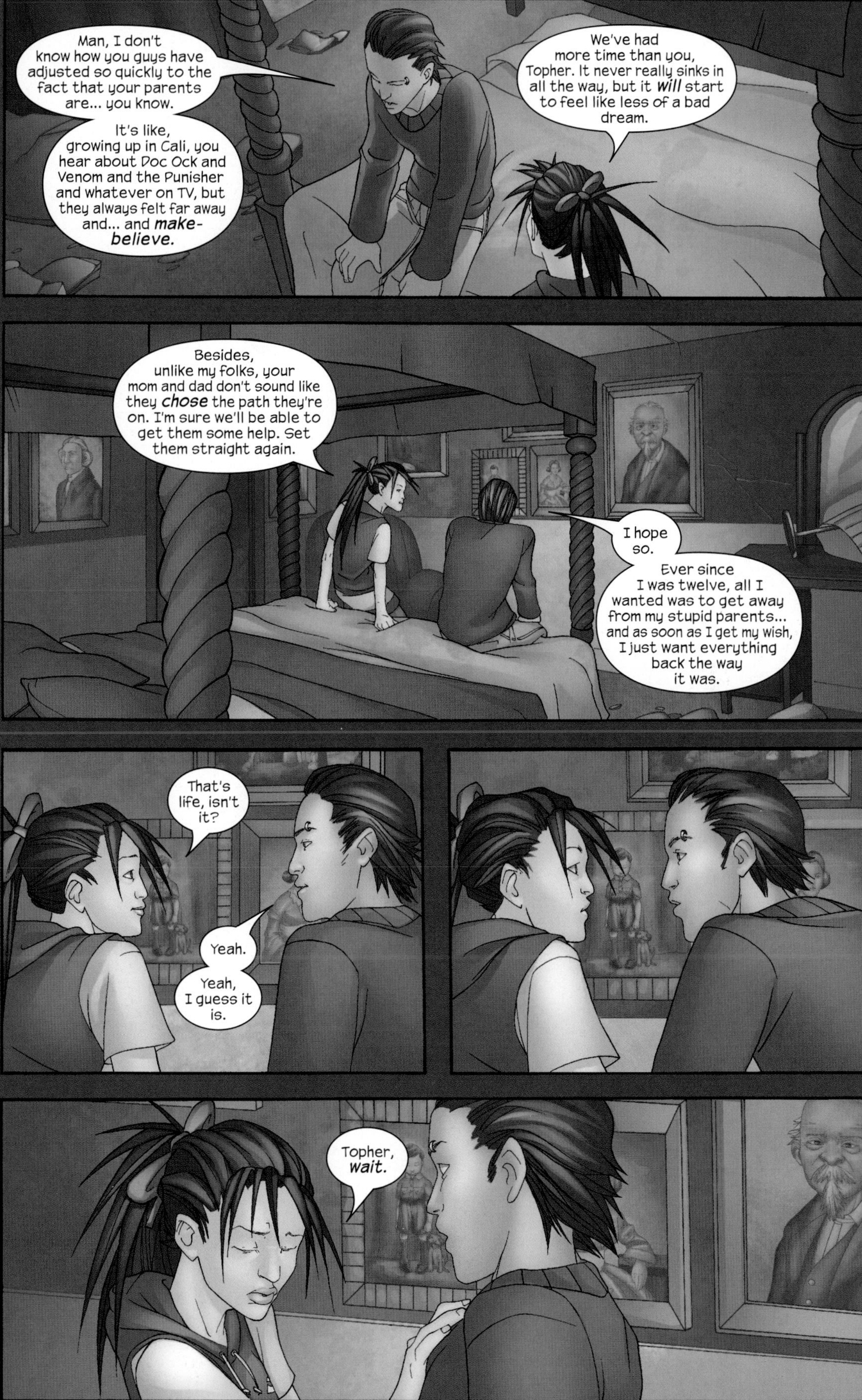
Man, I don't know how you guys have adjusted so quickly to the fact that your parents are... you know.
It's like, growing up in Cali, you hear about Doc Ock and Venom and the Punisher and whatever on TV, but they always felt far away and... and *make-believe.*
We've had more time than you, Topher. It never really sinks in all the way, but it *will* start to feel like less of a bad dream.
Besides, unlike my folks, your mom and dad don't sound like they *chose* the path they're on. I'm sure we'll be able to get them some help. Set them straight again.
I hope so.
Ever since I was twelve, all I wanted was to get away from my stupid parents... and as soon as I get my wish, I just want everything back the way it was.
That's life, isn't it?
Yeah.
Yeah, I guess it is.
Topher, *wait.*

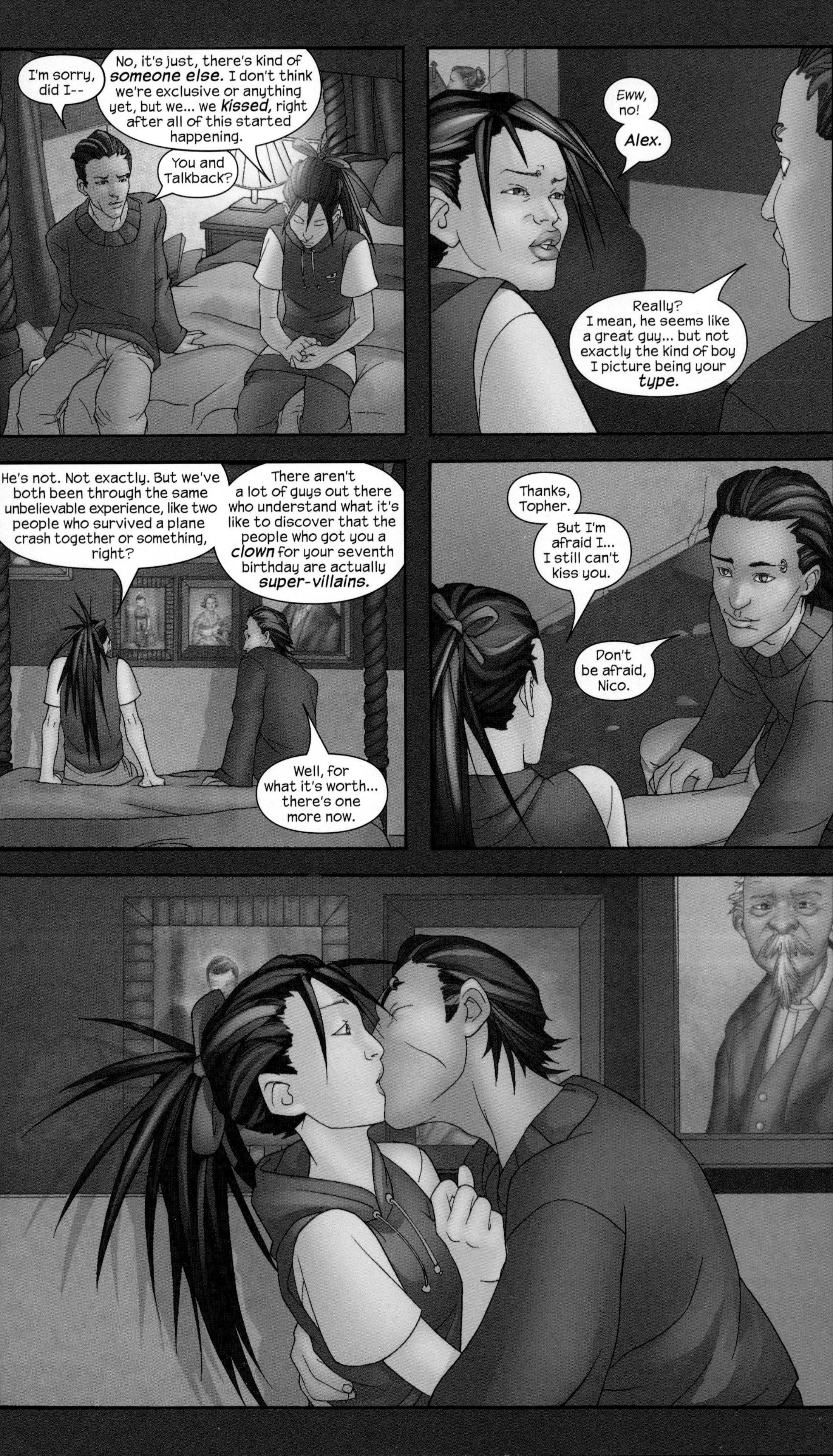
I'm sorry, did I--
No, it's just, there's kind of *someone else.* I don't think we're exclusive or anything yet, but we... we *kissed,* right after all of this started happening.
You and Talkback?
Eww, no!
Alex.
Really? I mean, he seems like a great guy... but not exactly the kind of boy I picture being your *type.*
He's not. Not exactly. But we've both been through the same unbelievable experience, like two people who survived a plane crash together or something, right?
There aren't a lot of guys out there who understand what it's like to discover that the people who got you a *clown* for your seventh birthday are actually *super-villains.*
Well, for what it's worth... there's one more now.
Thanks, Topher.
But I'm afraid I... I still can't kiss you.
Don't be afraid, Nico.

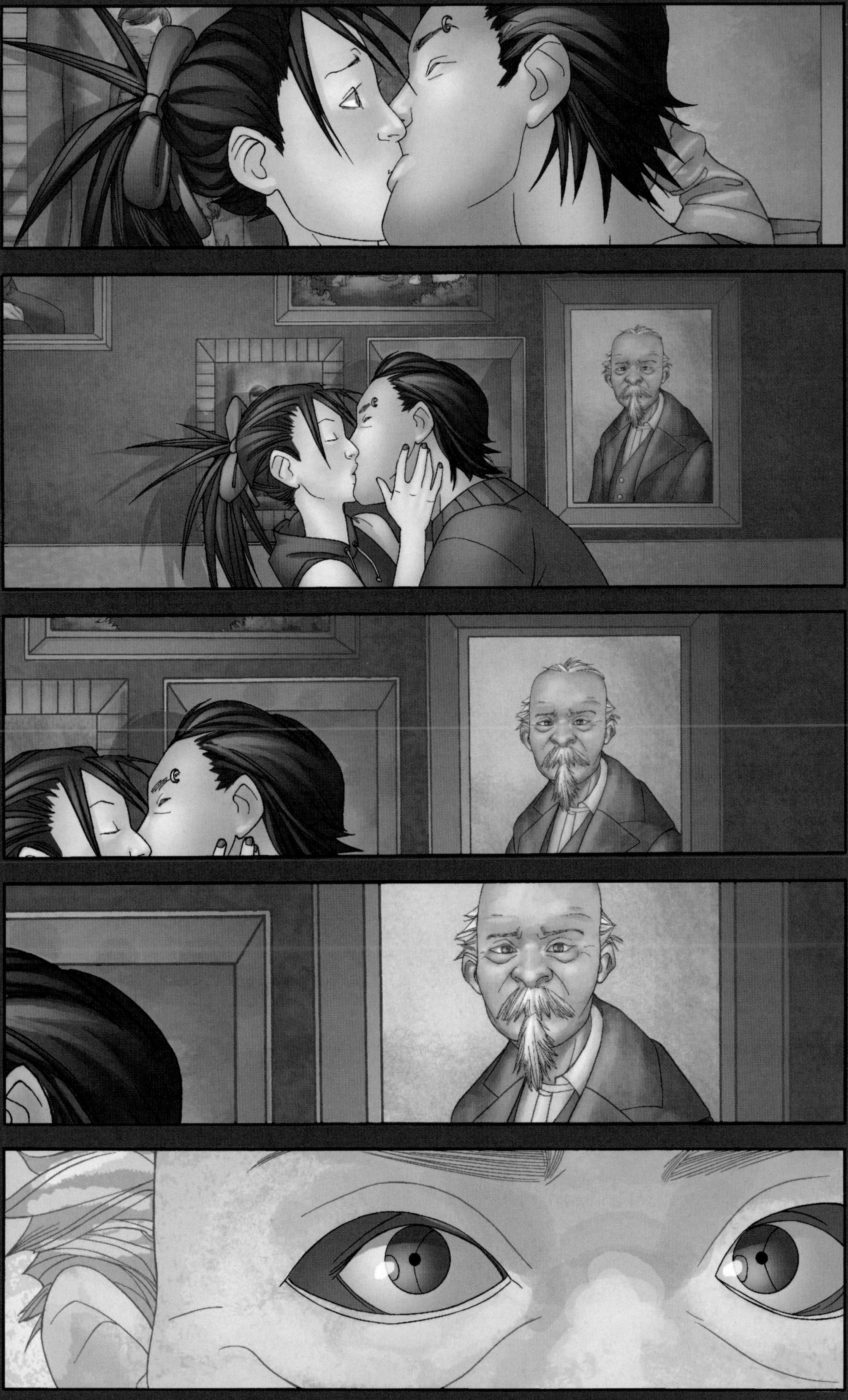

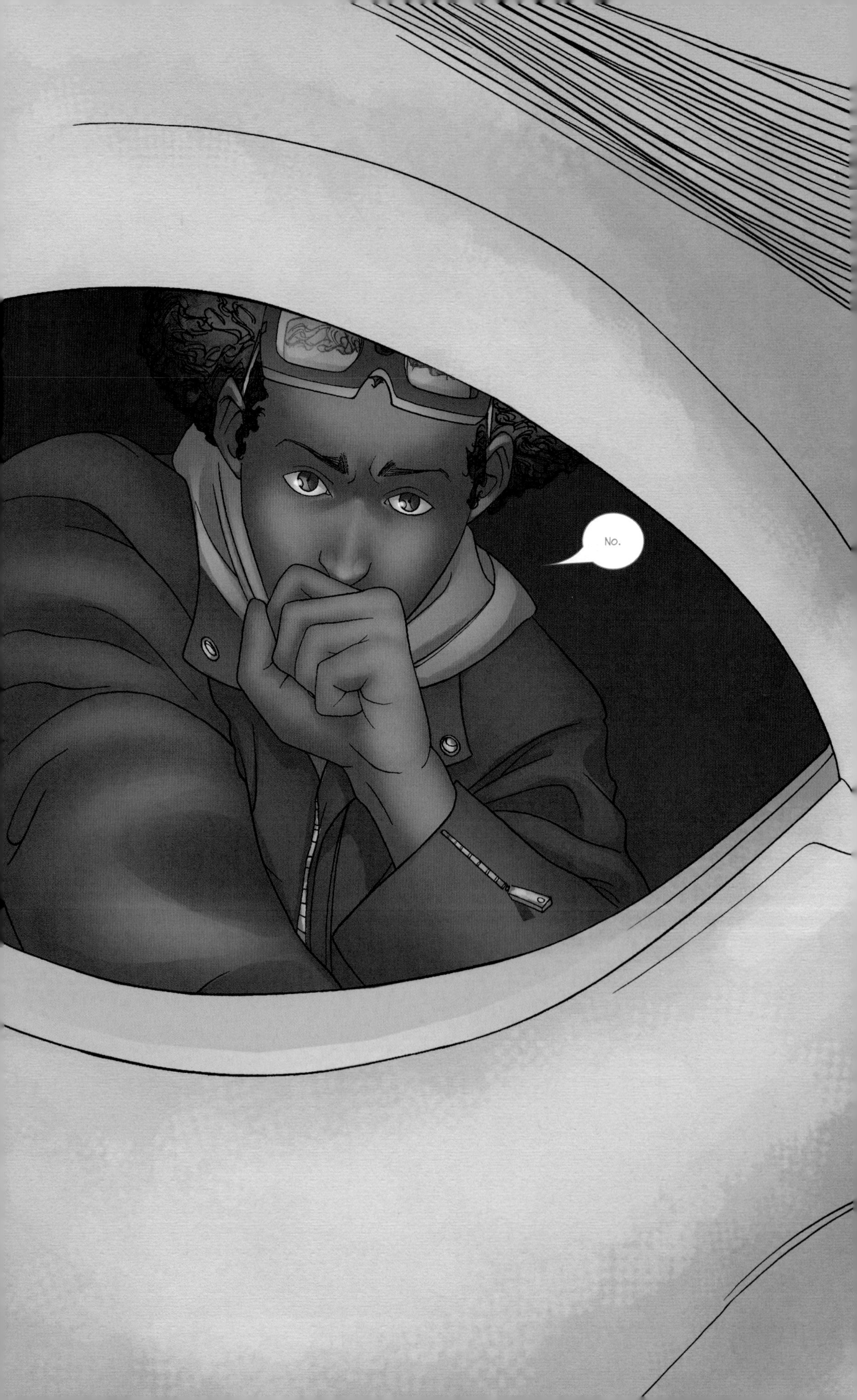
No.

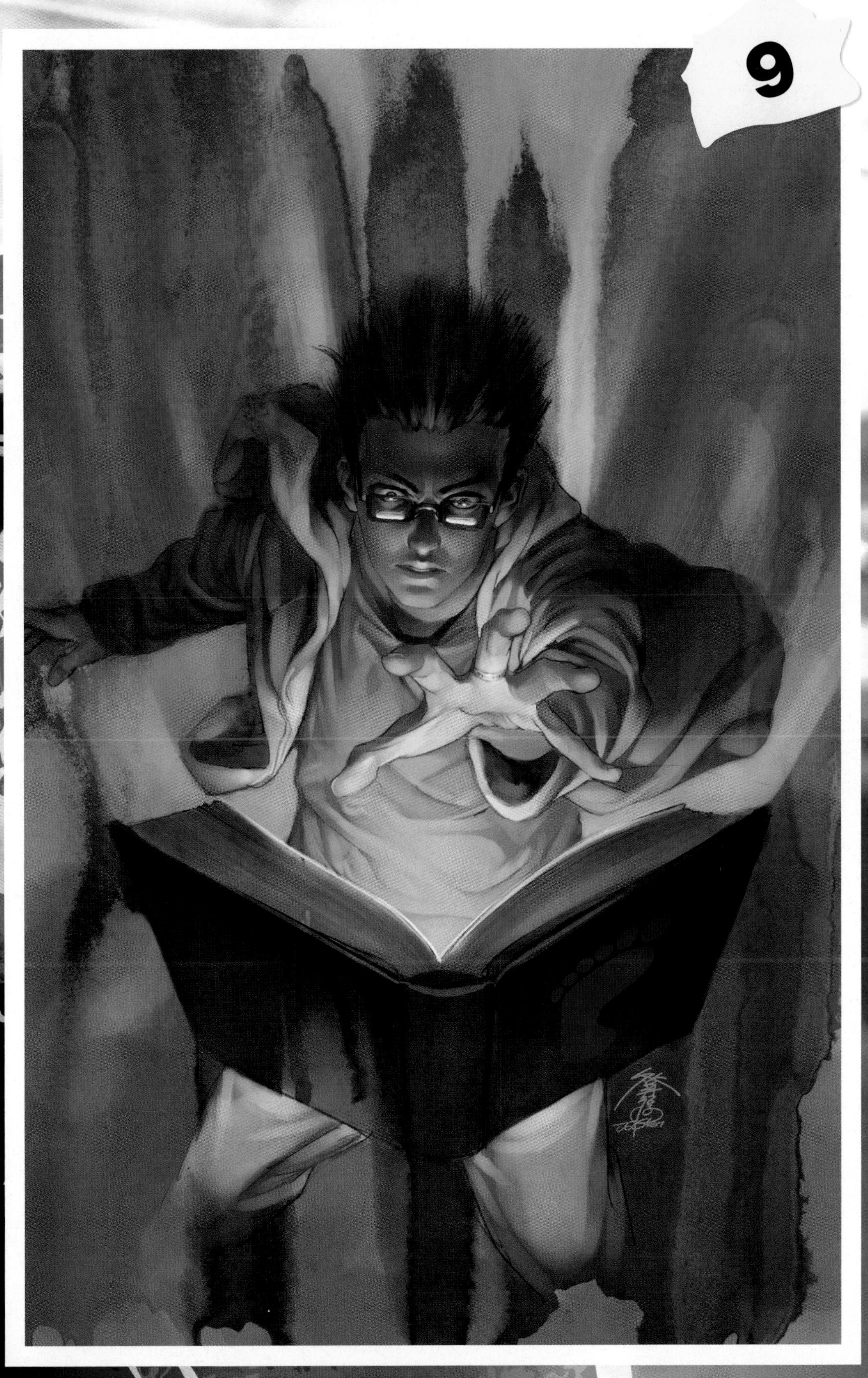
9

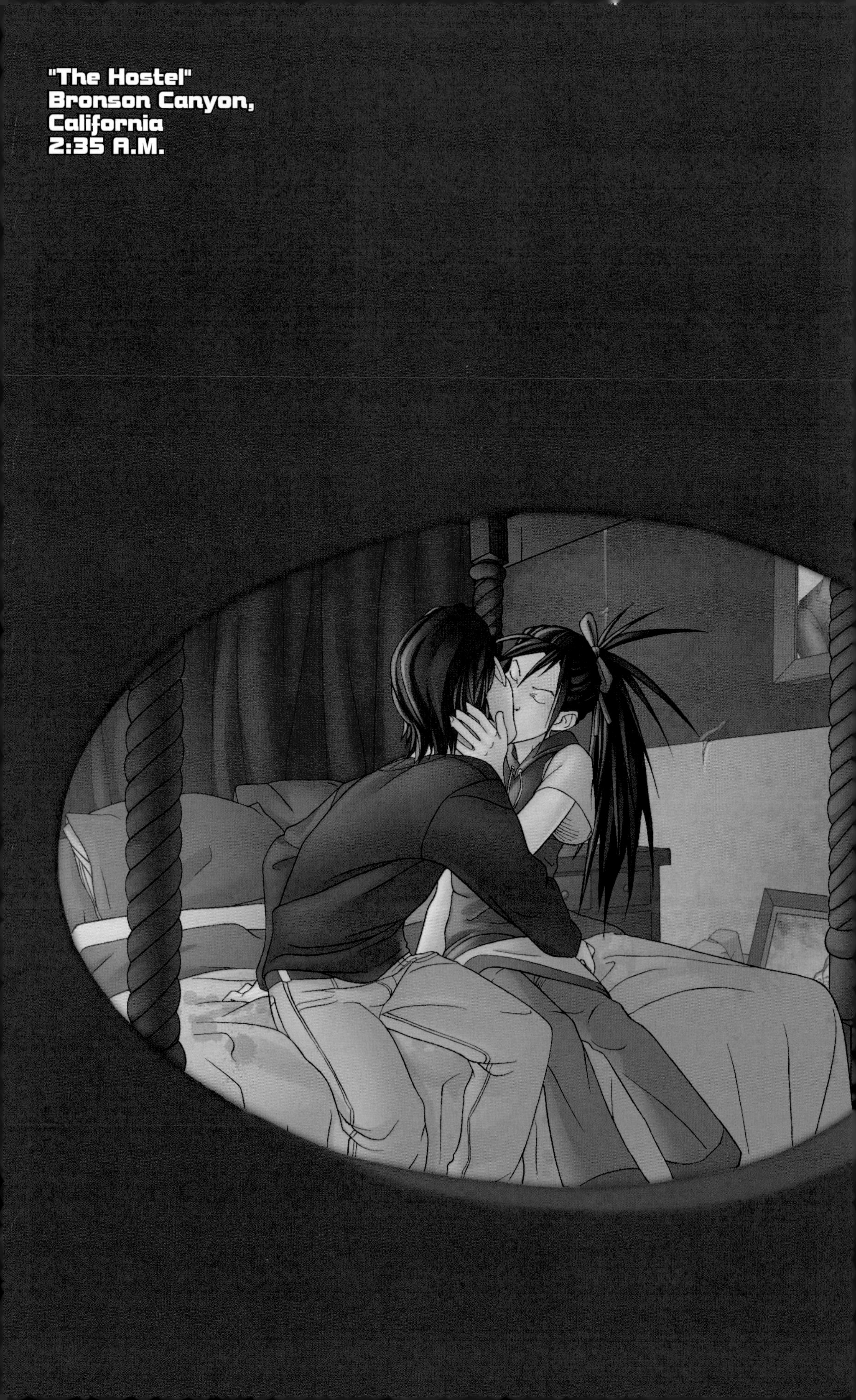
"The Hostel"
Bronson Canyon,
California
2:35 A.M.

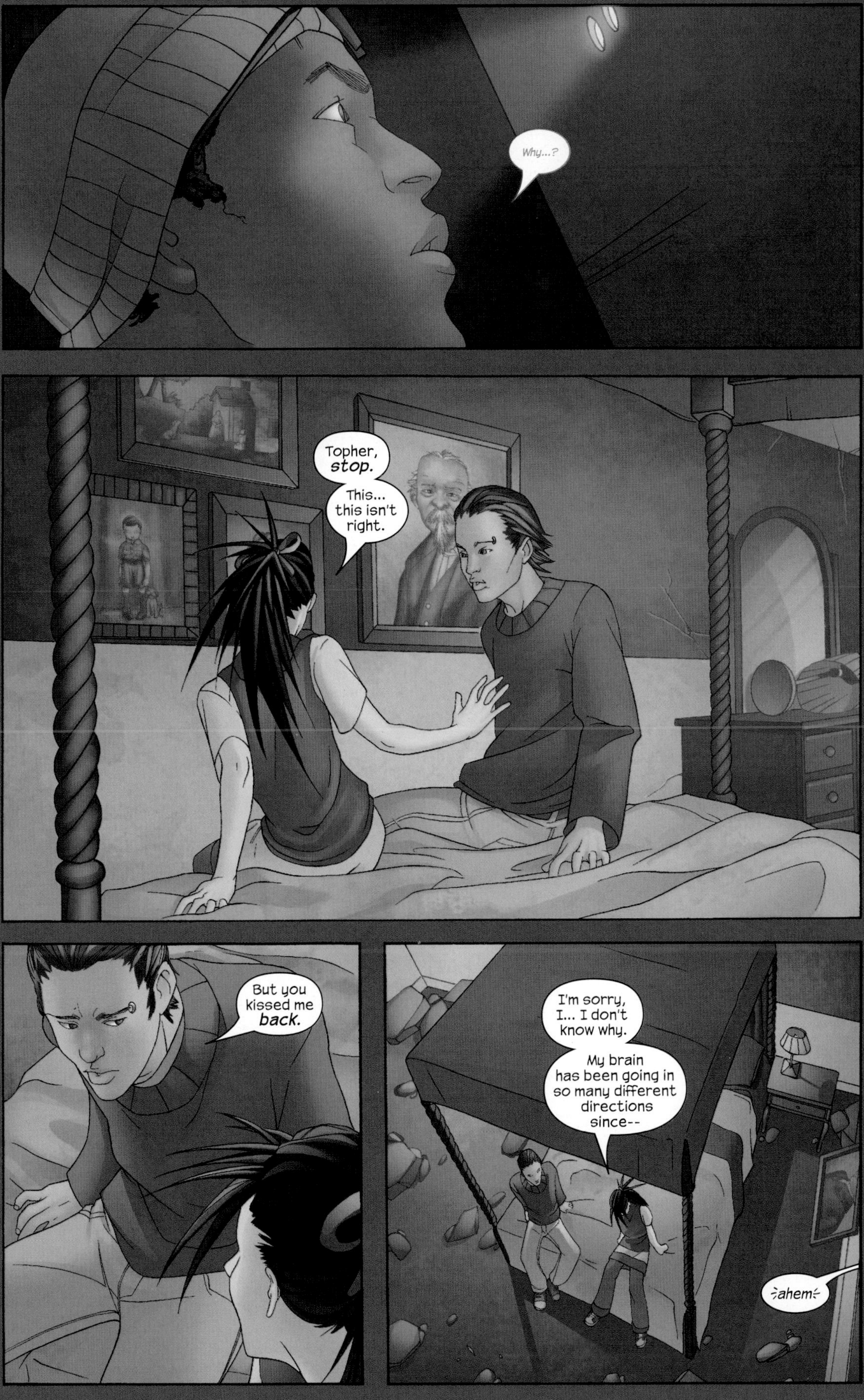
Why...?
Topher, *stop.*
This... this isn't right.
But you kissed me *back.*
I'm sorry, I... I don't know why.
My brain has been going in so many different directions since--
ahem

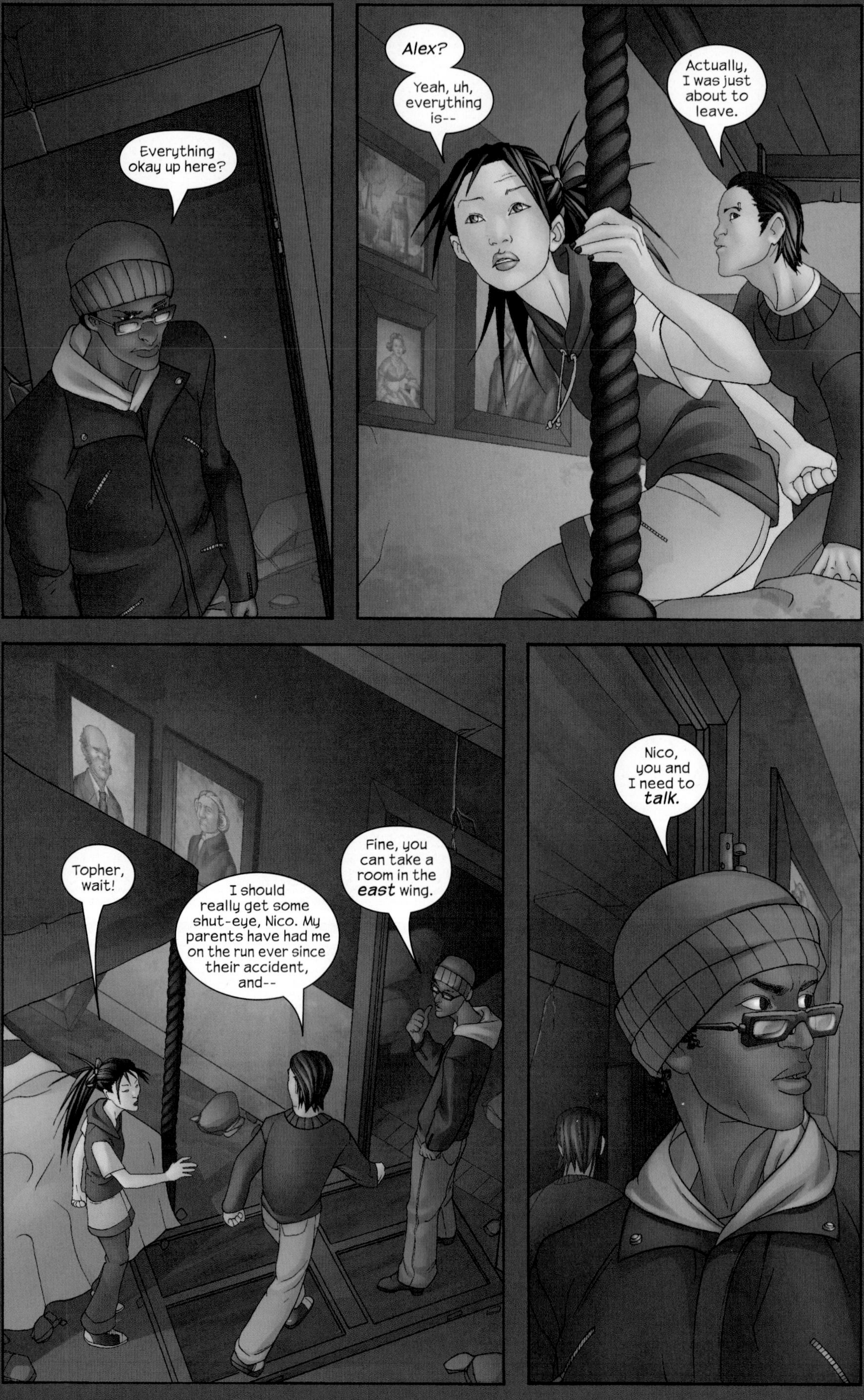
Everything okay up here?
Alex?
Yeah, uh, everything is--
Actually, I was just about to leave.
Topher, wait!
I should really get some shut-eye, Nico. My parents have had me on the run ever since their accident, and--
Fine, you can take a room in the *east* wing.
Nico, you and I need to *talk.*

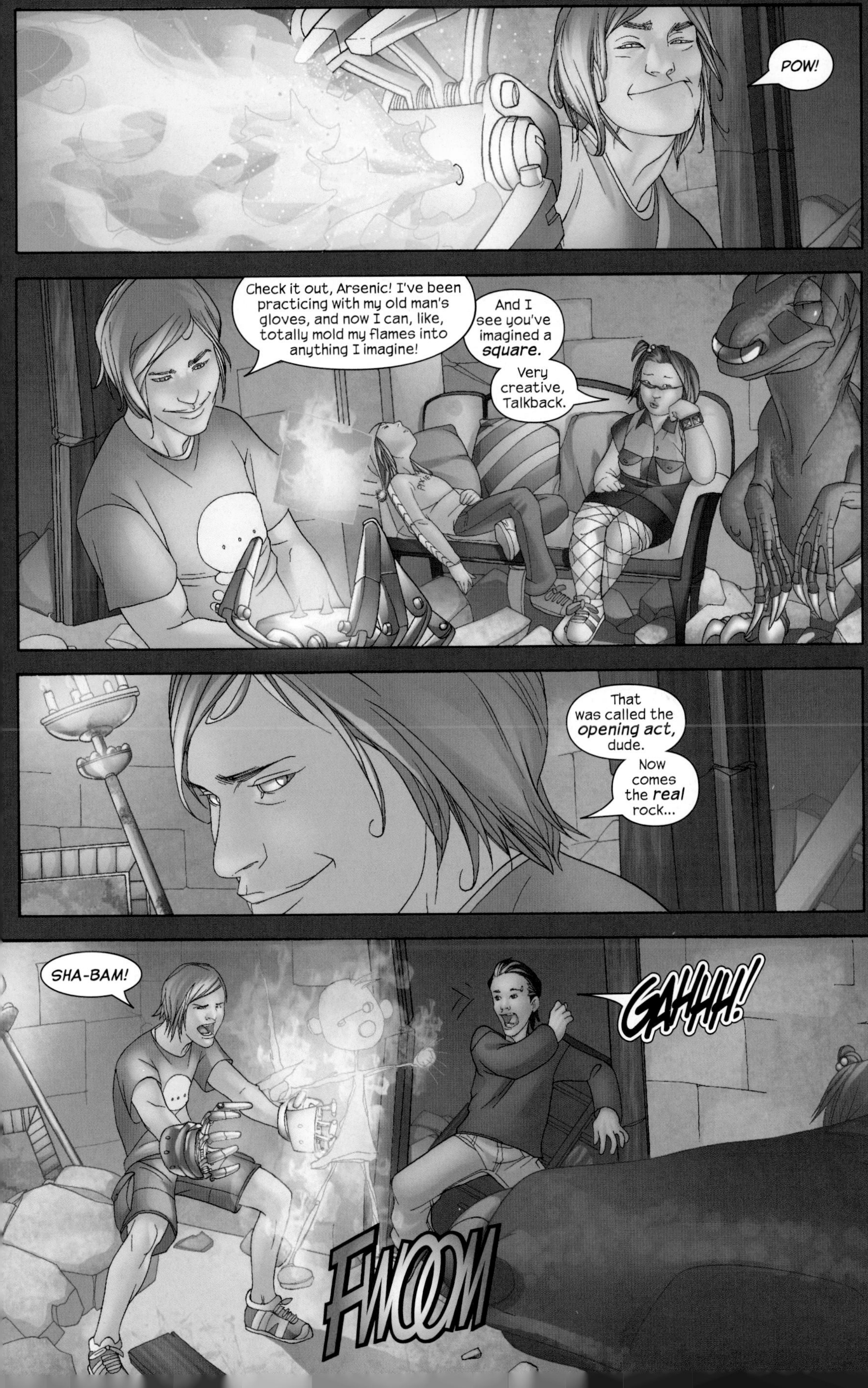
POW!
Check it out, Arsenic! I've been practicing with my old man's gloves, and now I can, like, totally mold my flames into anything I imagine!
And I see you've imagined a **square.**
Very creative, Talkback.
That was called the *opening act,* dude.
Now comes the *real* rock...
SHA-BAM!
GAHHH!
FWOOM

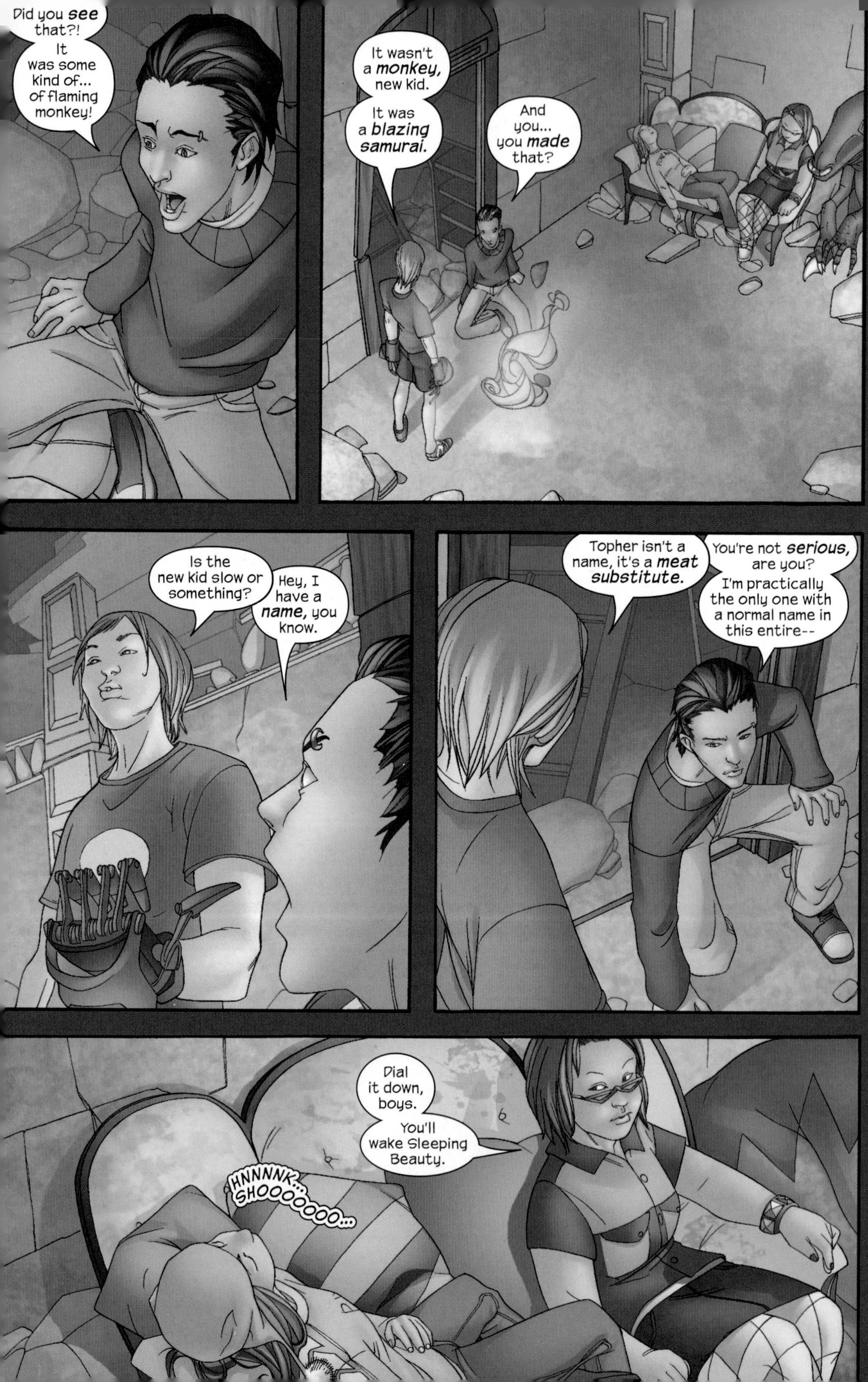
Did you see that?! It was some kind of... of flaming monkey!
It wasn't a monkey, new kid.
It was a blazing samurai.
And you... you made that?
Is the new kid slow or something?
Hey, I have a name, you know.
Topher isn't a name, it's a meat substitute.
You're not serious, are you?
I'm practically the only one with a normal name in this entire--
Dial it down, boys.
You'll wake Sleeping Beauty.
HNNNNK... SHOOOOOOO...

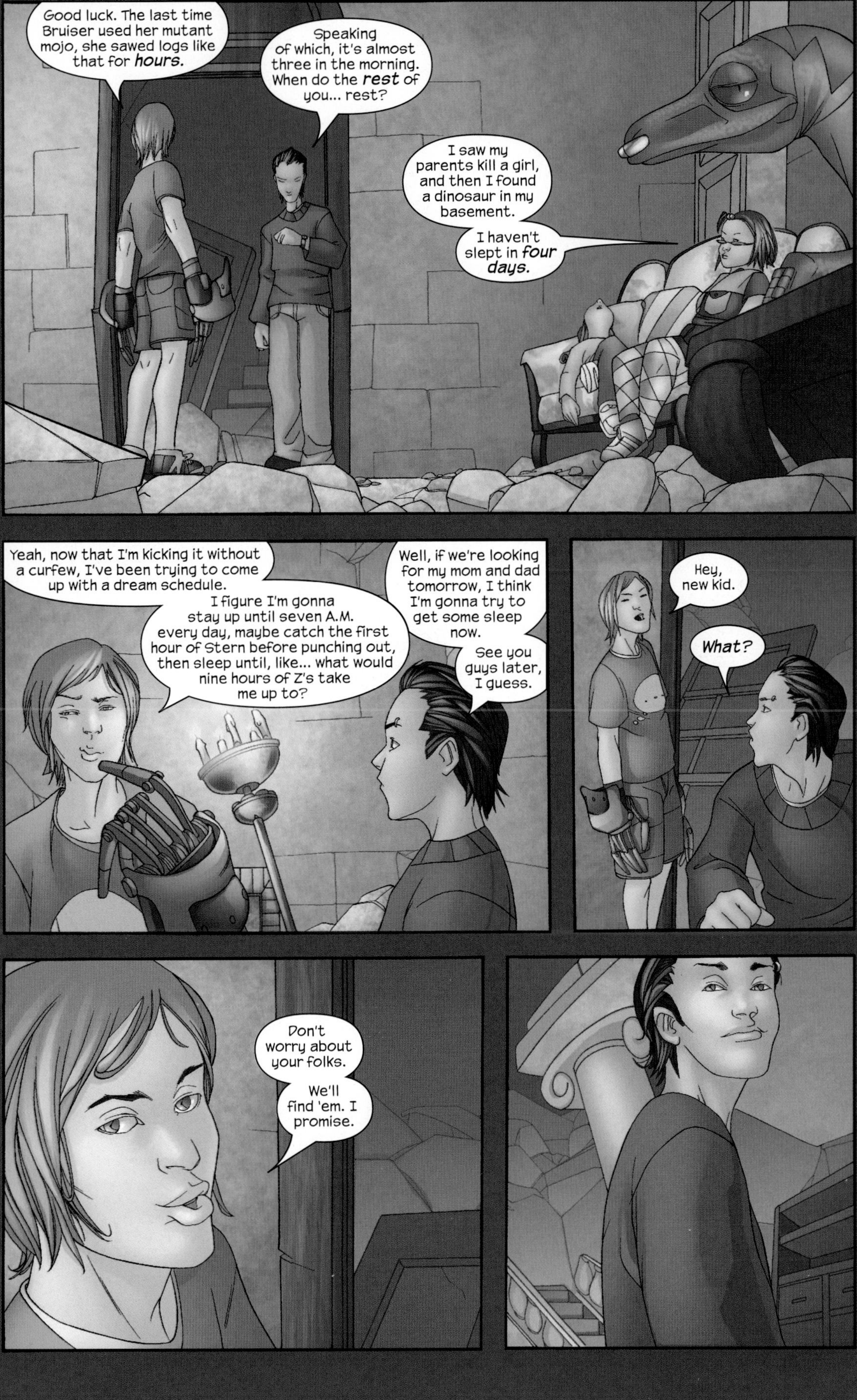
Good luck. The last time Bruiser used her mutant mojo, she sawed logs like that for *hours.*
Speaking of which, it's almost three in the morning. When do the *rest* of you... rest?
I saw my parents kill a girl, and then I found a dinosaur in my basement.
I haven't slept in *four days.*
Yeah, now that I'm kicking it without a curfew, I've been trying to come up with a dream schedule.
I figure I'm gonna stay up until seven A.M. every day, maybe catch the first hour of Stern before punching out, then sleep until, like... what would nine hours of Z's take me up to?
Well, if we're looking for my mom and dad tomorrow, I think I'm gonna try to get some sleep now.
See you guys later, I guess.
Hey, new kid.
What?
Don't worry about your folks.
We'll find 'em. I promise.

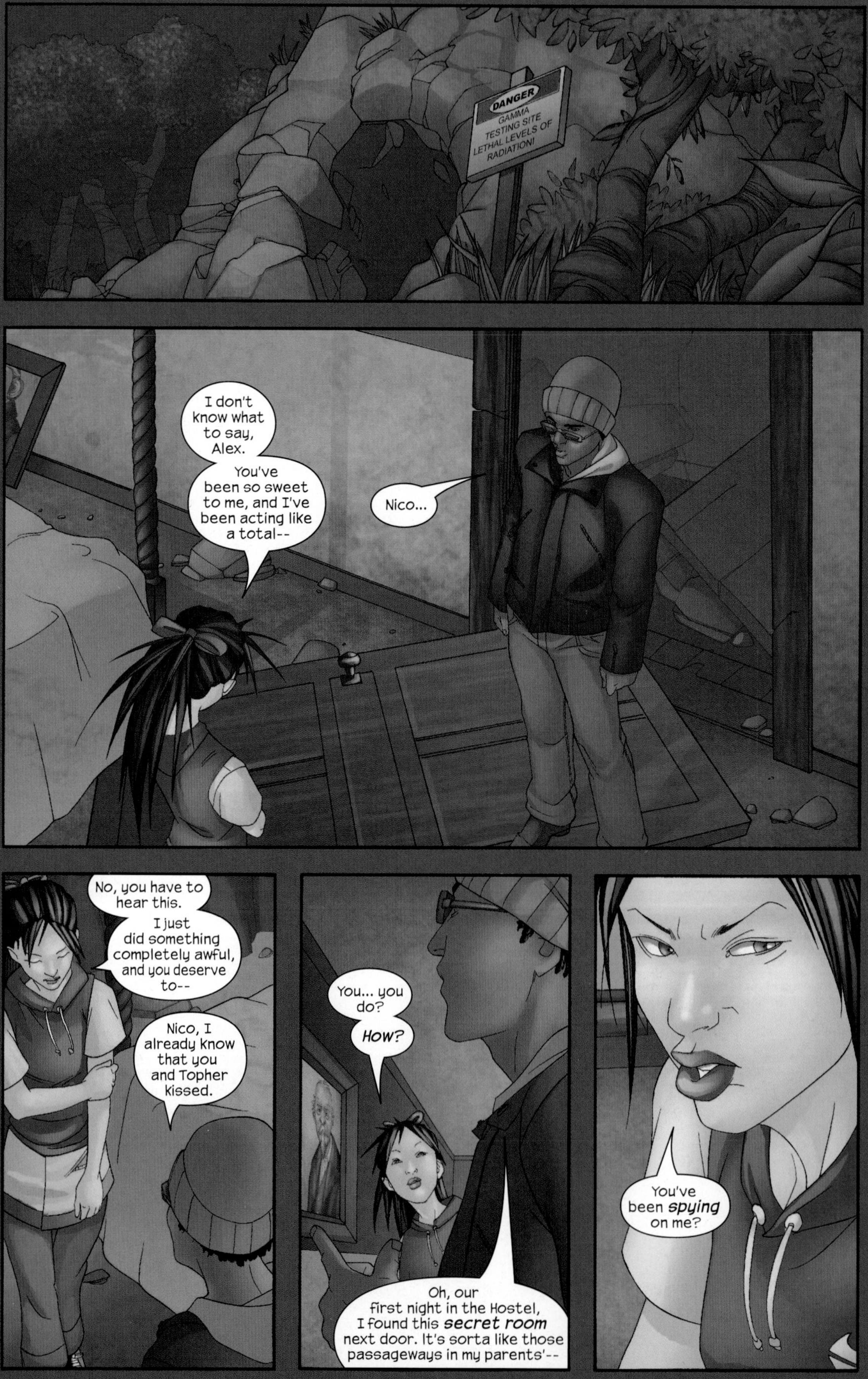
DANGER
GAMMA TESTING SITE
LETHAL LEVELS OF RADIATION!
I don't know what to say, Alex.
You've been so sweet to me, and I've been acting like a total--
Nico...
No, you have to hear this.
I just did something completely awful, and you deserve to--
Nico, I already know that you and Topher kissed.
You... you do?
HOW?
Oh, our first night in the Hostel, I found this secret room next door. It's sorta like those passageways in my parents'--
You've been spying on me?

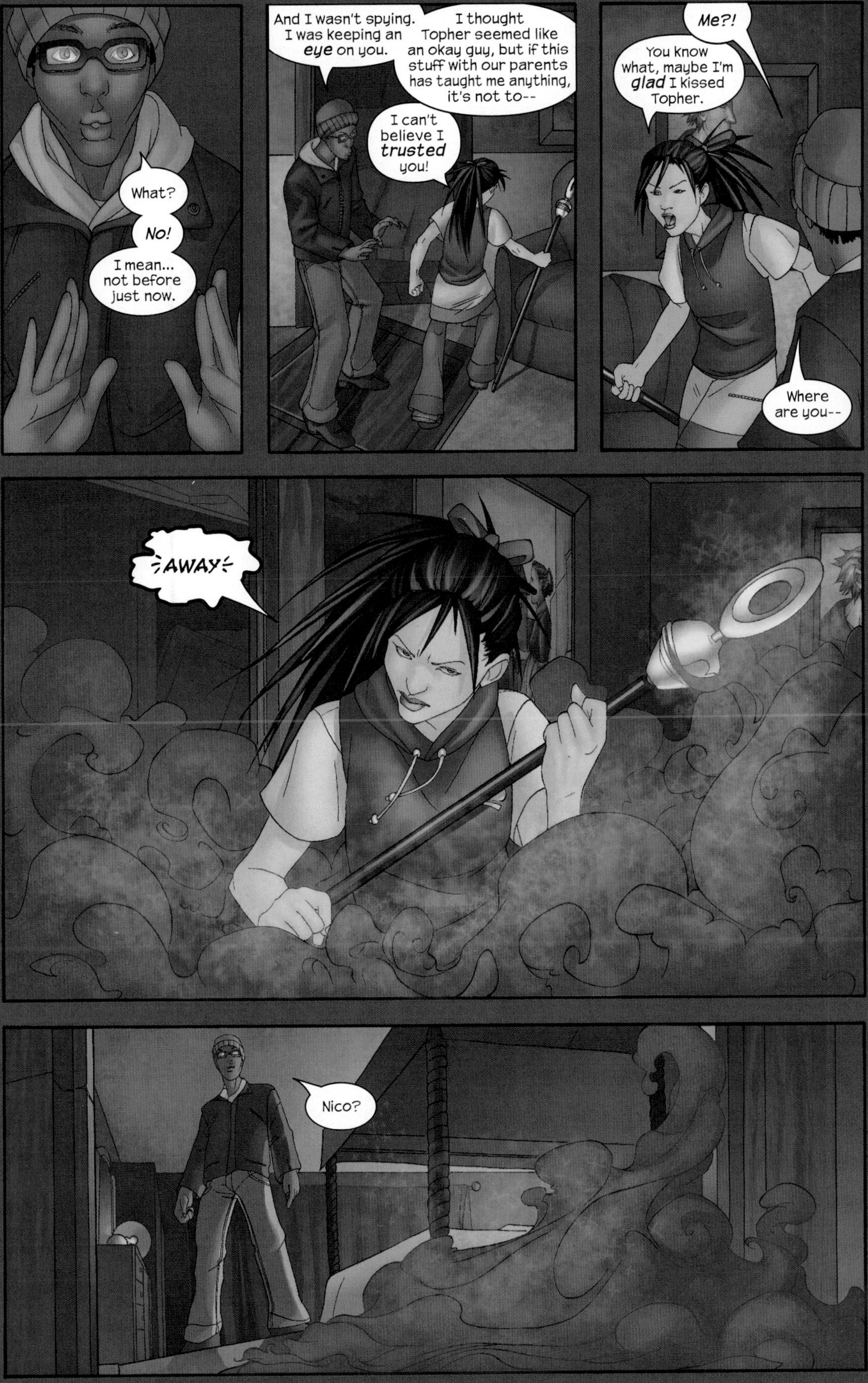
What?
No!
I mean... not before just now.
And I wasn't spying. I was keeping an eye on you.
I thought Topher seemed like an okay guy, but if this stuff with our parents has taught me anything, it's not to--
I can't believe I trusted you!
Me?!
You know what, maybe I'm glad I kissed Topher.
Where are you--
AWAY
Nico?

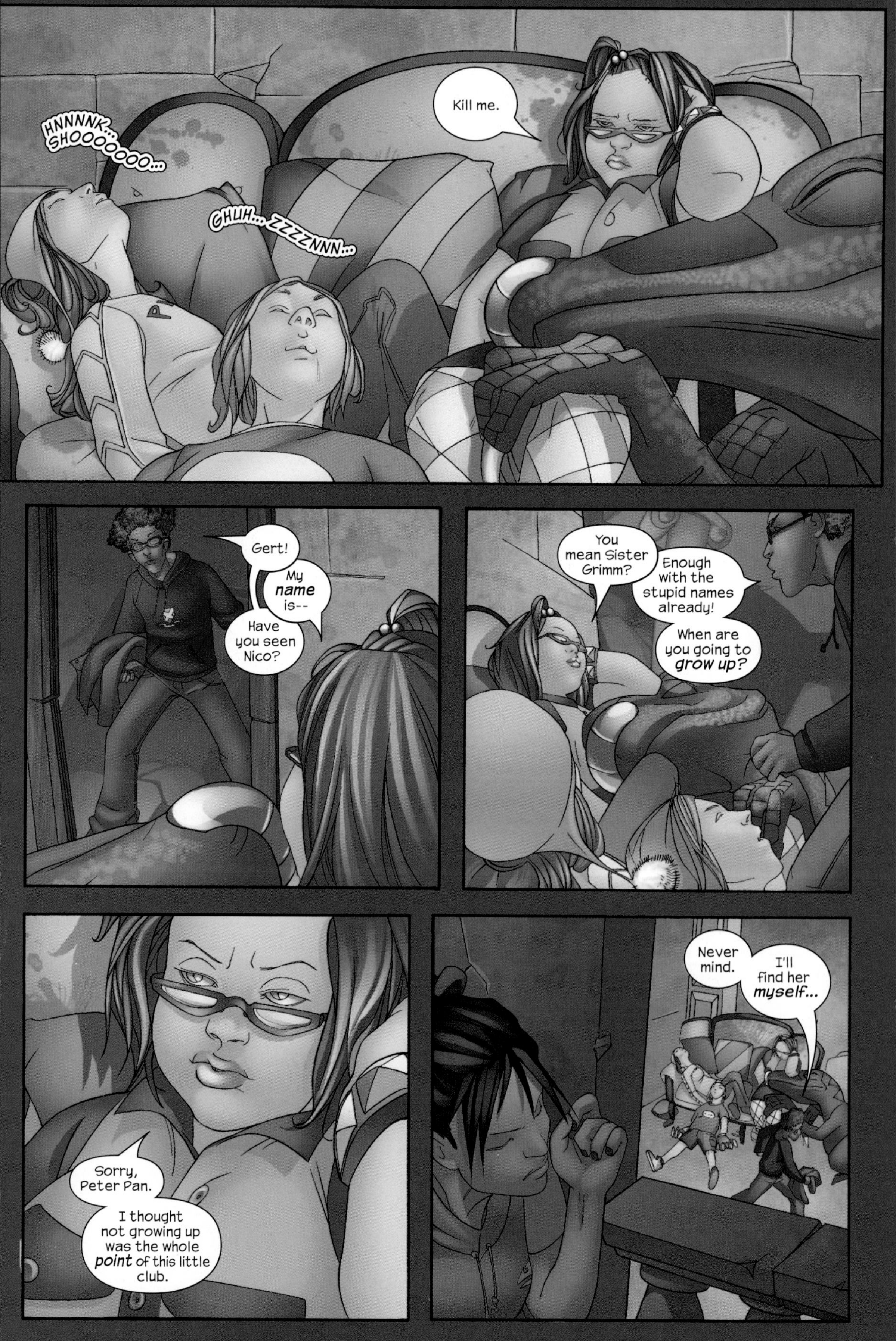
Kill me.
HNNNNK... SHOOOOOOO...
GHUH... ZZZZNNN...
Gert!
My *name* is--
Have you seen Nico?
You mean Sister Grimm?
Enough with the stupid names already!
When are you going to *grow up?*
Sorry, Peter Pan.
I thought not growing up was the whole *point* of this little club.
Never mind.
I'll find her *myself...*

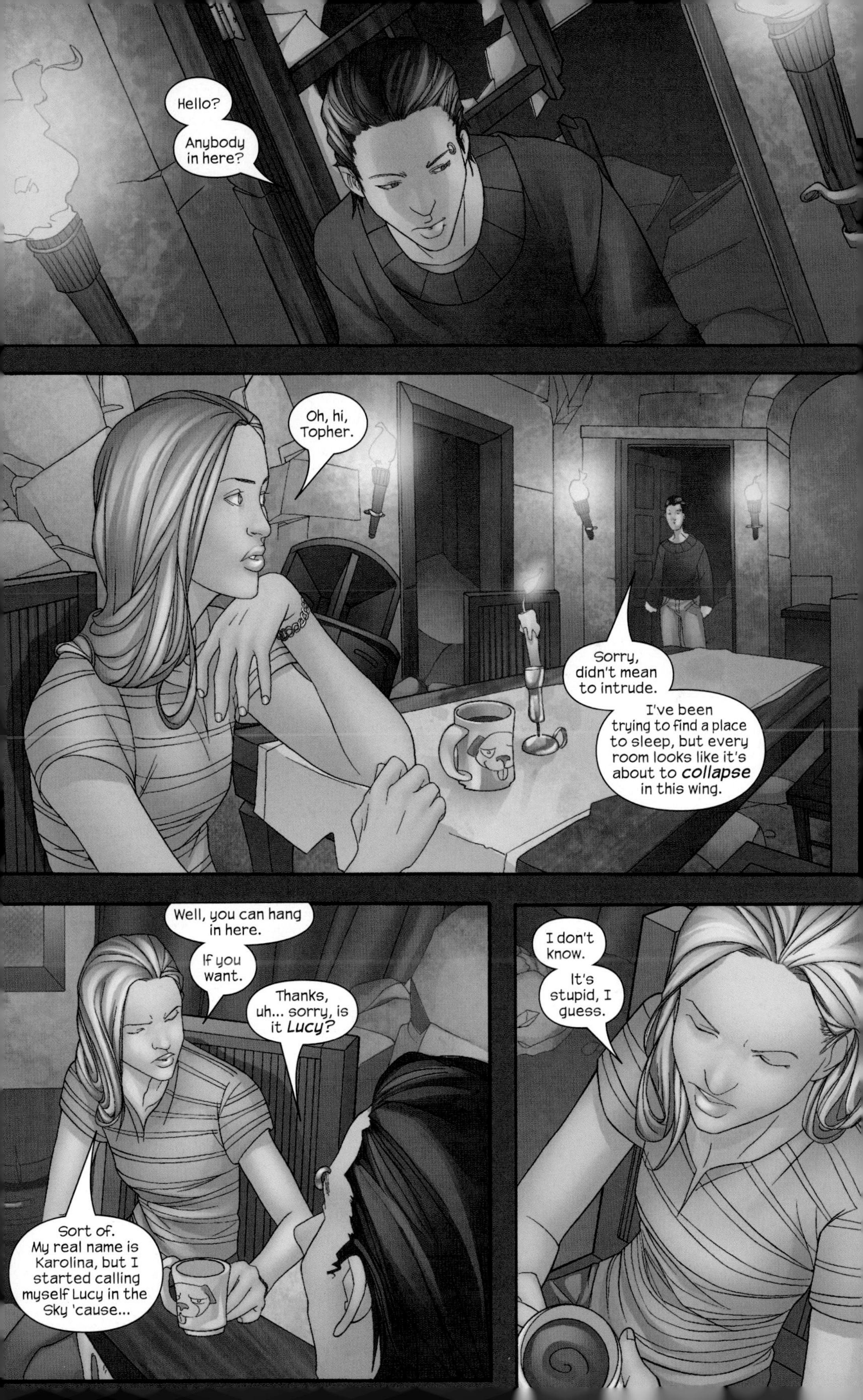
Hello?
Anybody in here?
Oh, hi, Topher.
Sorry, didn't mean to intrude.
I've been trying to find a place to sleep, but every room looks like it's about to *collapse* in this wing.
Well, you can hang in here.
If you want.
Thanks, uh... sorry, is it *Lucy?*
Sort of. My real name is Karolina, but I started calling myself Lucy in the Sky 'cause...
I don't know.
It's stupid, I guess.

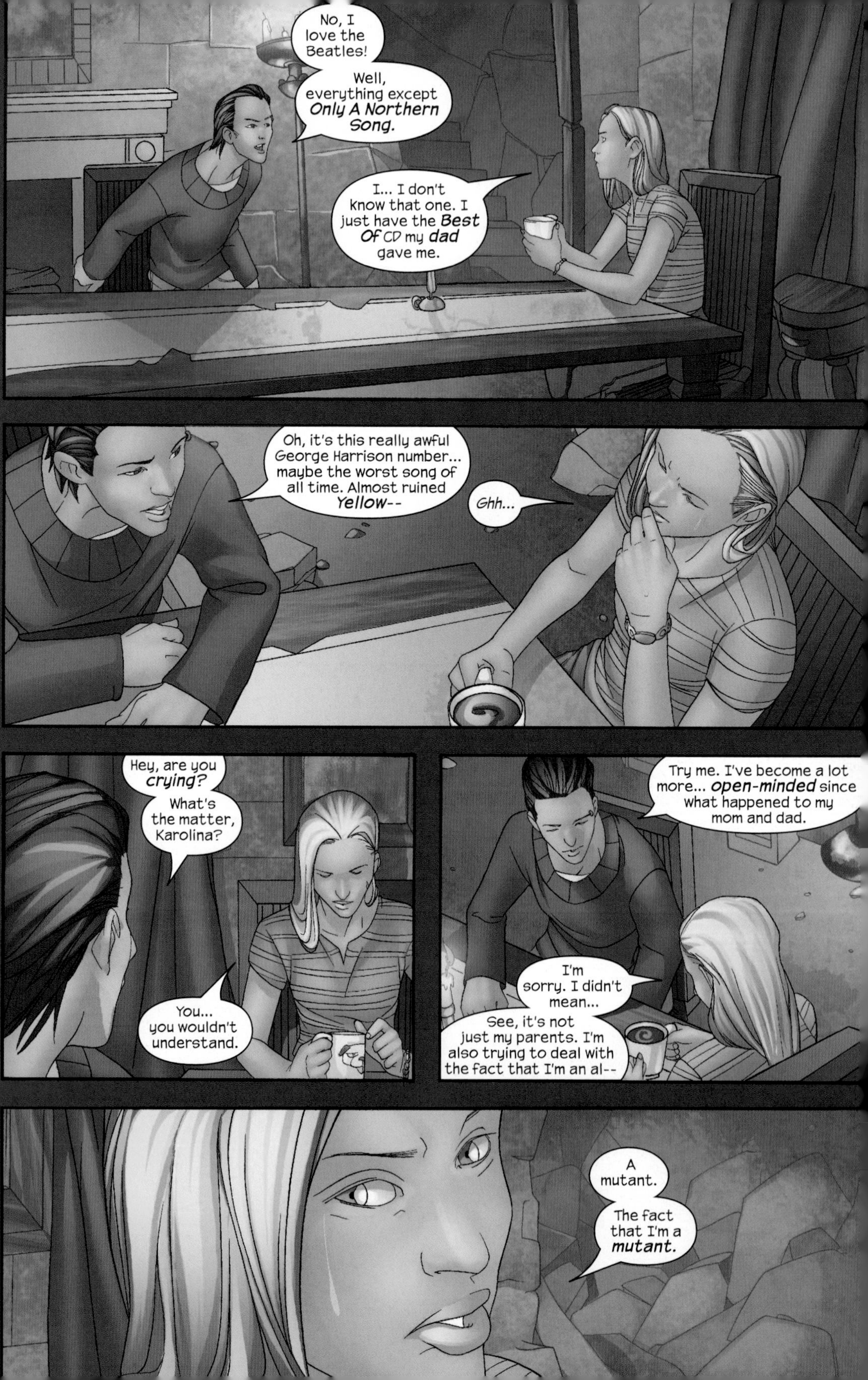
No, I love the Beatles!
Well, everything except *Only A Northern Song.*
I... I don't know that one. I just have the *Best Of* CD my *dad* gave me.
Oh, it's this really awful George Harrison number... maybe the worst song of all time. Almost ruined *Yellow*--
Ghh...
Hey, are you *crying?*
What's the matter, Karolina?
You... you wouldn't understand.
Try me. I've become a lot more... *open-minded* since what happened to my mom and dad.
I'm sorry. I didn't mean...
See, it's not just my parents. I'm also trying to deal with the fact that I'm an al--
A mutant.
The fact that I'm a *mutant.*

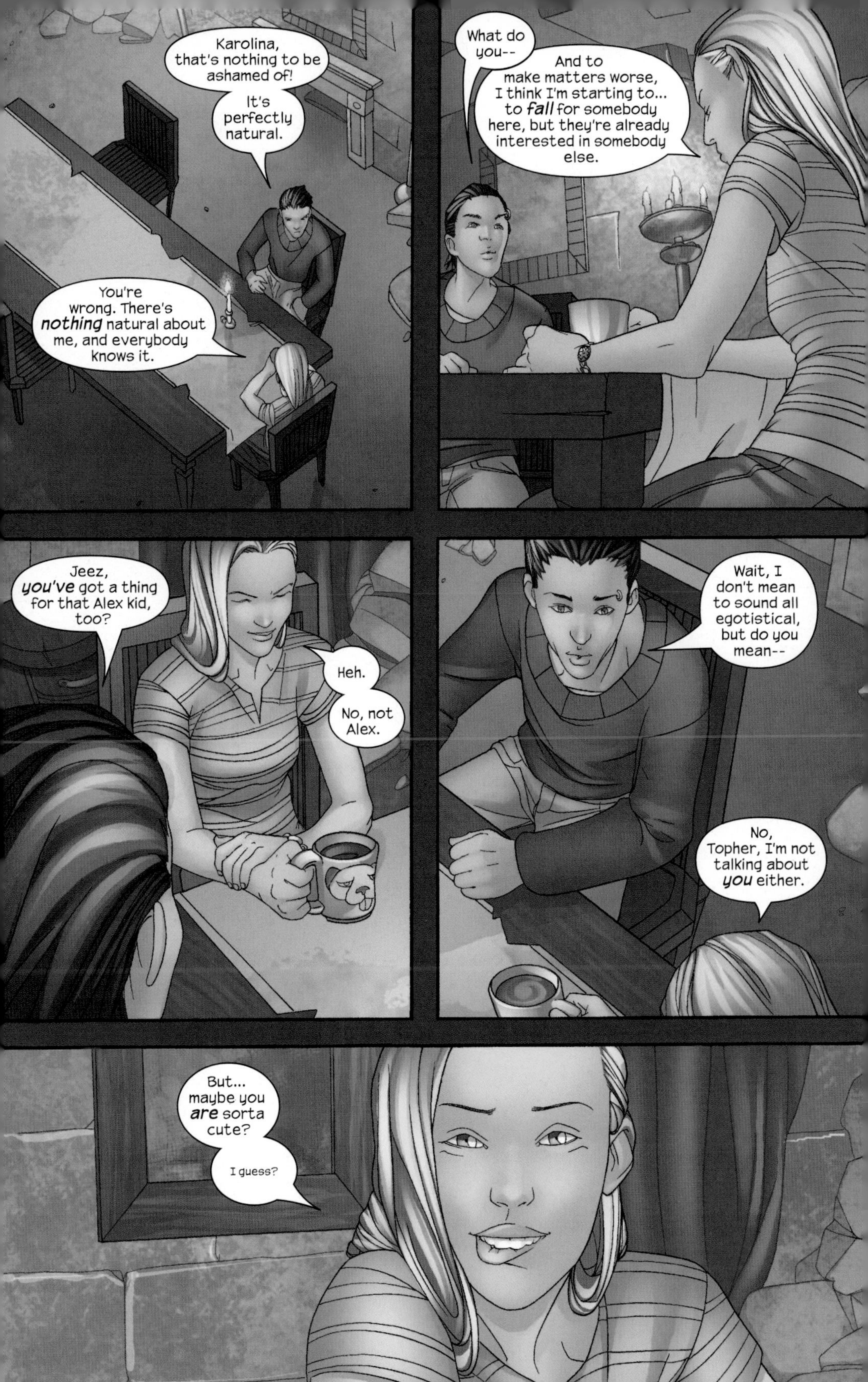

Karolina, that's nothing to be ashamed of!
It's perfectly natural.
You're wrong. There's *nothing* natural about me, and everybody knows it.
What do you--
And to make matters worse, I think I'm starting to... to *fall* for somebody here, but they're already interested in somebody else.
Jeez, *you've* got a thing for that Alex kid, too?
Heh.
No, not Alex.
Wait, I don't mean to sound all egotistical, but do you mean--
No, Topher, I'm not talking about *you* either.
But... maybe you *are* sorta cute?
I guess?

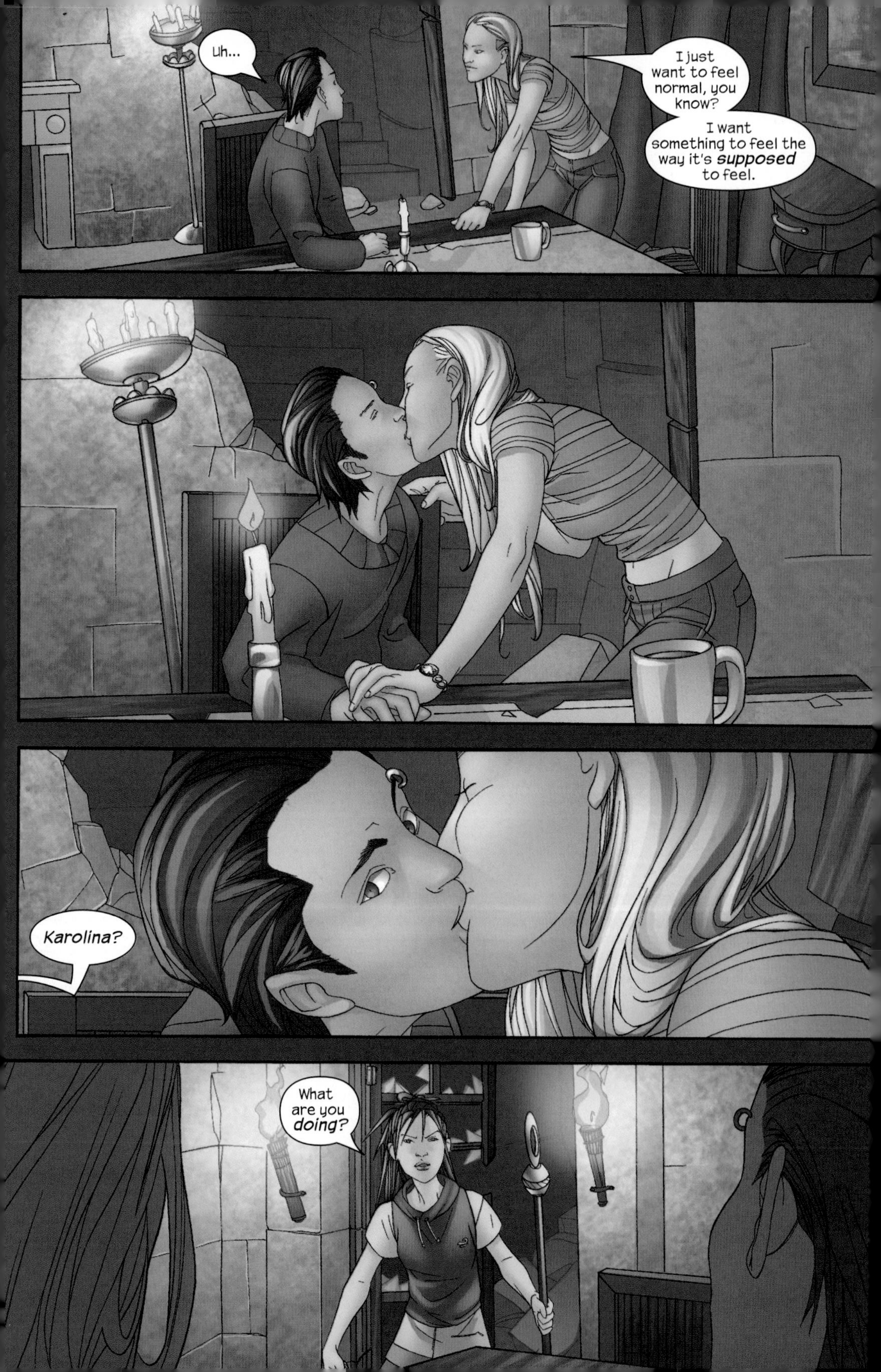
Uh...
I just want to feel normal, you know?
I want something to feel the way it's *supposed* to feel.
Karolina?
What are you *doing?*

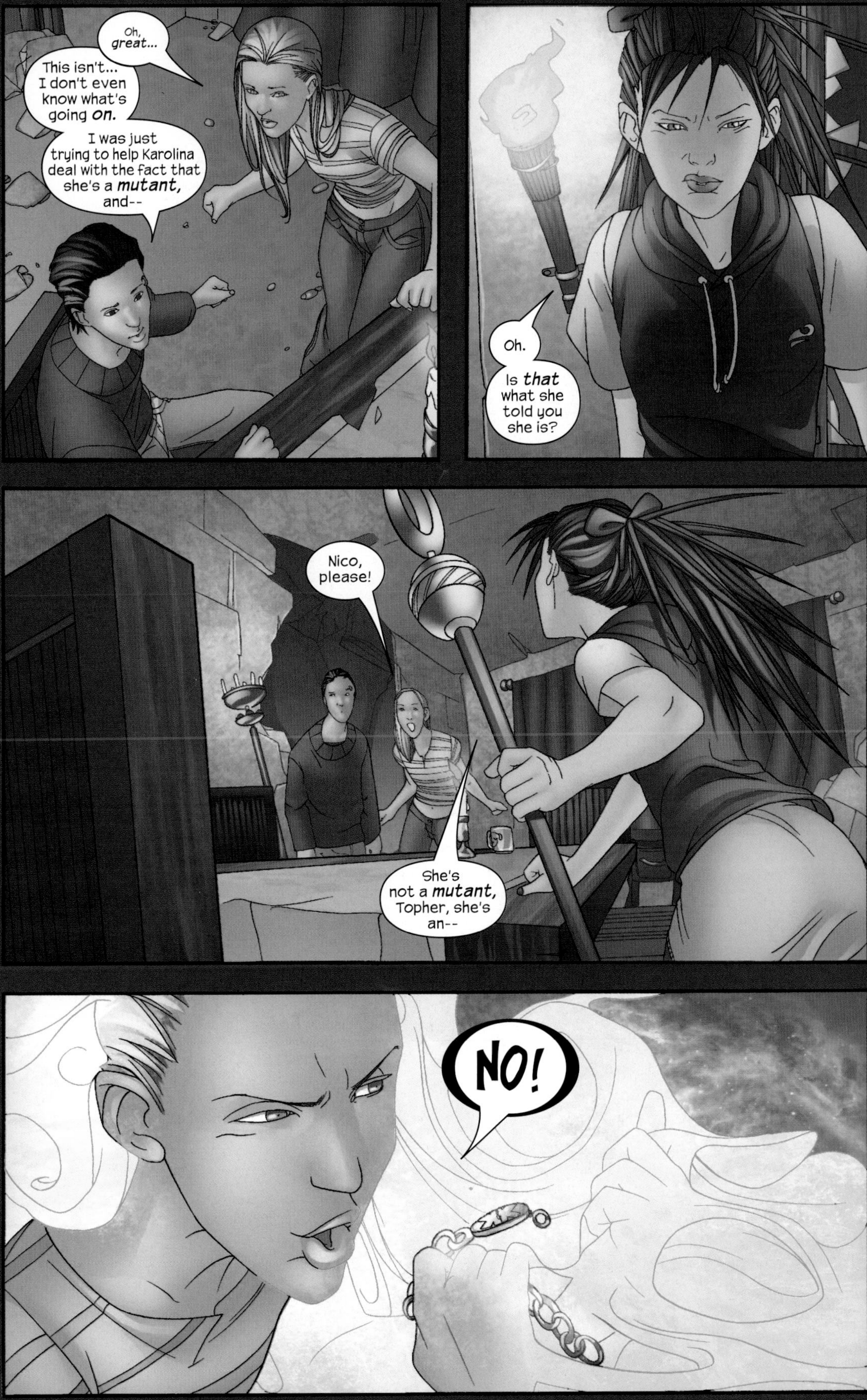
Oh, great...
This isn't... I don't even know what's going on.
I was just trying to help Karolina deal with the fact that she's a mutant, and--
Oh.
Is that what she told you she is?
Nico, please!
She's not a mutant, Topher, she's an--
NO!

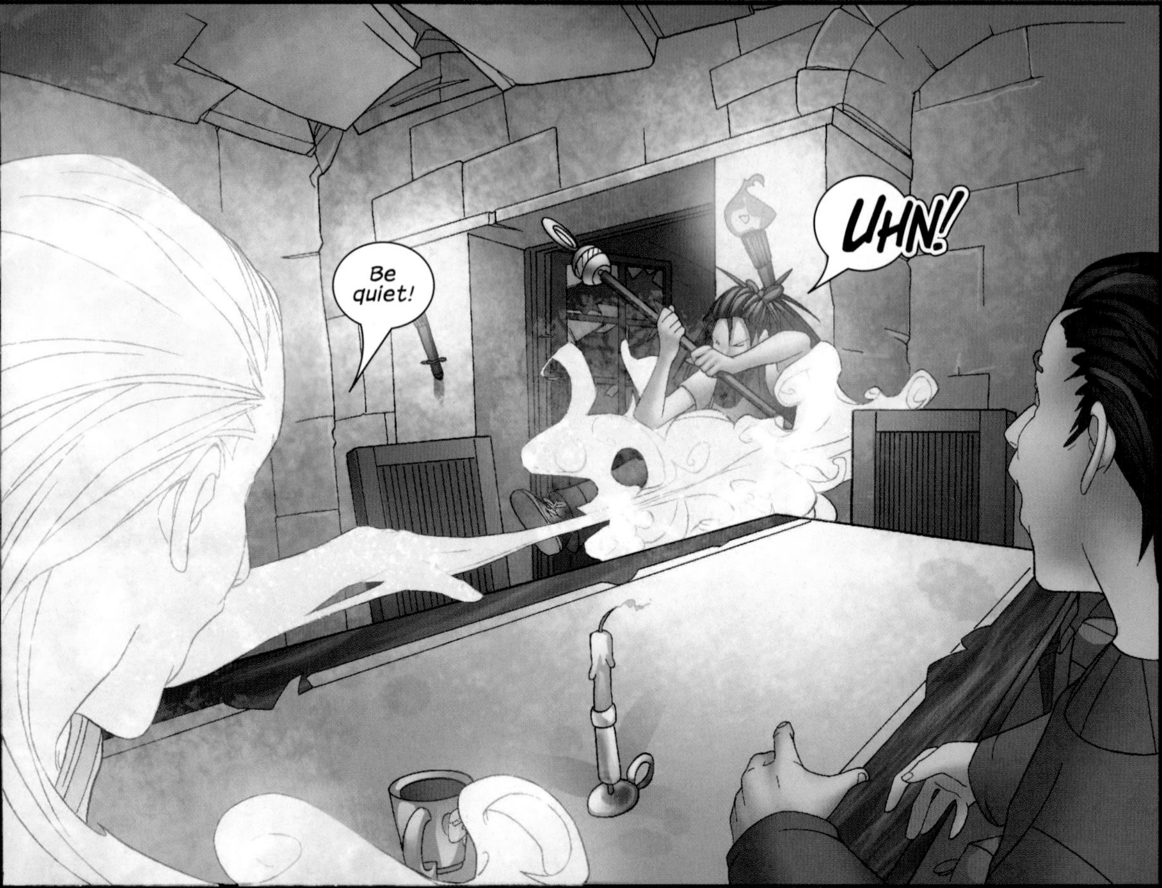
Be quiet!
UHN!
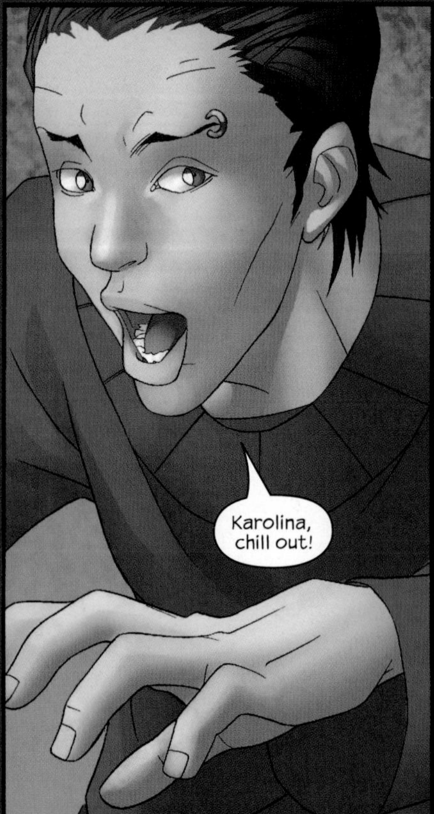
Karolina, chill out!
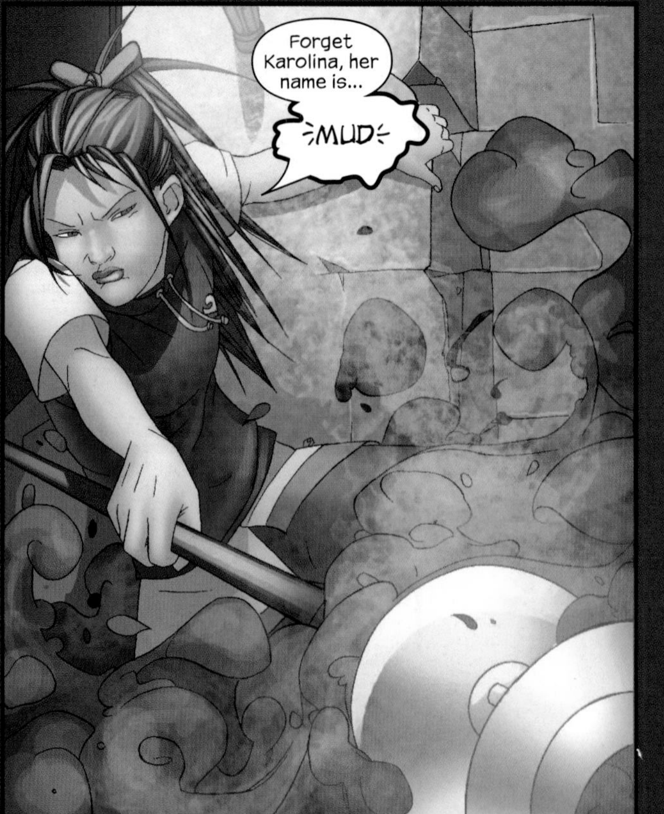
Forget Karolina, her name is...
MUD

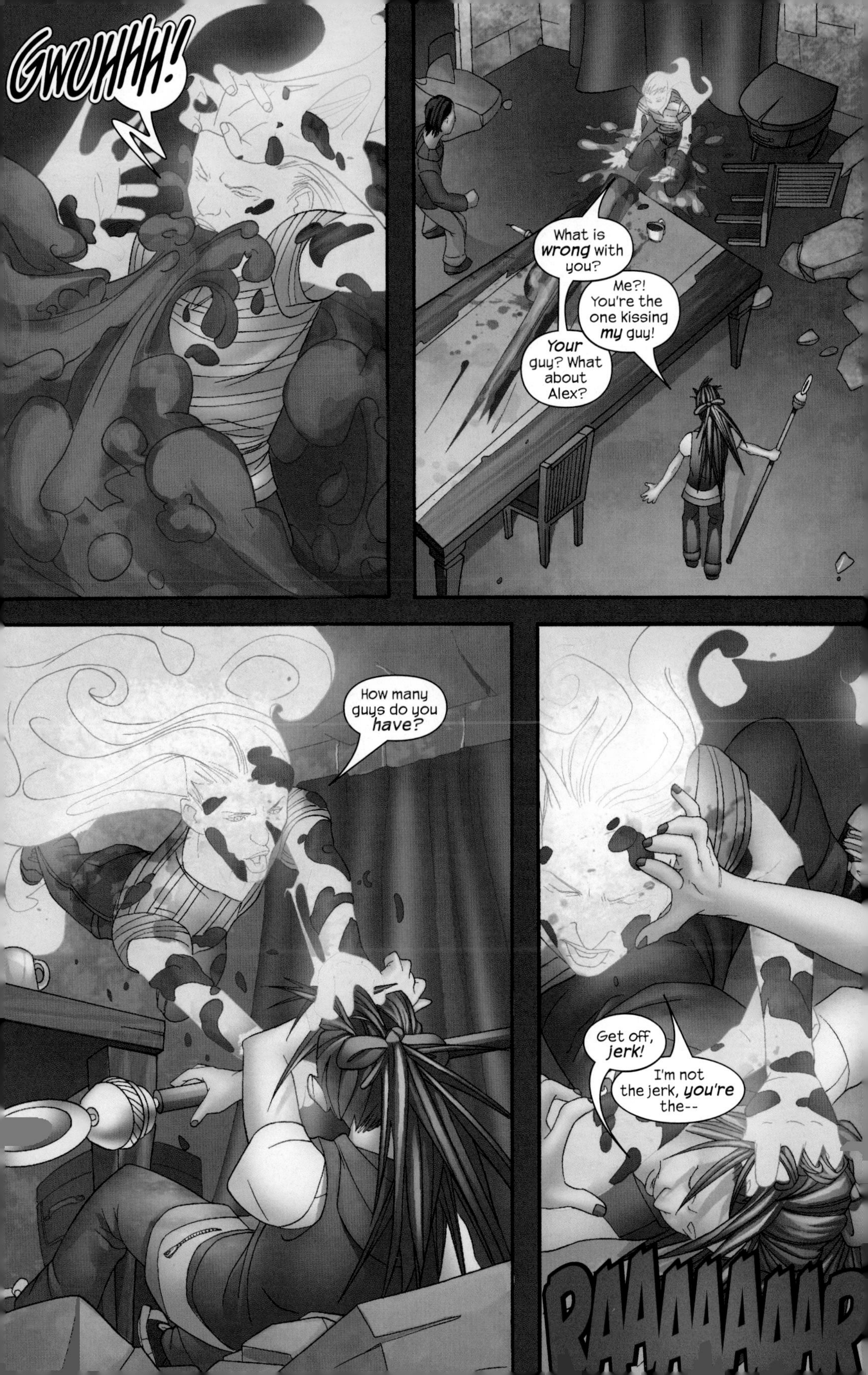
GWUHHH!
What is *wrong* with you?
Me?! You're the one kissing *my* guy!
Your guy? What about Alex?
How many guys do you *have?*
Get off, *jerk!*
I'm not the jerk, *you're* the--
RAAAAAAR

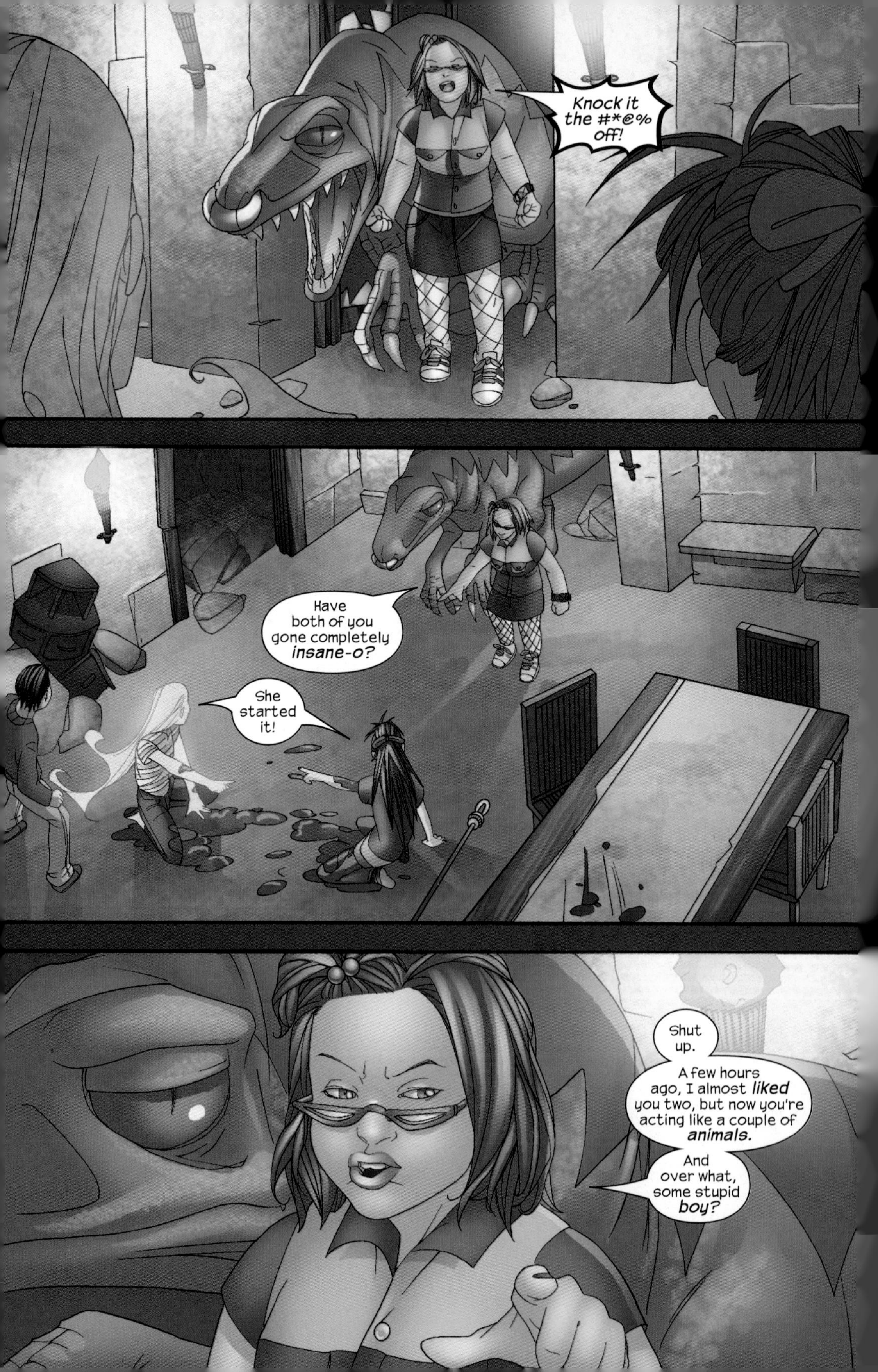
Knock it the #*@% off!
Have both of you gone completely insane-o?
She started it!
Shut up.
A few hours ago, I almost liked you two, but now you're acting like a couple of animals.
And over what, some stupid boy?

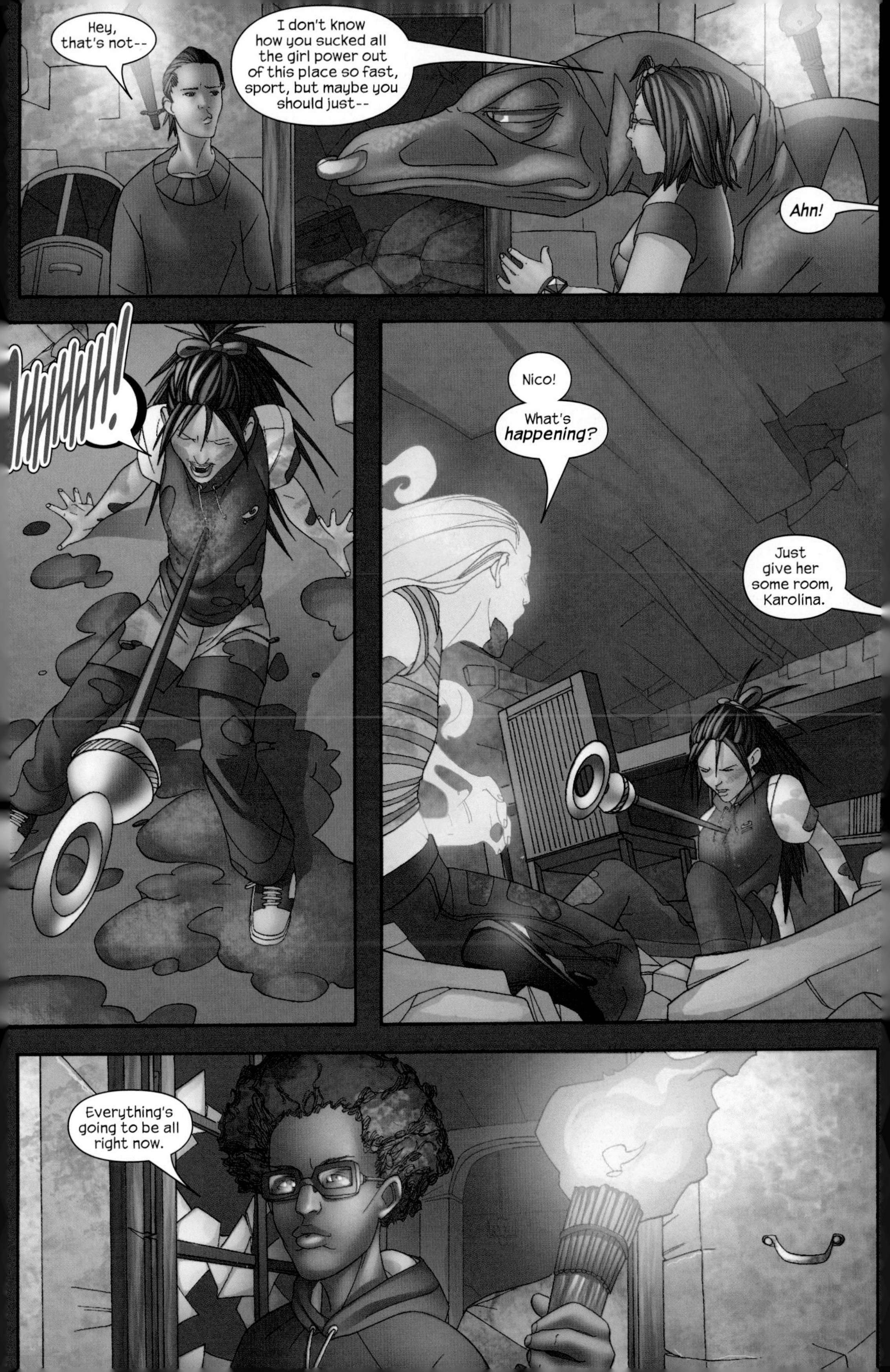
Hey, that's not--
I don't know how you sucked all the girl power out of this place so fast, sport, but maybe you should just--
Ahn!
Nico!
What's *happening*?
Just give her some room, Karolina.
Everything's going to be all right now.

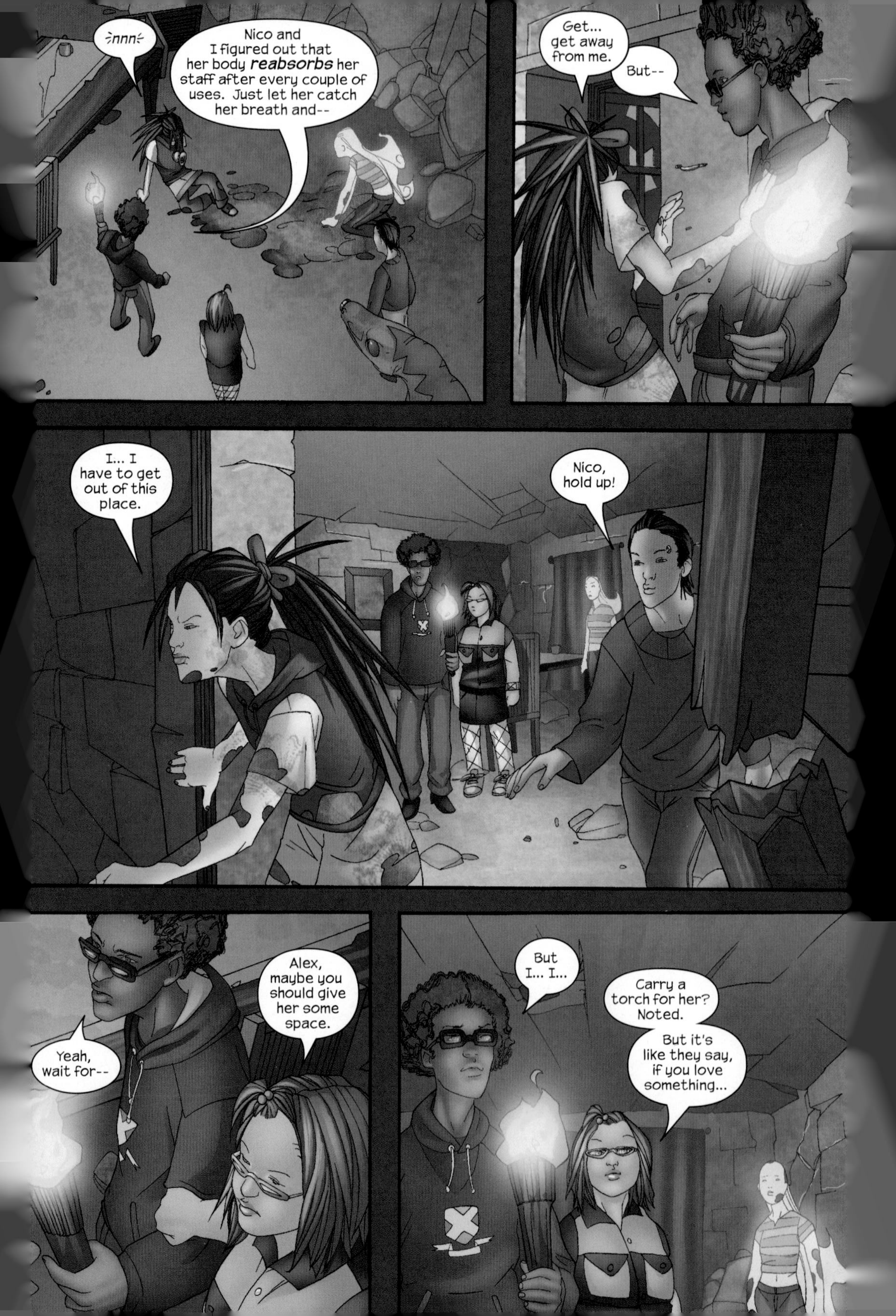

nnn
Nico and I figured out that her body ***reabsorbs*** her staff after every couple of uses. Just let her catch her breath and--
Get... get away from me.
But--
I... I have to get out of this place.
Nico, hold up!
Alex, maybe you should give her some space.
Yeah, wait for--
But I... I...
Carry a torch for her? Noted.
But it's like they say, if you love something...

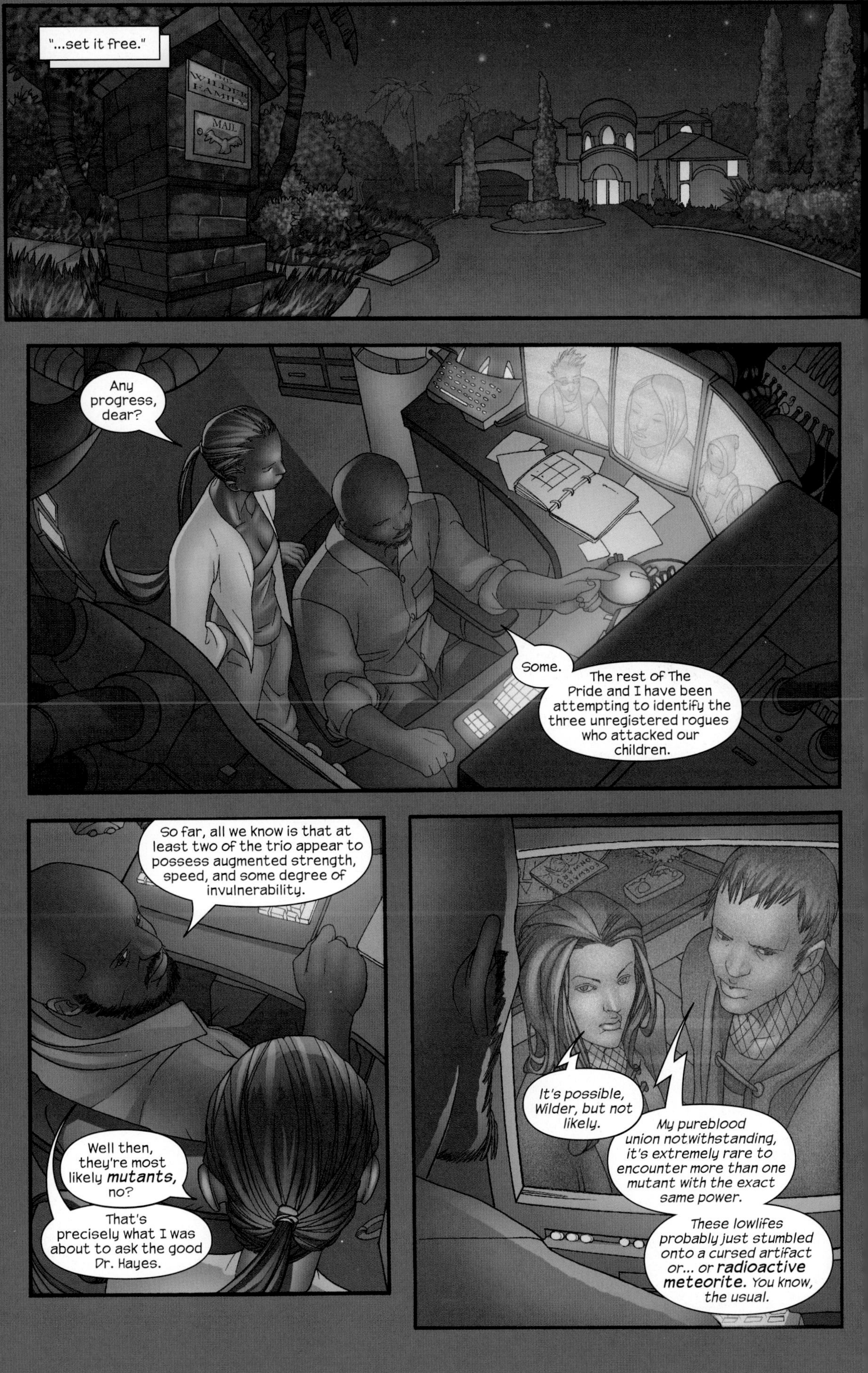
"...set it free."
THE WILDER FAMILY
MAIL
Any progress, dear?
Some.
The rest of The Pride and I have been attempting to identify the three unregistered rogues who attacked our children.
So far, all we know is that at least two of the trio appear to possess augmented strength, speed, and some degree of invulnerability.
Well then, they're most likely *mutants,* no?
That's precisely what I was about to ask the good Dr. Hayes.
It's possible, Wilder, but not likely.
My pureblood union notwithstanding, it's extremely rare to encounter more than one mutant with the exact same power.
These lowlifes probably just stumbled onto a cursed artifact or... or **radioactive meteorite.** You know, the usual.

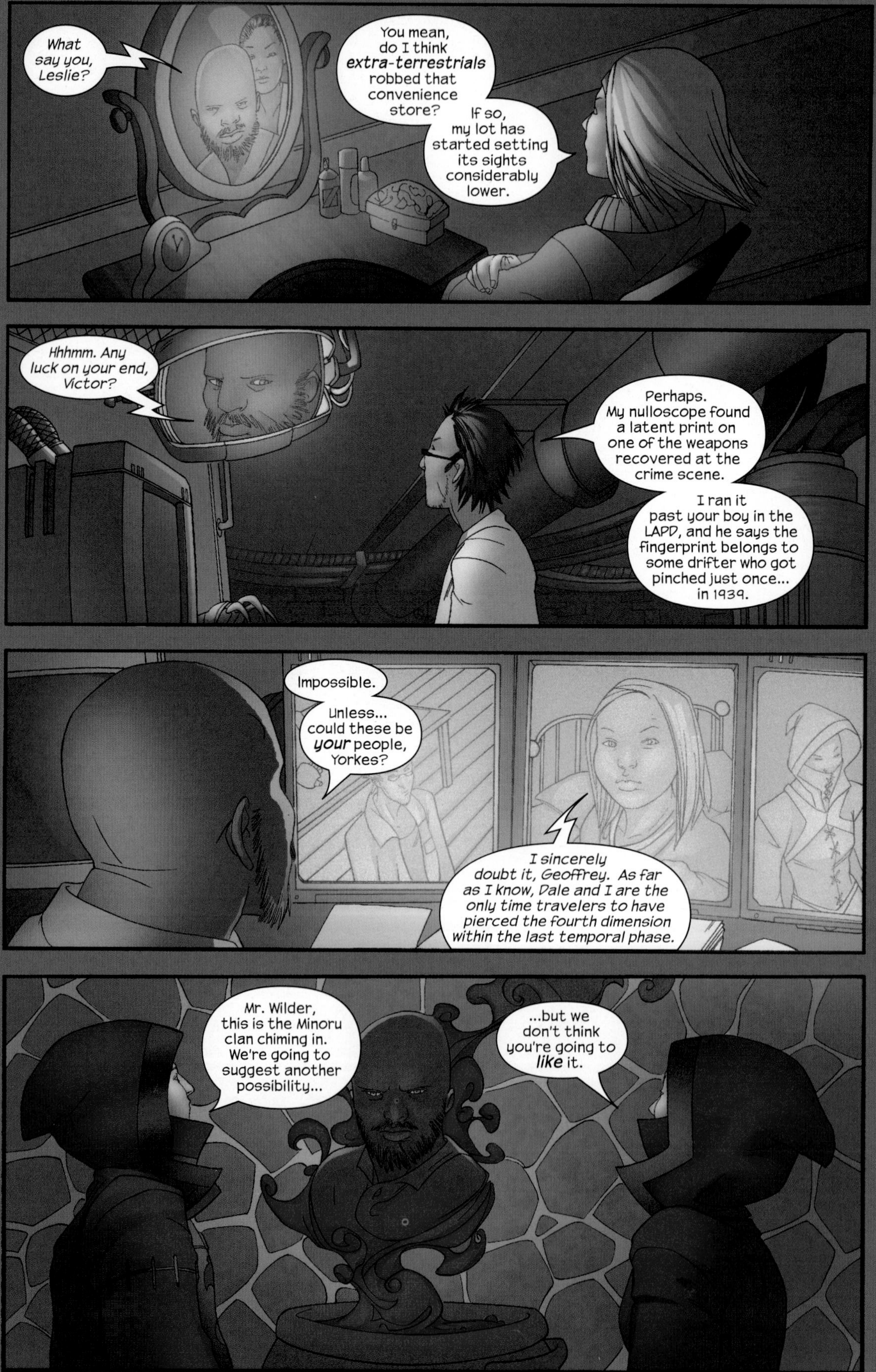
What say you, Leslie?
You mean, do I think extra-terrestrials robbed that convenience store?
If so, my lot has started setting its sights considerably lower.
Hhhmm. Any luck on your end, Victor?
Perhaps. My nulloscope found a latent print on one of the weapons recovered at the crime scene.
I ran it past your boy in the LAPD, and he says the fingerprint belongs to some drifter who got pinched just once... in 1939.
Impossible.
Unless... could these be your people, Yorkes?
I sincerely doubt it, Geoffrey. As far as I know, Dale and I are the only time travelers to have pierced the fourth dimension within the last temporal phase.
Mr. Wilder, this is the Minoru clan chiming in. We're going to suggest another possibility...
...but we don't think you're going to like it.

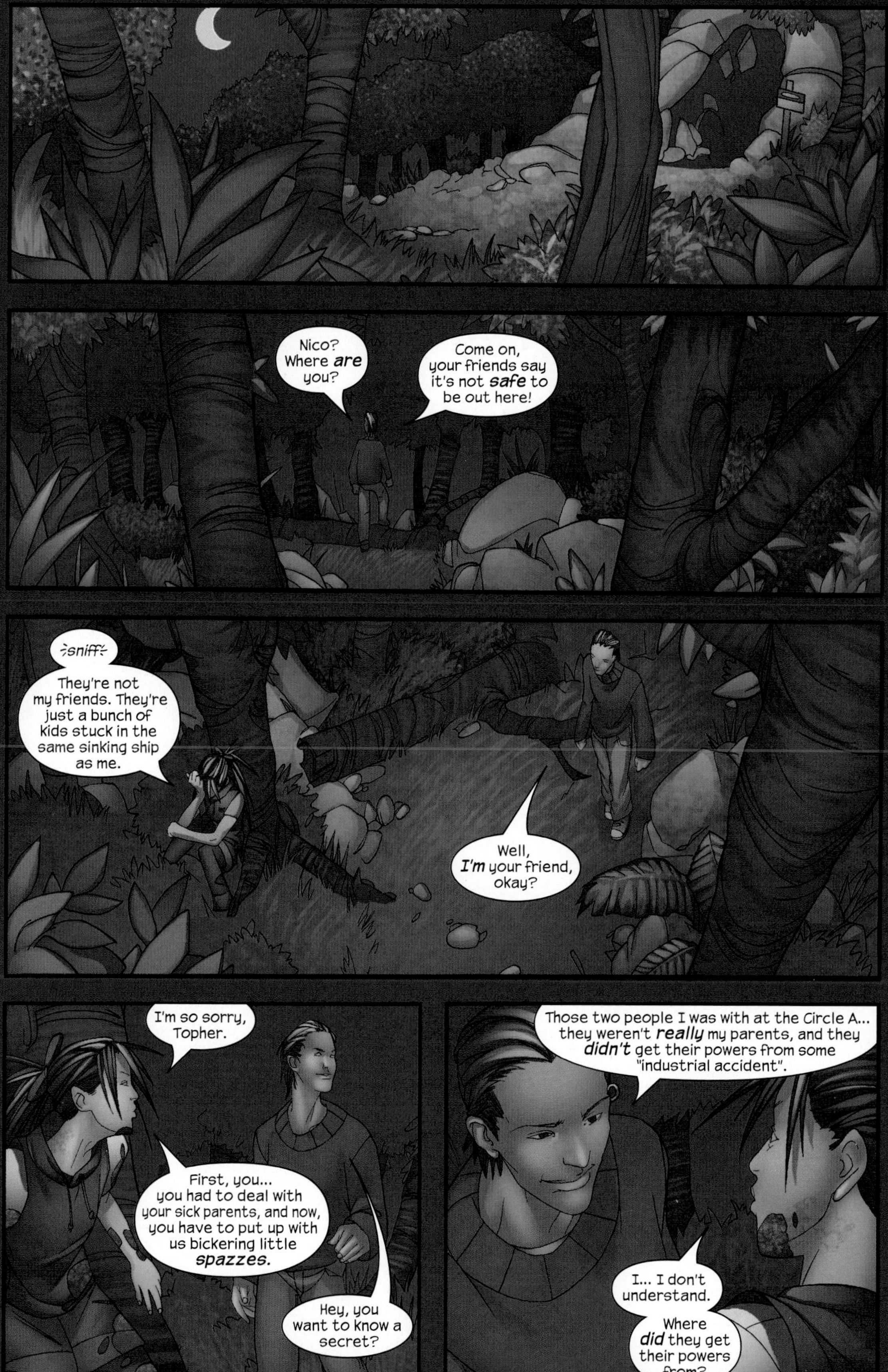
Nico? Where are you?
Come on, your friends say it's not safe to be out here!
sniff
They're not my friends. They're just a bunch of kids stuck in the same sinking ship as me.
Well, I'm your friend, okay?
I'm so sorry, Topher.
First, you... you had to deal with your sick parents, and now, you have to put up with us bickering little spazzes.
Hey, you want to know a secret?
Those two people I was with at the Circle A... they weren't really my parents, and they didn't get their powers from some "industrial accident".
I... I don't understand.
Where did they get their powers from?

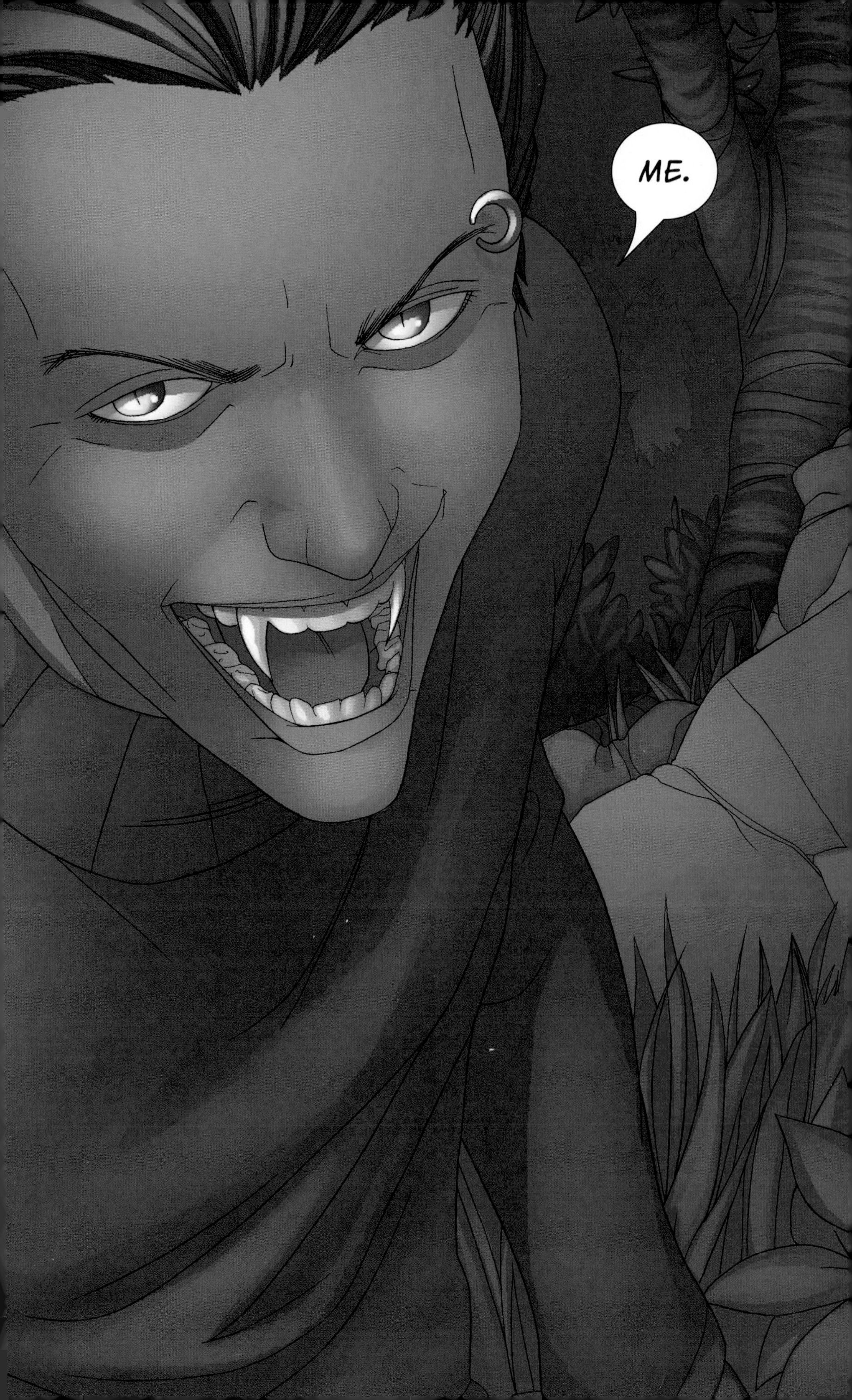
ME.

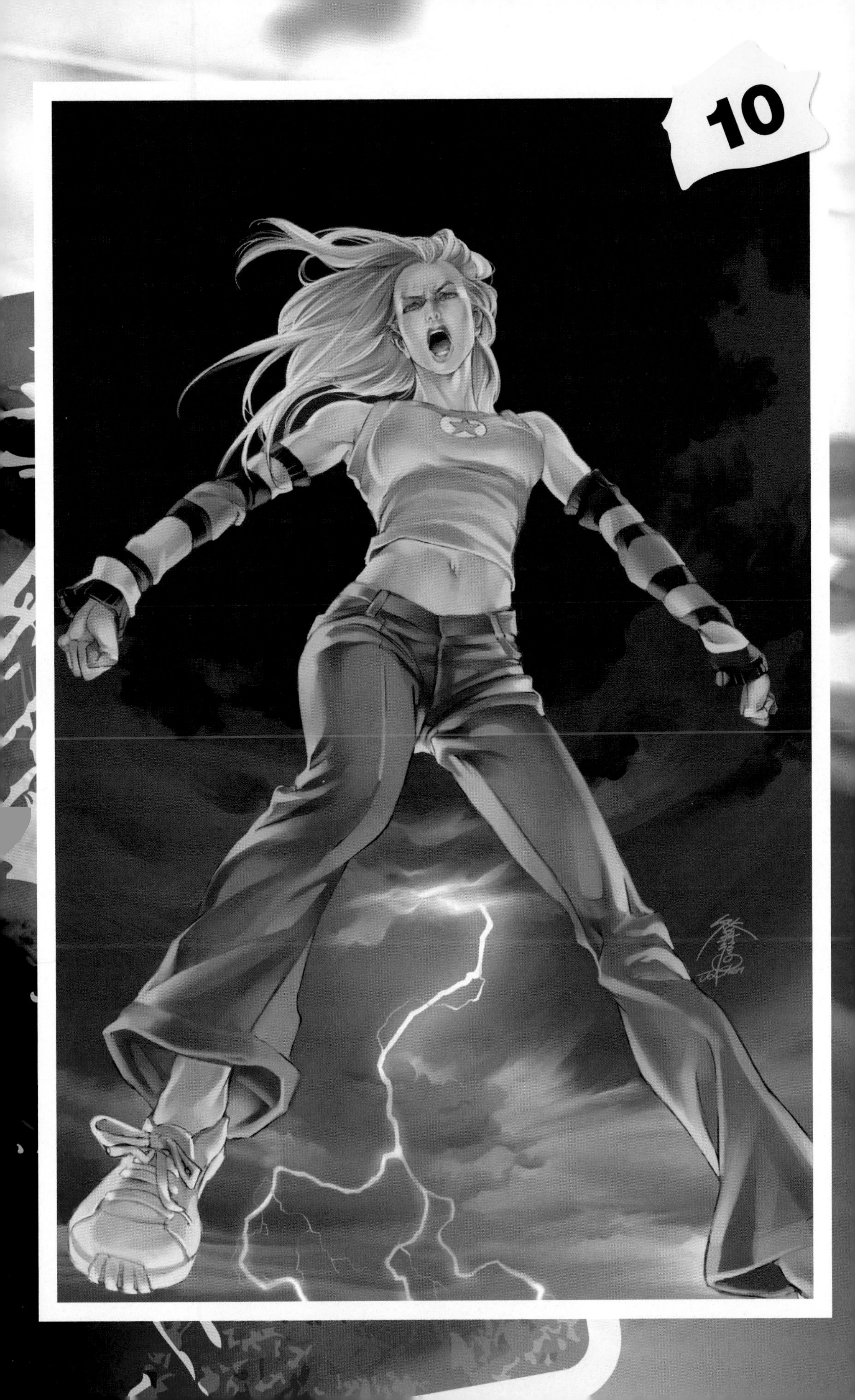
10

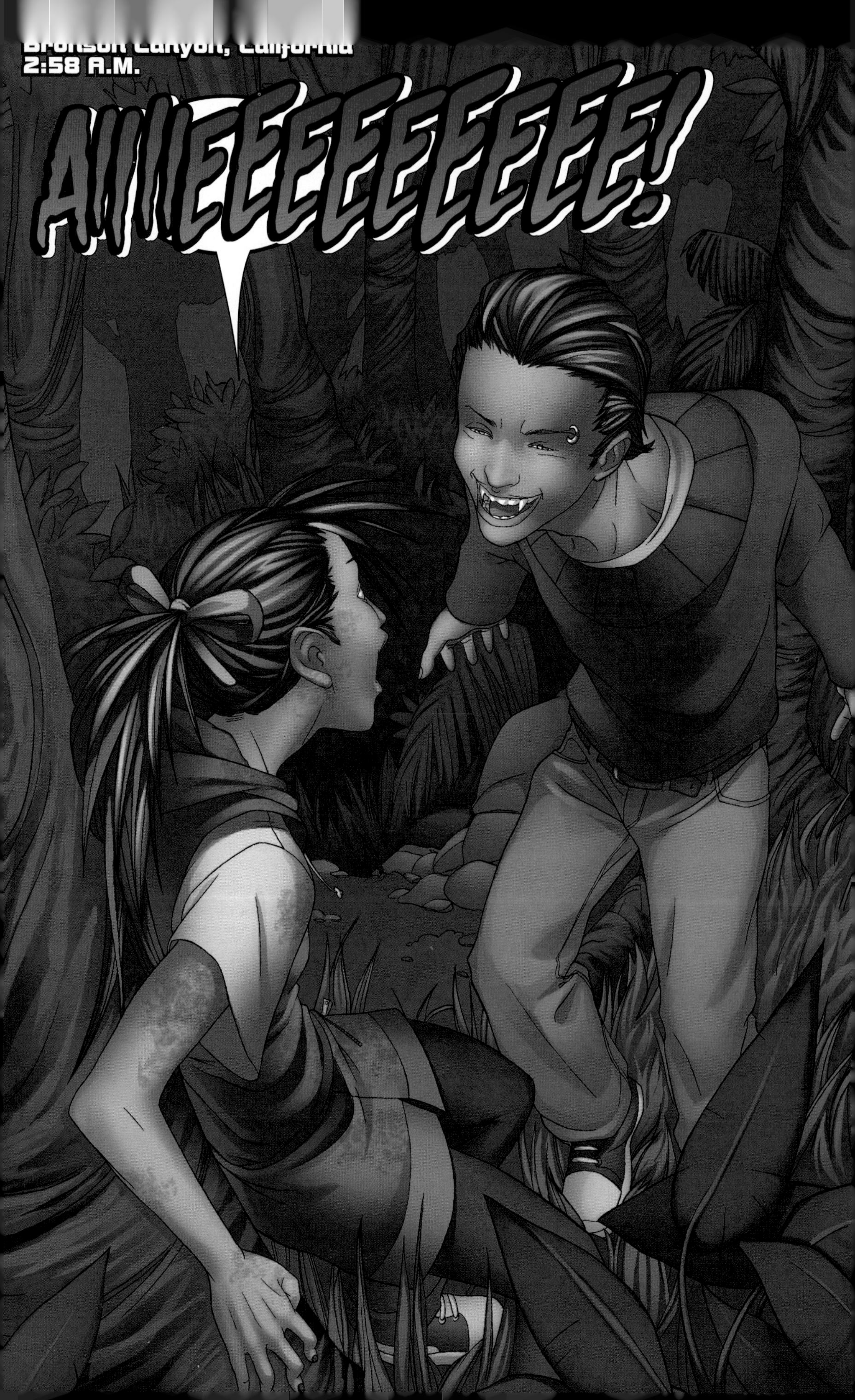
Bronson Canyon, California
2:58 A.M.
AIIEEEEEEEEEE!

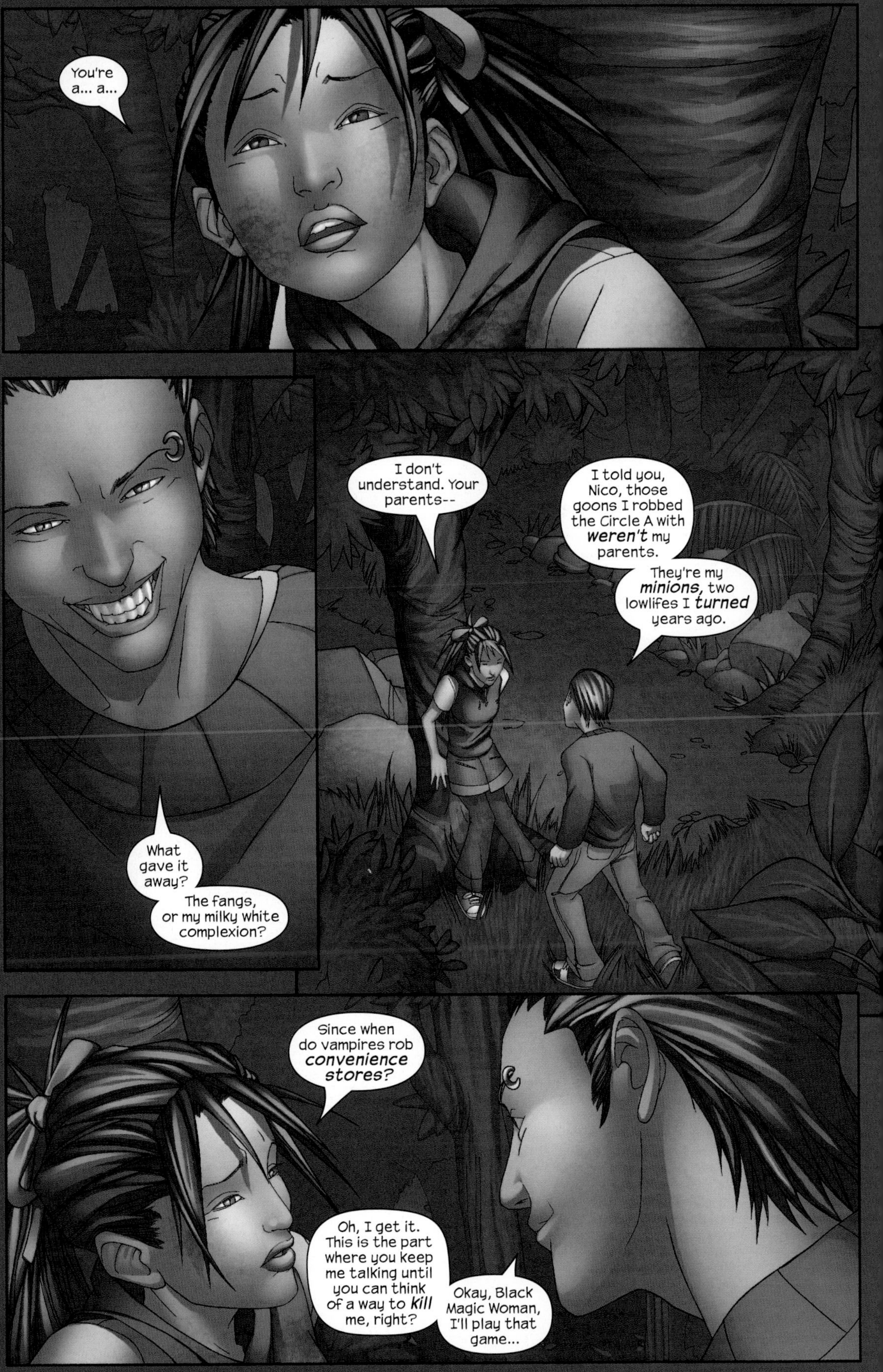
You're a... a...
What gave it away?
The fangs, or my milky white complexion?
I don't understand. Your parents--
I told you, Nico, those goons I robbed the Circle A with *weren't* my parents.
They're my *minions,* two lowlifes I *turned* years ago.
Since when do vampires rob *convenience stores?*
Oh, I get it. This is the part where you keep me talking until you can think of a way to *kill* me, right?
Okay, Black Magic Woman, I'll play that game...

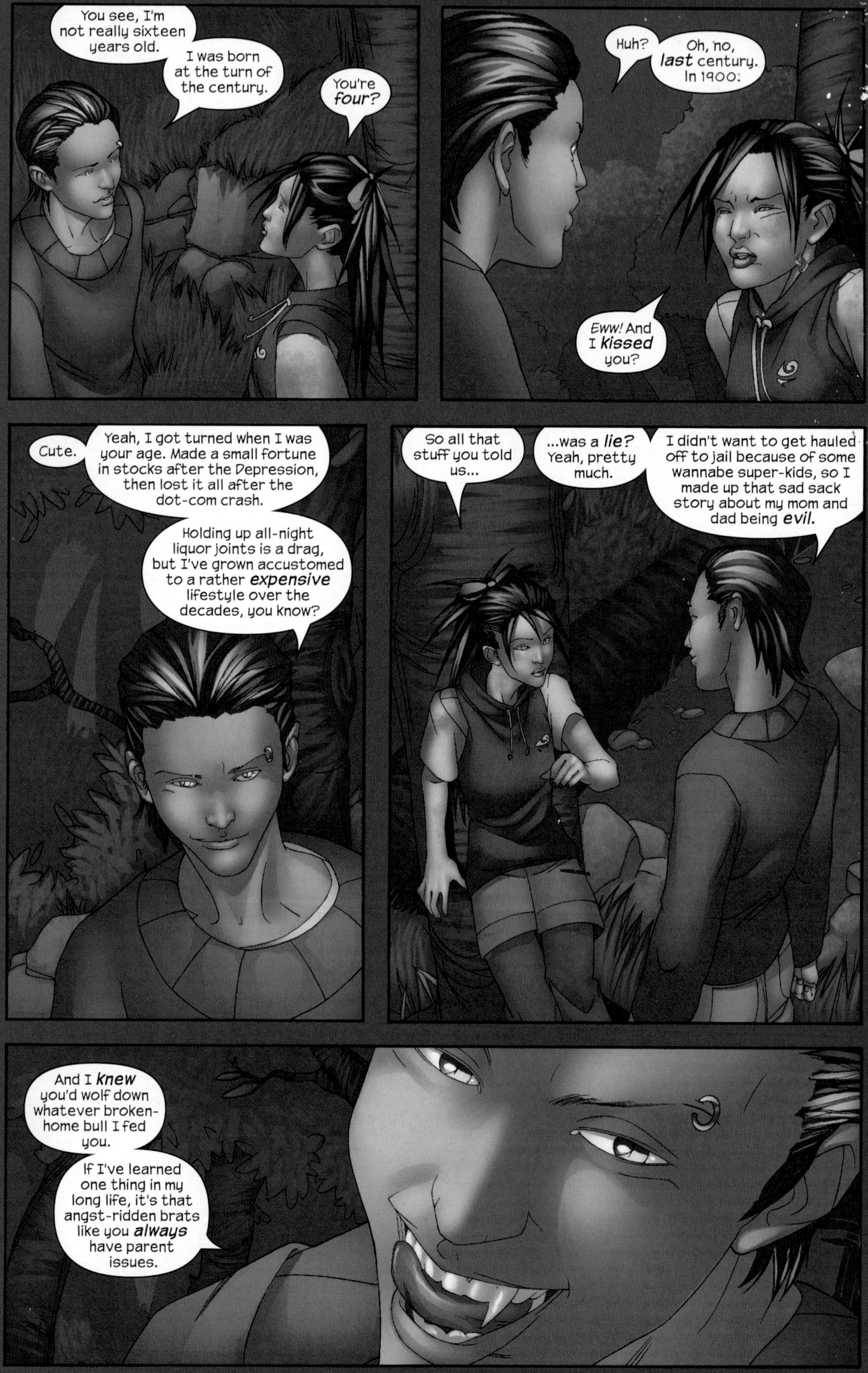
You see, I'm not really sixteen years old.
I was born at the turn of the century.
You're *four?*
Huh?
Oh, no, *last* century. In 1900.
Eww! And I *kissed* you?
Cute.
Yeah, I got turned when I was your age. Made a small fortune in stocks after the Depression, then lost it all after the dot-com crash.
Holding up all-night liquor joints is a drag, but I've grown accustomed to a rather *expensive* lifestyle over the decades, you know?
So all that stuff you told us...
...was a *lie?* Yeah, pretty much.
I didn't want to get hauled off to jail because of some wannabe super-kids, so I made up that sad sack story about my mom and dad being *evil.*
And I *knew* you'd wolf down whatever broken-home bull I fed you.
If I've learned one thing in my long life, it's that angst-ridden brats like you *always* have parent issues.

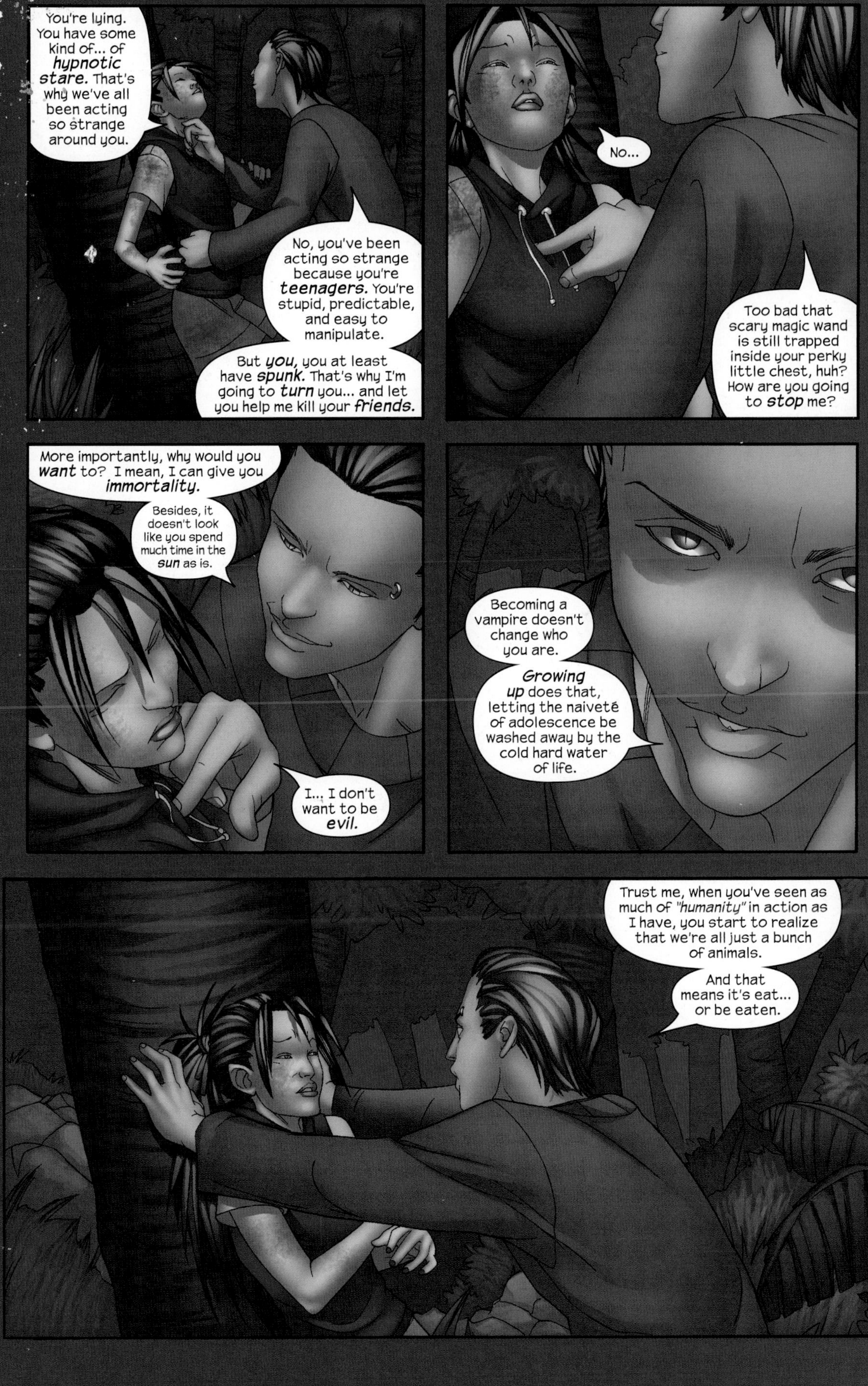

You're lying. You have some kind of... of hypnotic stare. That's why we've all been acting so strange around you.
No, you've been acting so strange because you're teenagers. You're stupid, predictable, and easy to manipulate.
But you, you at least have spunk. That's why I'm going to turn you... and let you help me kill your friends.
No...
Too bad that scary magic wand is still trapped inside your perky little chest, huh? How are you going to stop me?
More importantly, why would you want to? I mean, I can give you immortality.
Besides, it doesn't look like you spend much time in the sun as is.
I... I don't want to be evil.
Becoming a vampire doesn't change who you are.
Growing up does that, letting the naiveté of adolescence be washed away by the cold hard water of life.
Trust me, when you've seen as much of "humanity" in action as I have, you start to realize that we're all just a bunch of animals.
And that means it's eat... or be eaten.

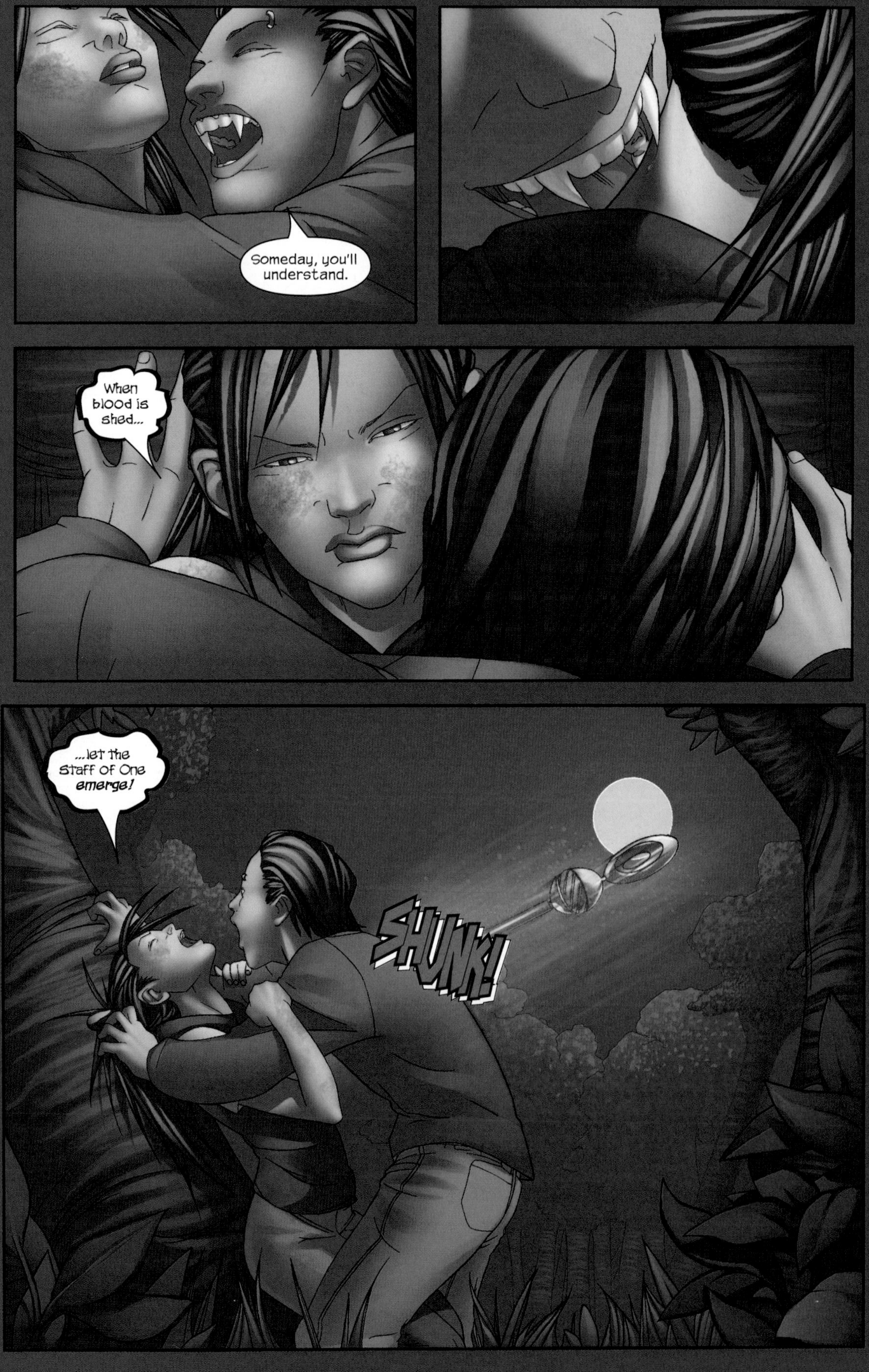
Someday, you'll understand.
When blood is shed...
...let the Staff Of One emerge!
SHUNK!

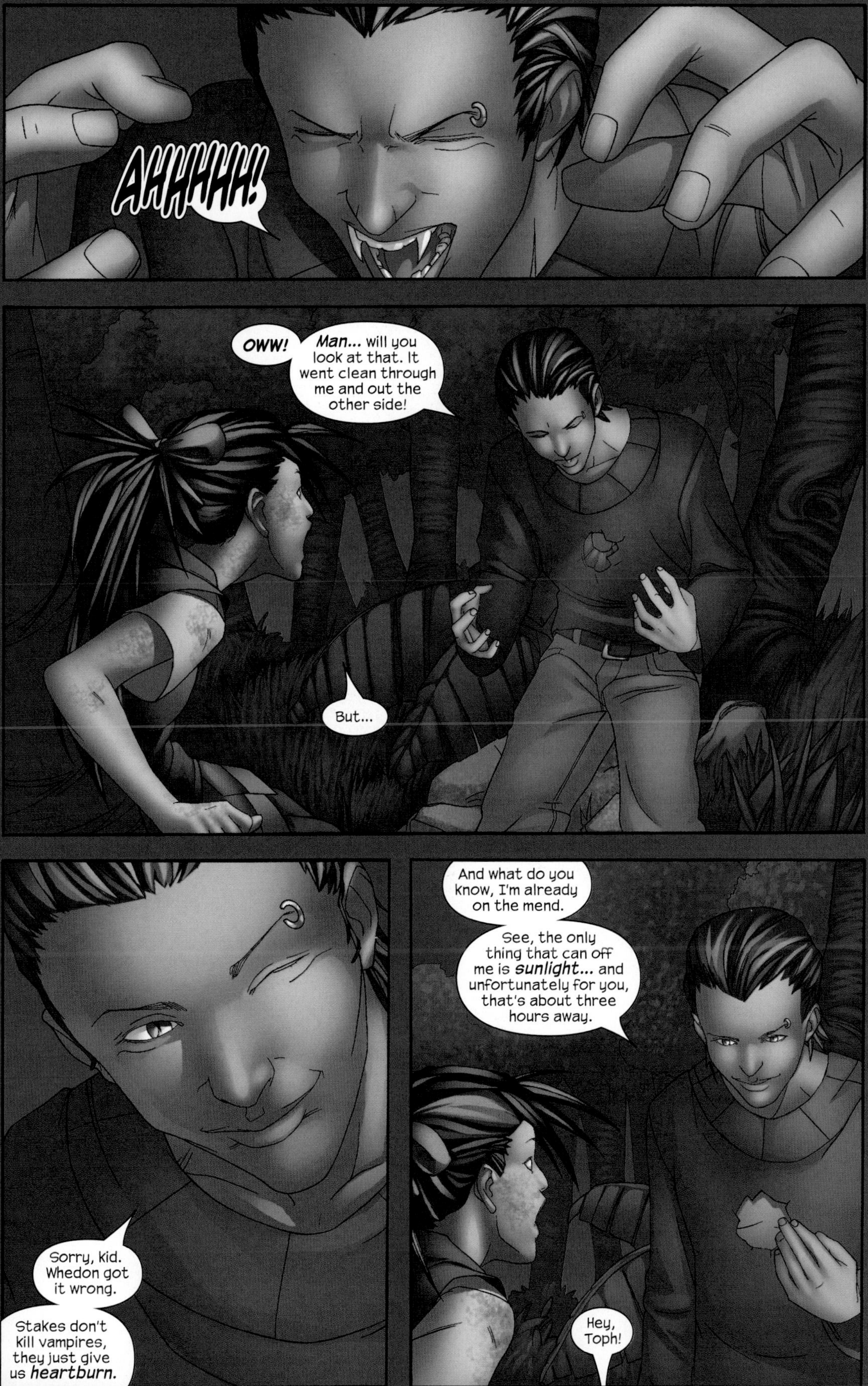
AHHHHH!
OWW!
Man... will you look at that. It went clean through me and out the other side!
But...
Sorry, kid. Whedon got it wrong.
Stakes don't kill vampires, they just give us heartburn.
And what do you know, I'm already on the mend.
See, the only thing that can off me is sunlight... and unfortunately for you, that's about three hours away.
Hey, Toph!

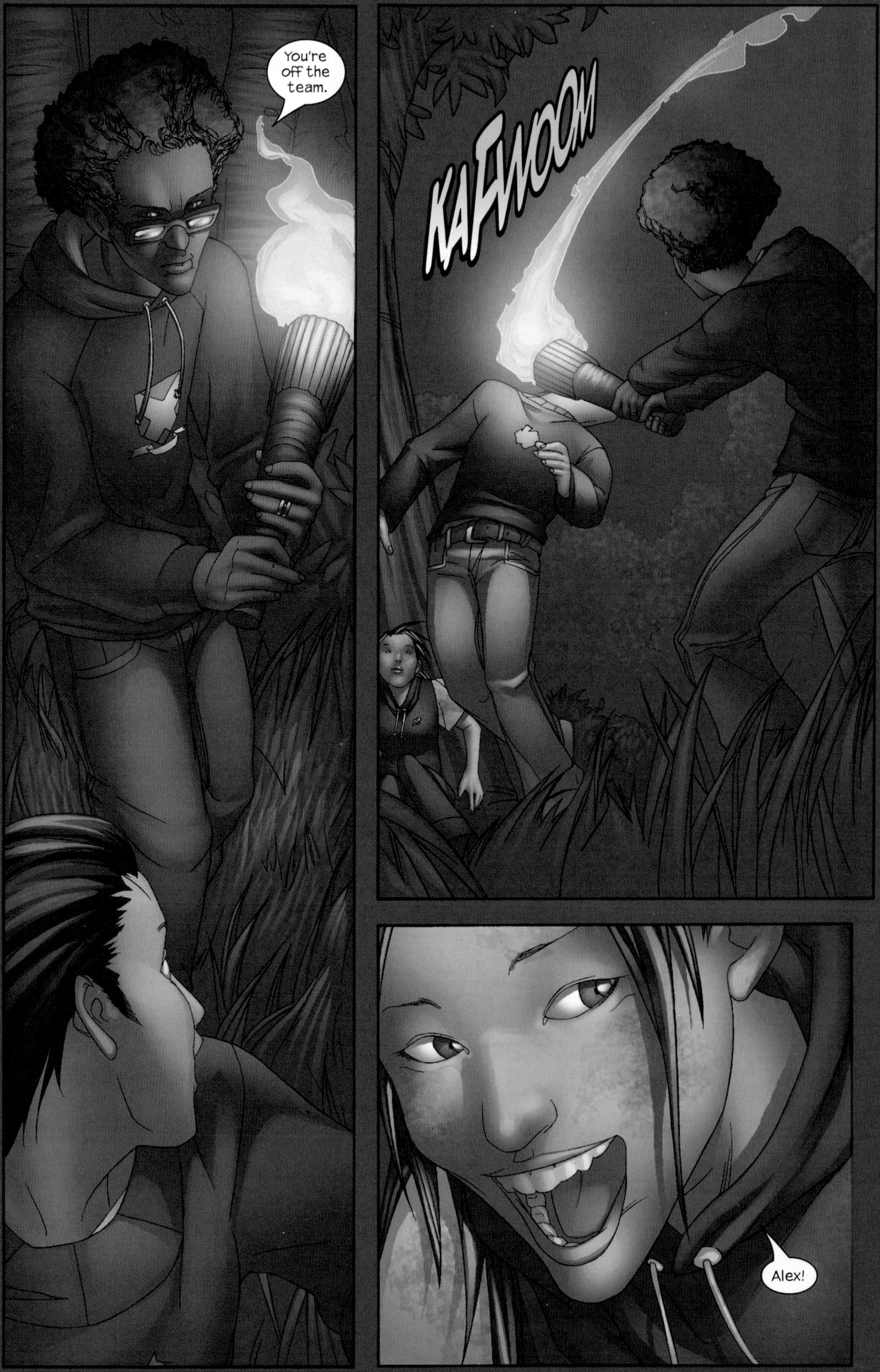
You're off the team.
KAFWOOM
Alex!

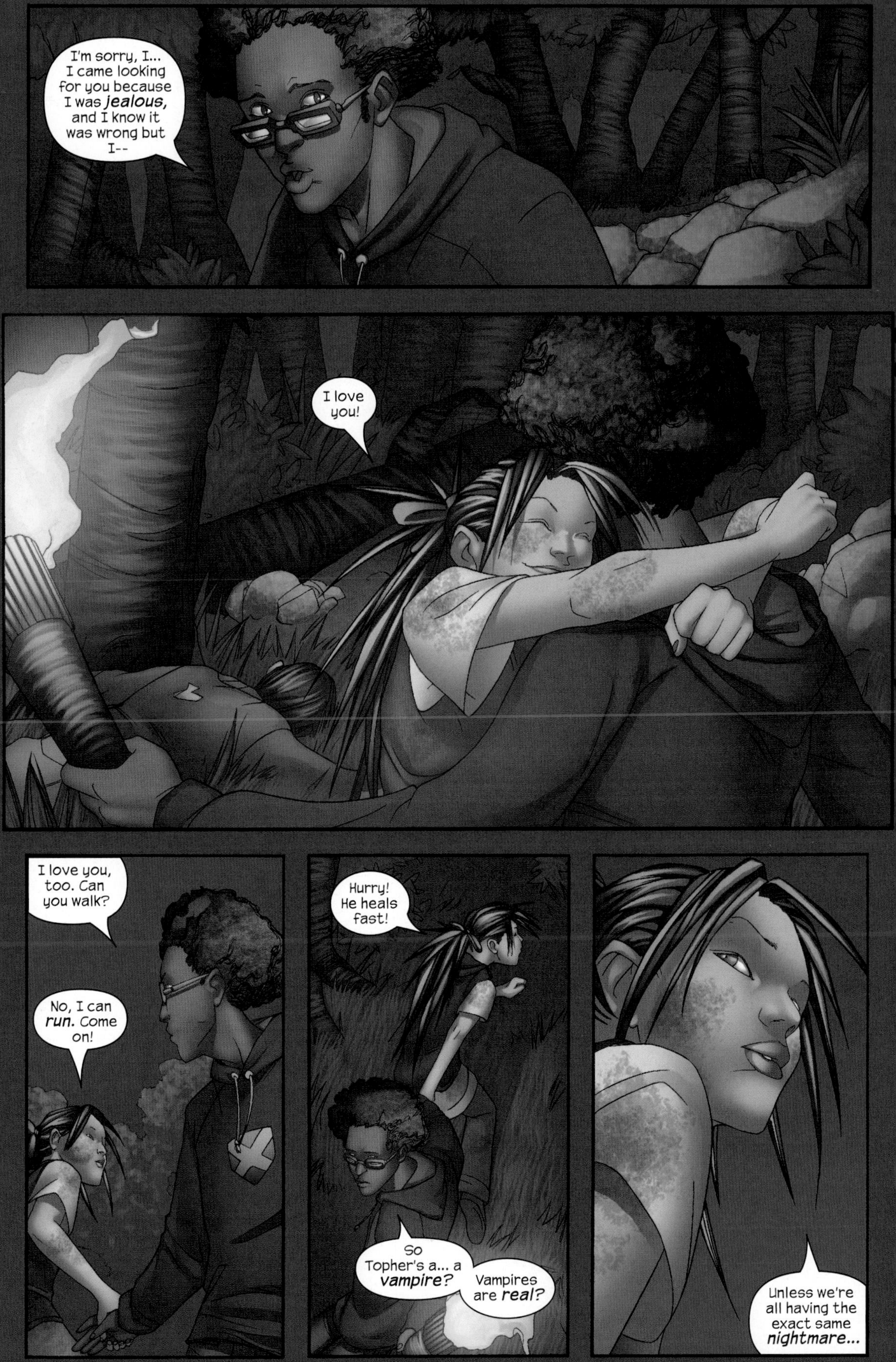
I'm sorry, I... I came looking for you because I was *jealous,* and I know it was wrong but I--
I love you!
I love you, too. Can you walk?
No, I can *run.* Come on!
Hurry! He heals fast!
So Topher's a... a *vampire?*
Vampires are *real?*
Unless we're all having the exact same *nightmare...*

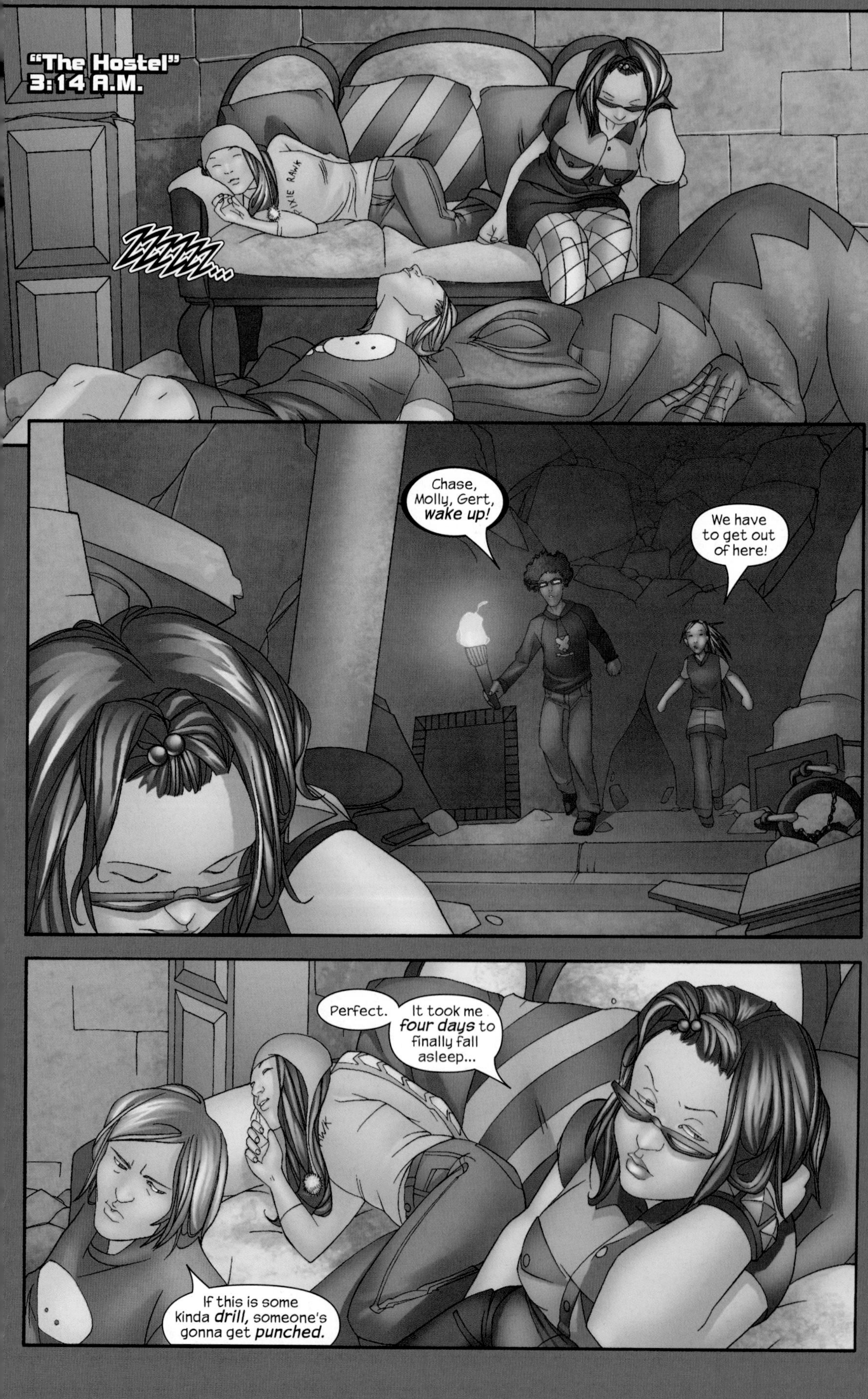
"The Hostel"
3:14 A.M.
PIXIE RAWK
ZZZZZ...
Chase, Molly, Gert, wake up!
We have to get out of here!
Perfect.
It took me four days to finally fall asleep...
If this is some kinda drill, someone's gonna get punched.

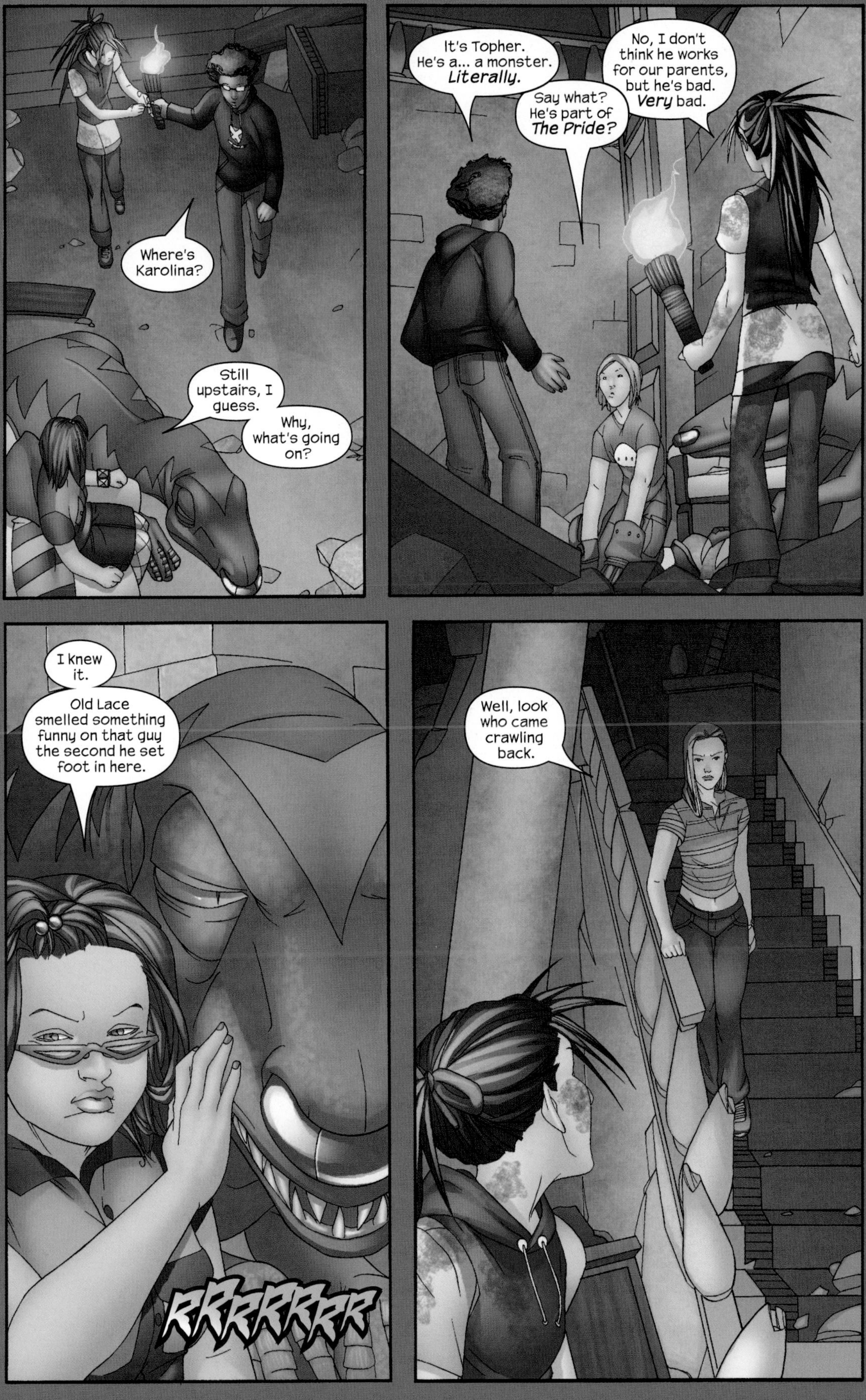
Where's Karolina?
Still upstairs, I guess.
Why, what's going on?
It's Topher. He's a... a monster. *Literally.*
Say what? He's part of *The Pride?*
No, I don't think he works for our parents, but he's bad. *Very* bad.
I knew it.
Old Lace smelled something funny on that guy the second he set foot in here.
RRRRRRR
Well, look who came crawling back.

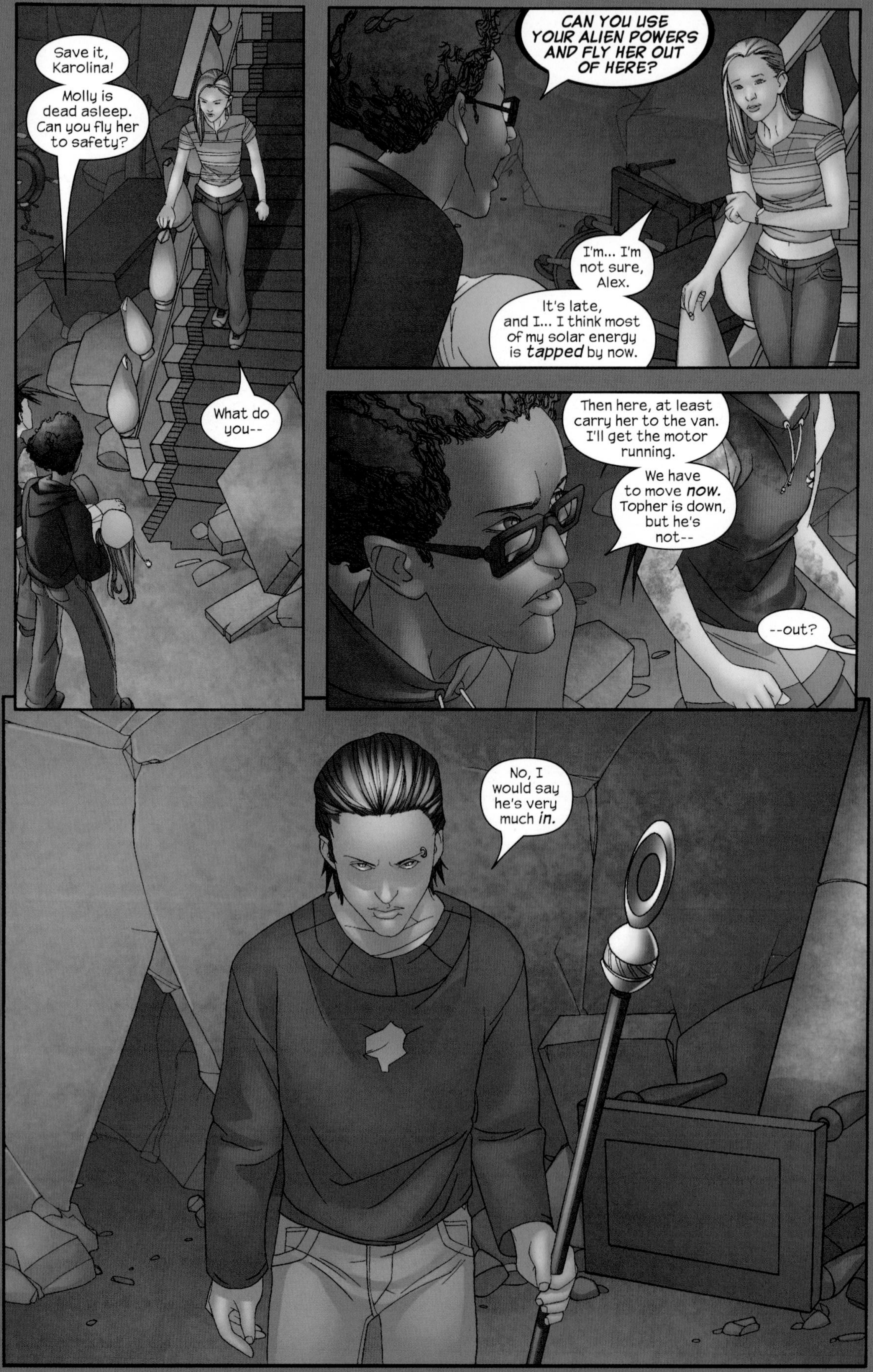
Save it, Karolina!
Molly is dead asleep. Can you fly her to safety?
What do you--
CAN YOU USE YOUR ALIEN POWERS AND FLY HER OUT OF HERE?
I'm... I'm not sure, Alex.
It's late, and I... I think most of my solar energy is tapped by now.
Then here, at least carry her to the van. I'll get the motor running.
We have to move now. Topher is down, but he's not--
--out?
No, I would say he's very much in.

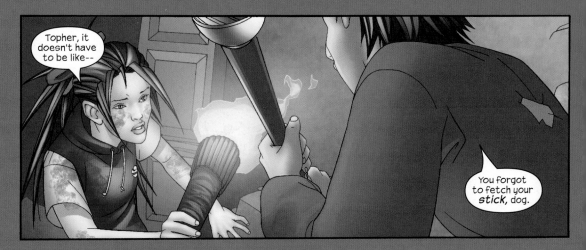

Topher, it doesn't have to be like--

You forgot to fetch your *stick*, dog.

THWACK

NO!

Are you really surprised to see me, Alex?

Did you honestly think a little *fire* was going to slow me down?

How about a *lot* of fire, new kid?

FWOOOOM

Poor Chase. You're even more stupid than your friends think you are.

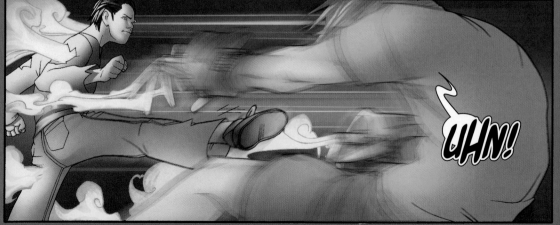

UHN!

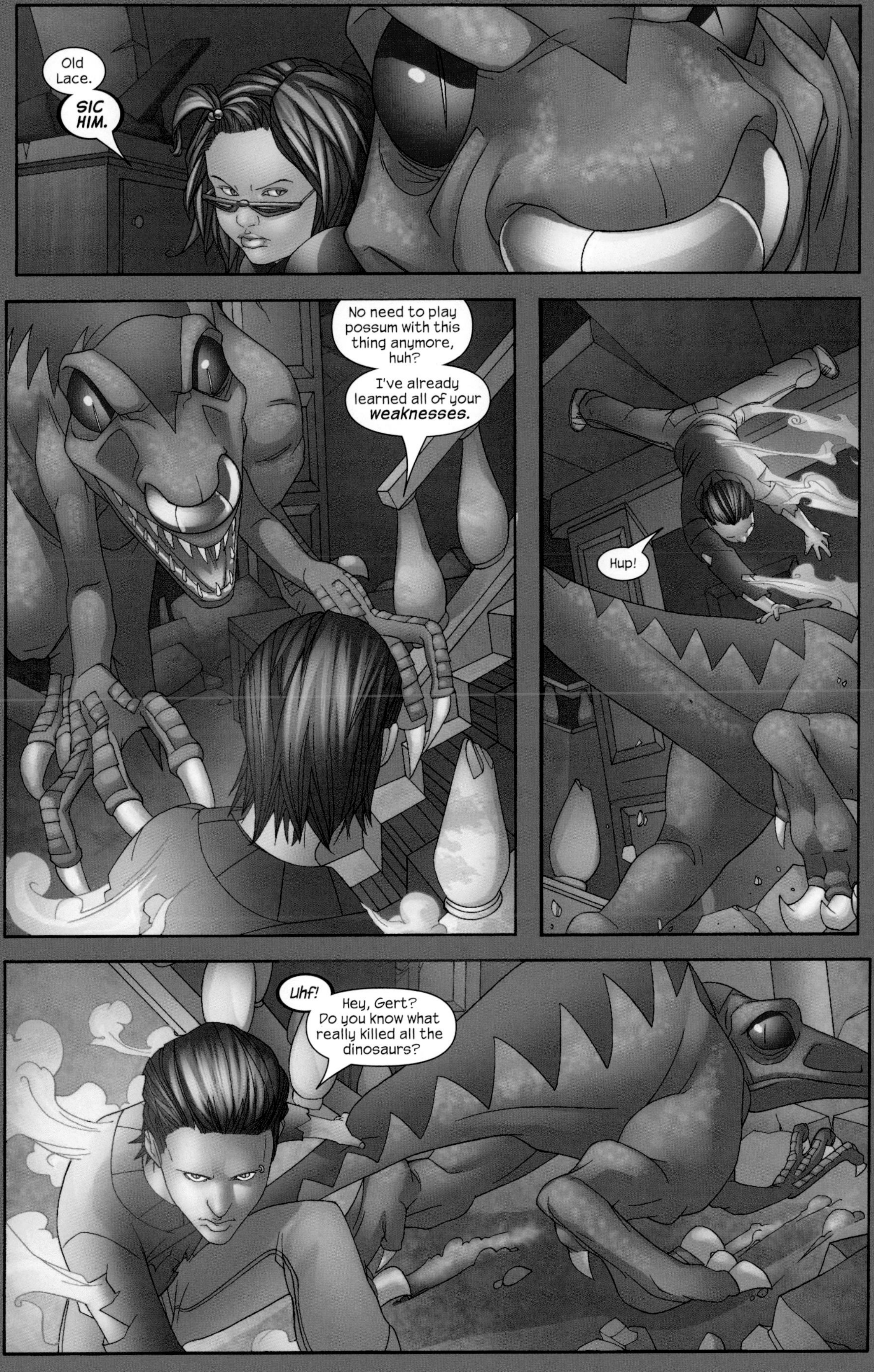
Old Lace.
SIC HIM.
No need to play possum with this thing anymore, huh?
I've already learned all of your weaknesses.
Hup!
Uhf!
Hey, Gert? Do you know what really killed all the dinosaurs?

Me neither.

But I bet it sounded something like...

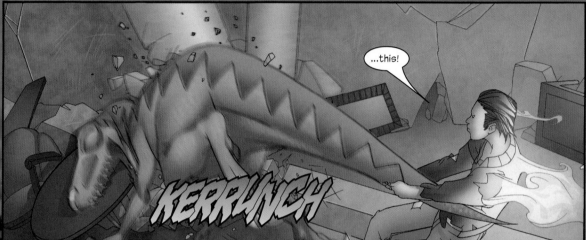

...this!

KERRUNCH

AHNNNN!

Ah yes, your empathic connection.

Lucky you, I forget what it's like to actually *feel* for another life...

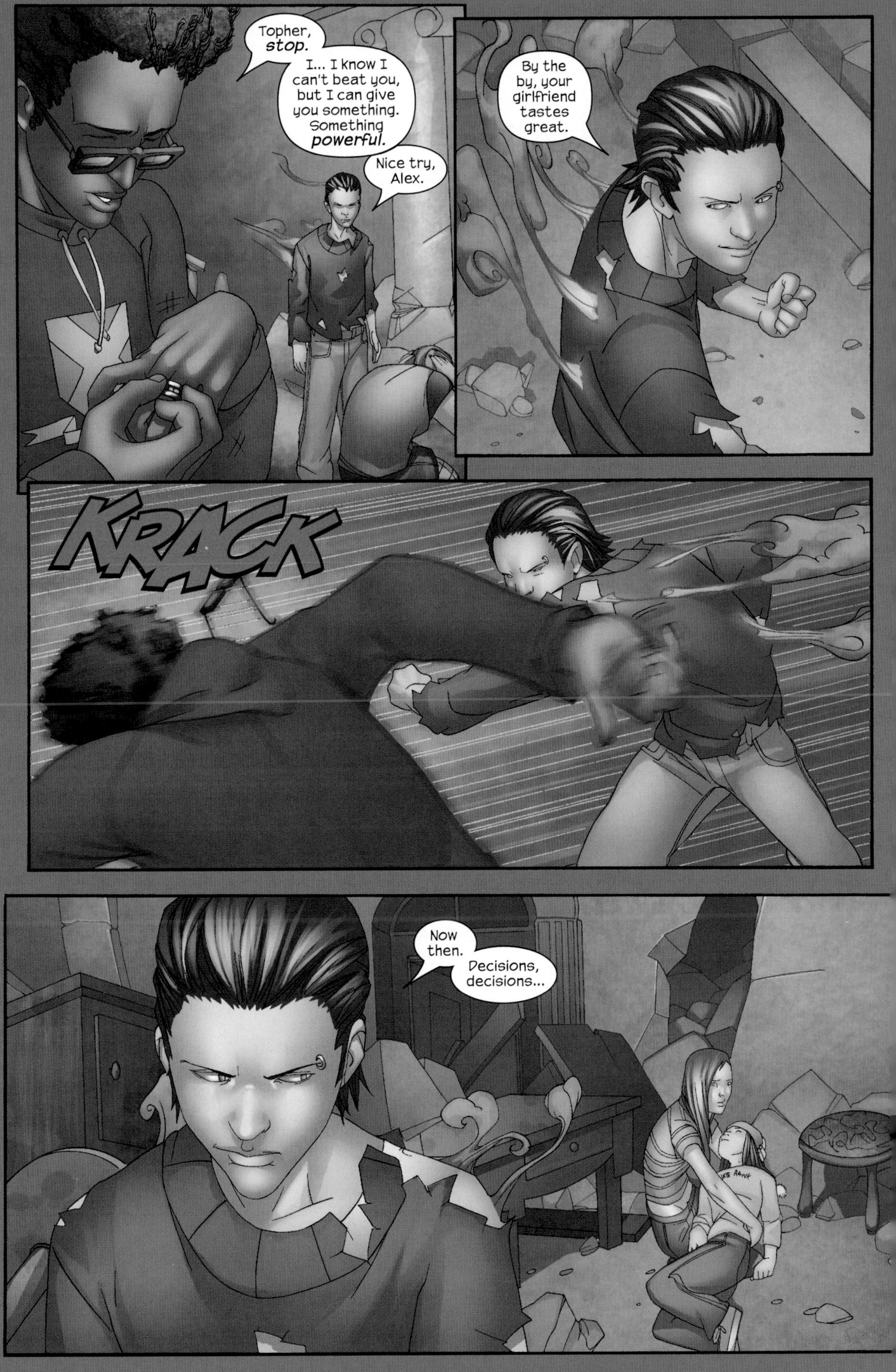
Topher, *stop.*
I... I know I can't beat you, but I can give you something. Something *powerful.*
Nice try, Alex.
By the by, your girlfriend tastes great.
KRACK
Now then.
Decisions, decisions...

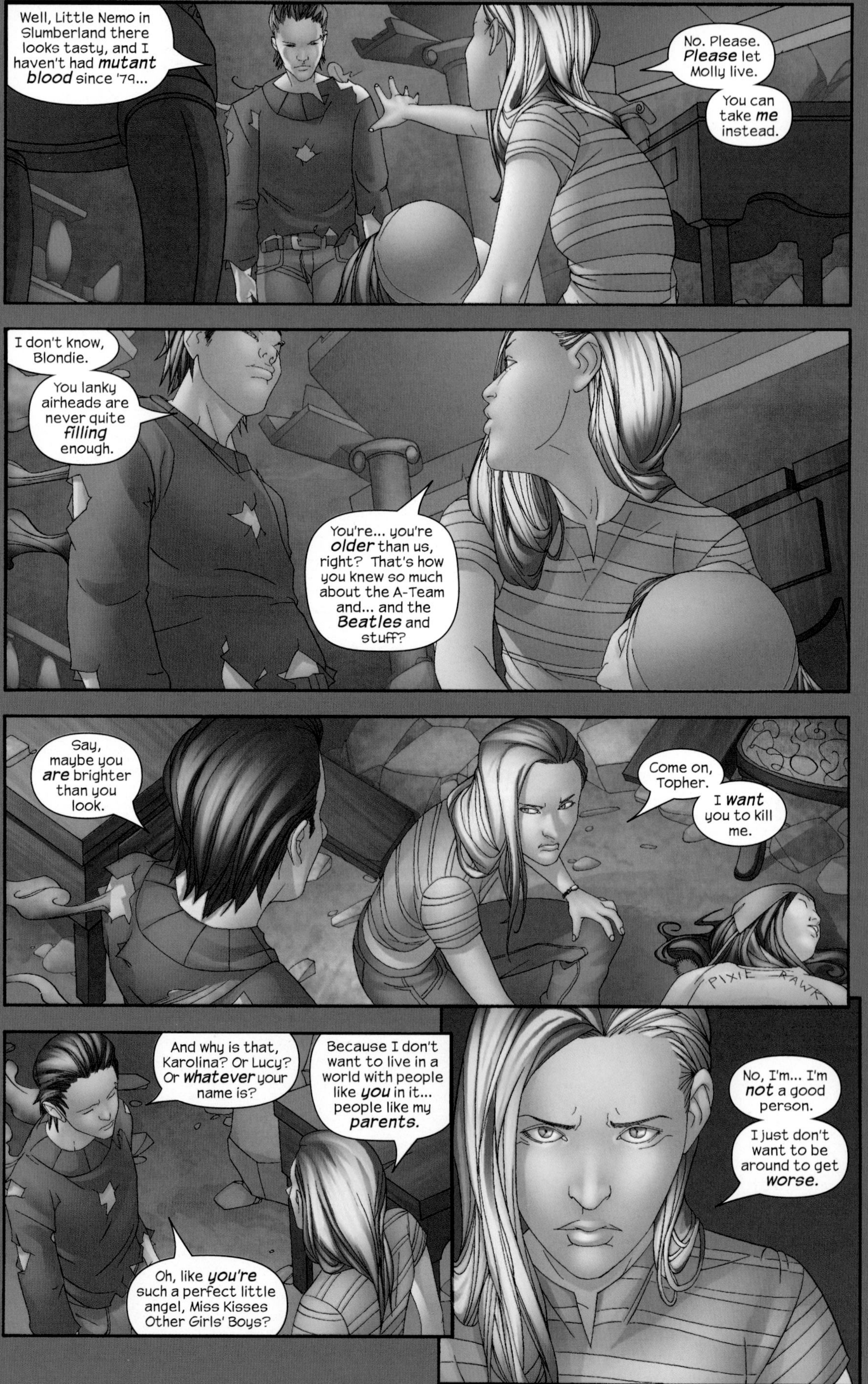
Well, Little Nemo in Slumberland there looks tasty, and I haven't had *mutant blood* since '79...
No. Please. *Please* let Molly live.
You can take *me* instead.
I don't know, Blondie.
You lanky airheads are never quite *filling* enough.
You're... you're *older* than us, right? That's how you knew so much about the A-Team and... and the *Beatles* and stuff?
Say, maybe you *are* brighter than you look.
Come on, Topher.
I *want* you to kill me.
PIXIE RAWK
And why is that, Karolina? Or Lucy? Or *whatever* your name is?
Because I don't want to live in a world with people like *you* in it... people like my *parents.*
Oh, like *you're* such a perfect little angel, Miss Kisses Other Girls' Boys?
No, I'm... I'm *not* a good person.
I just don't want to be around to get *worse.*

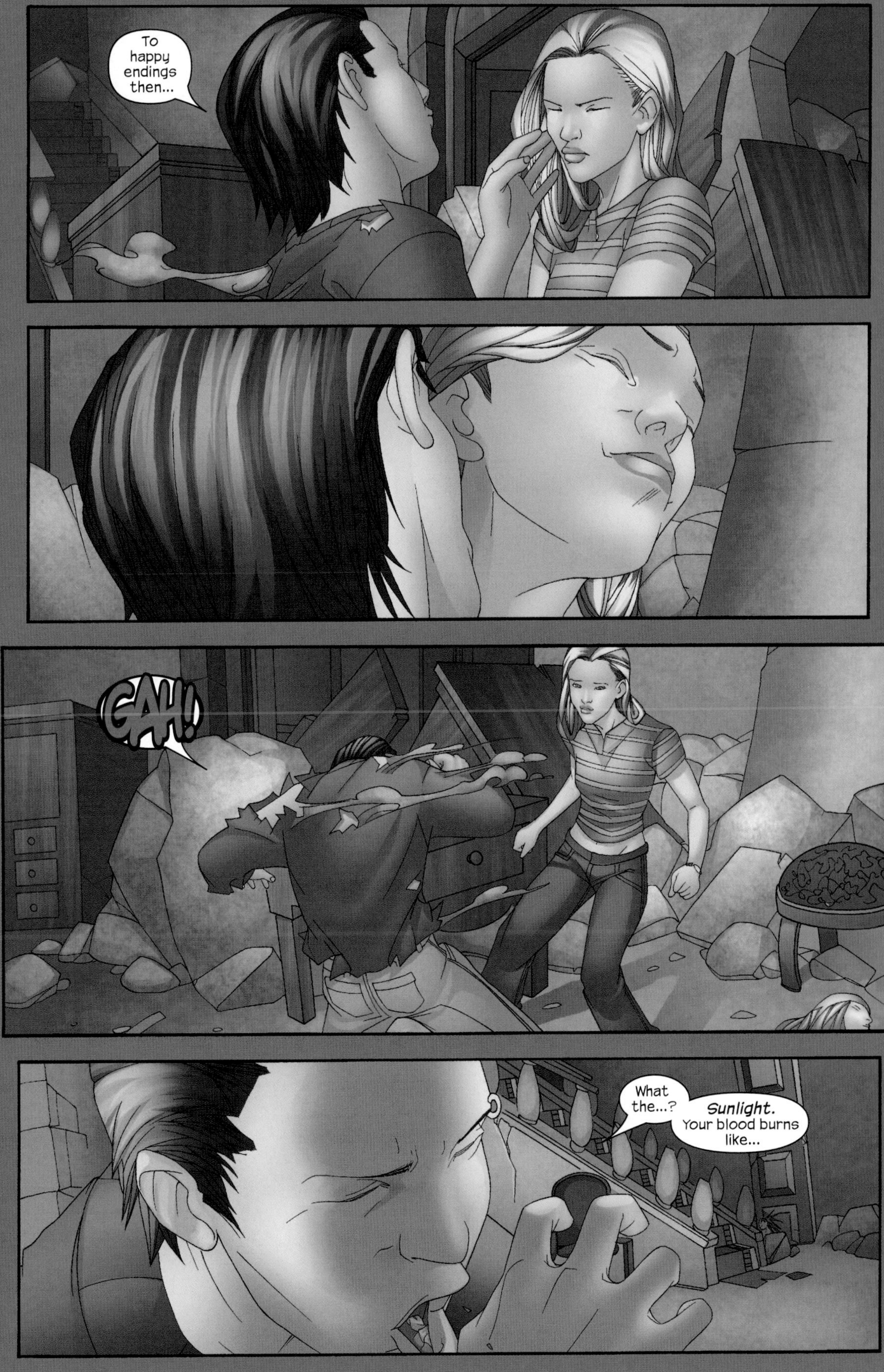
To happy endings then...
GAH!
What the...?
Sunlight. Your blood burns like...

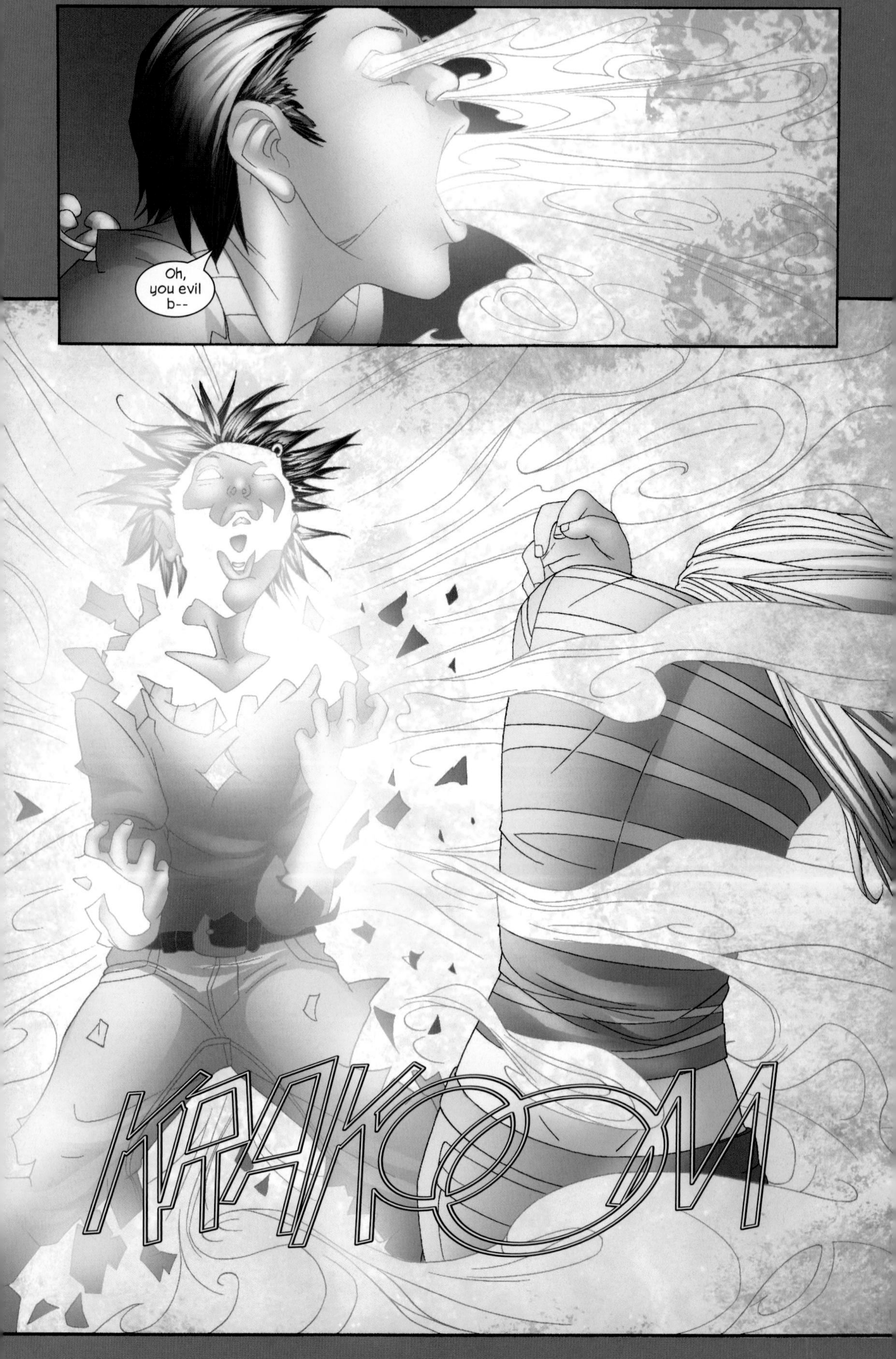
Oh, you evil b--
KRAKOOM

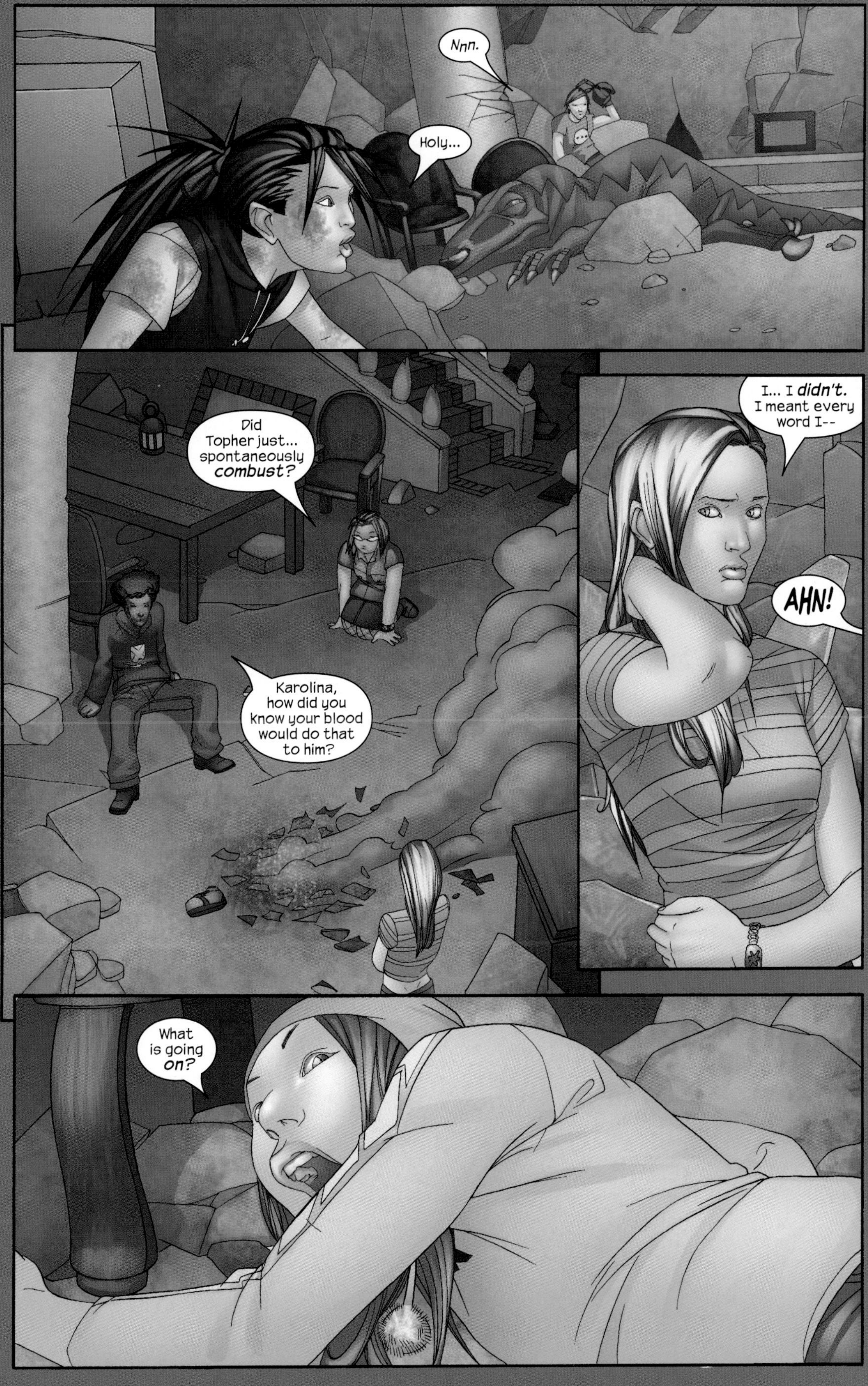
Nnn.
Holy...
Did Topher just... spontaneously combust?
Karolina, how did you know your blood would do that to him?
I... I didn't. I meant every word I--
AHN!
What is going on?

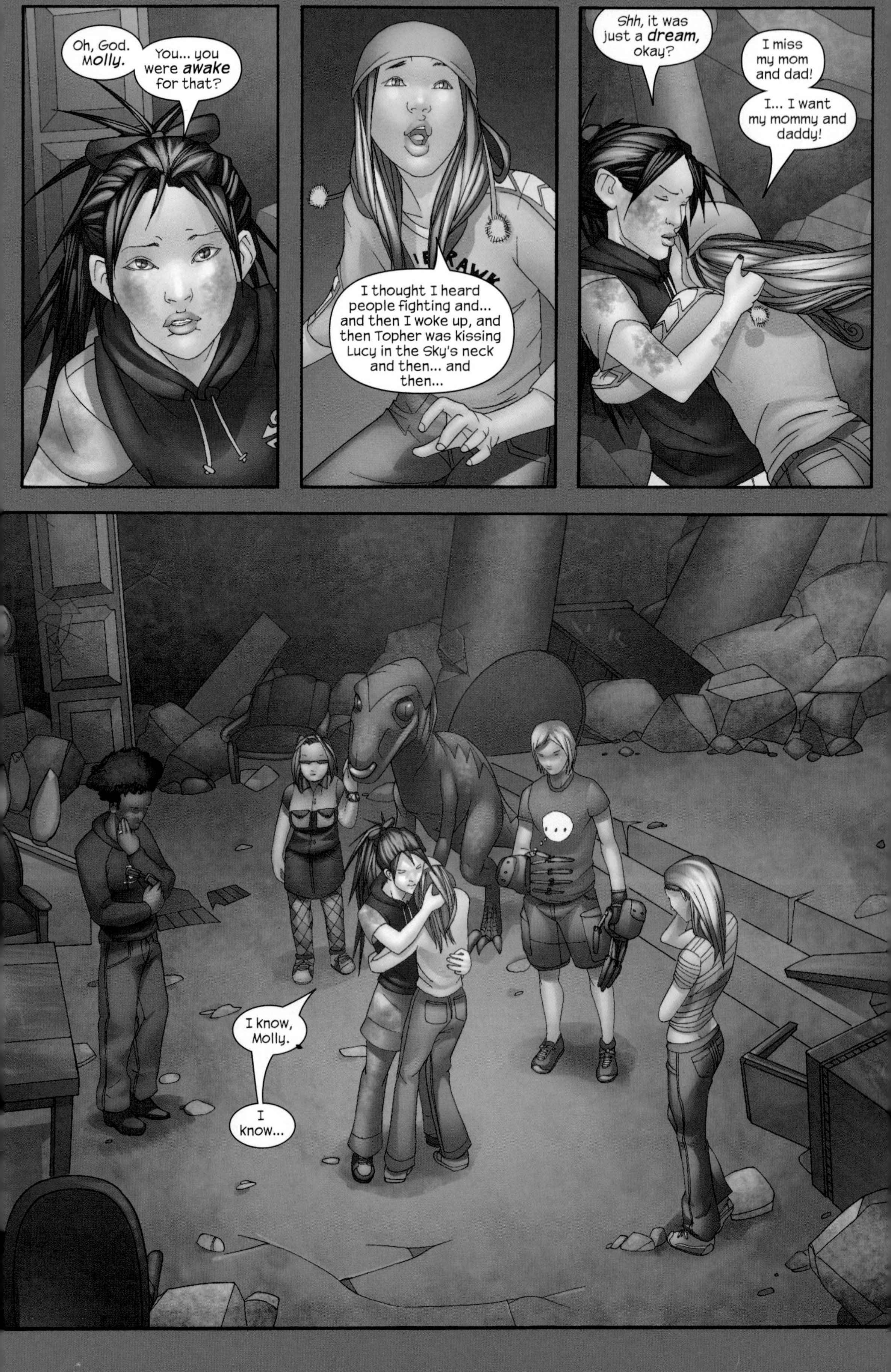

Oh, God. Molly.
You... you were awake for that?
I thought I heard people fighting and... and then I woke up, and then Topher was kissing Lucy in the Sky's neck and then... and then...
RAWK
Shh, it was just a dream, okay?
I miss my mom and dad!
I... I want my mommy and daddy!
I know, Molly.
I know...

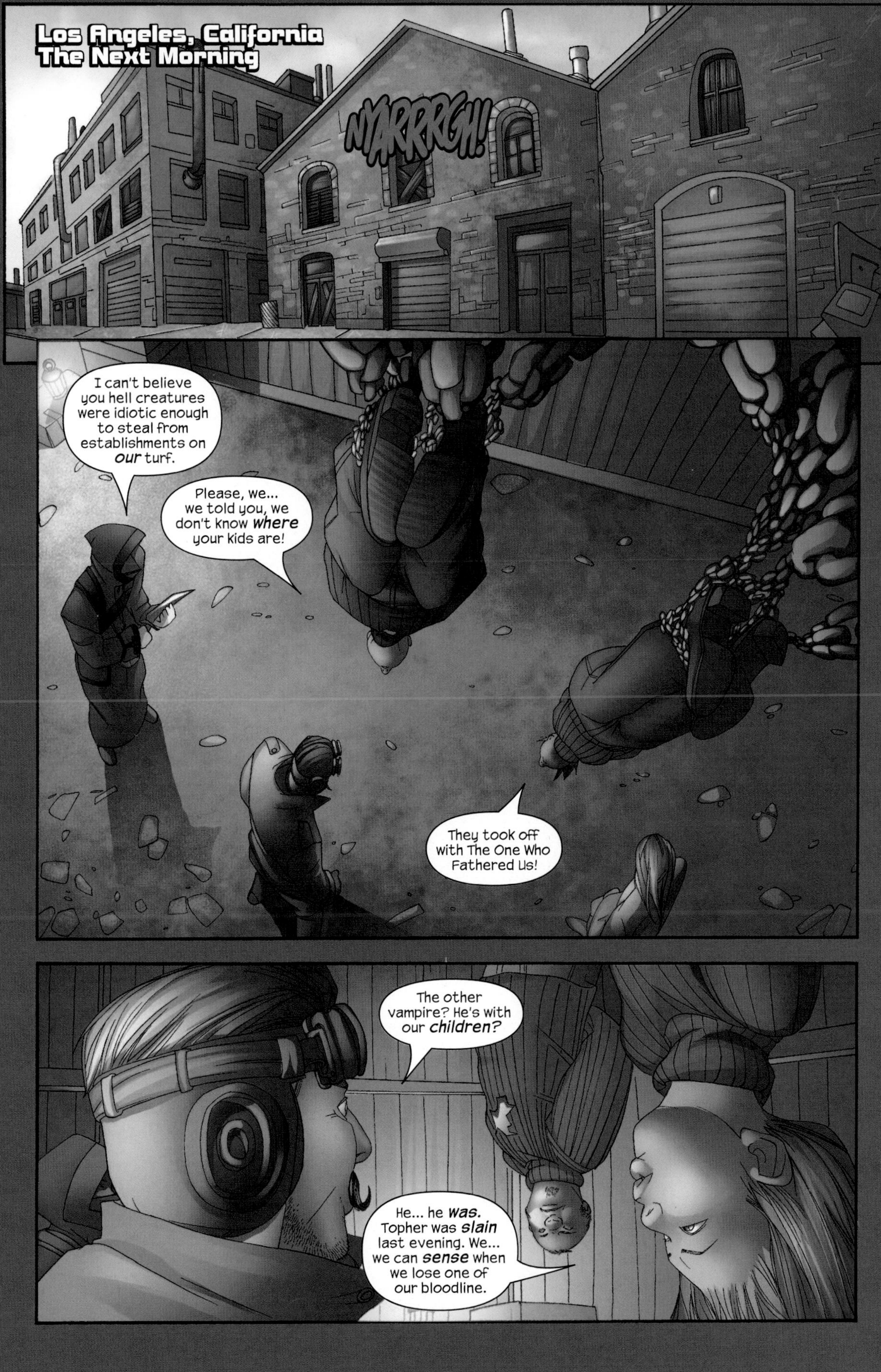

Los Angeles, California
The Next Morning
NYARRRGH!
I can't believe you hell creatures were idiotic enough to steal from establishments on our turf.
Please, we... we told you, we don't know where your kids are!
They took off with The One Who Fathered Us!
The other vampire? He's with our children?
He... he was. Topher was slain last evening. We... we can sense when we lose one of our bloodline.

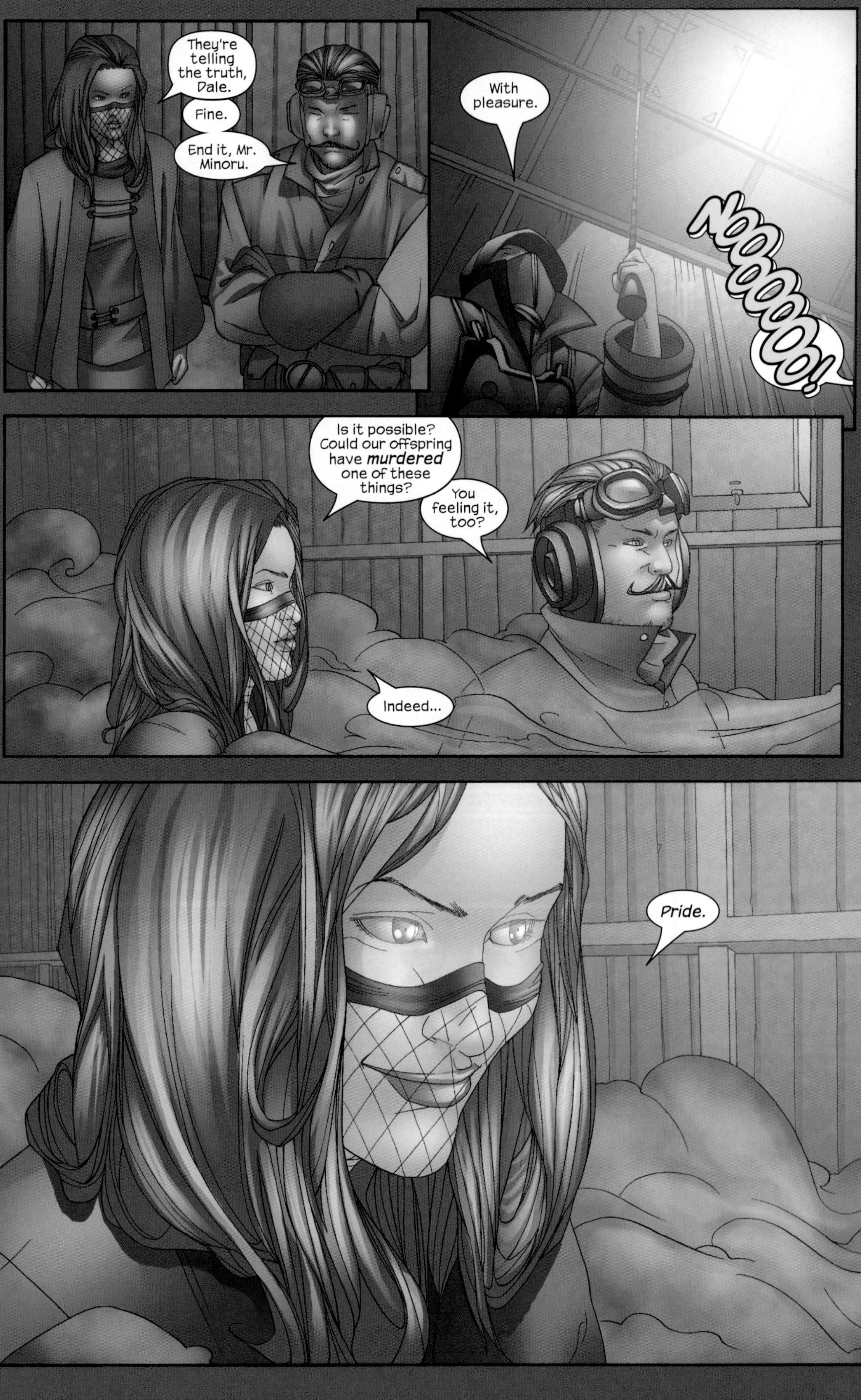
They're telling the truth, Dale.
Fine.
End it, Mr. Minoru.
With pleasure.
NOOOOOOO!
Is it possible? Could our offspring have *murdered* one of these things?
You feeling it, too?
Indeed...
Pride.

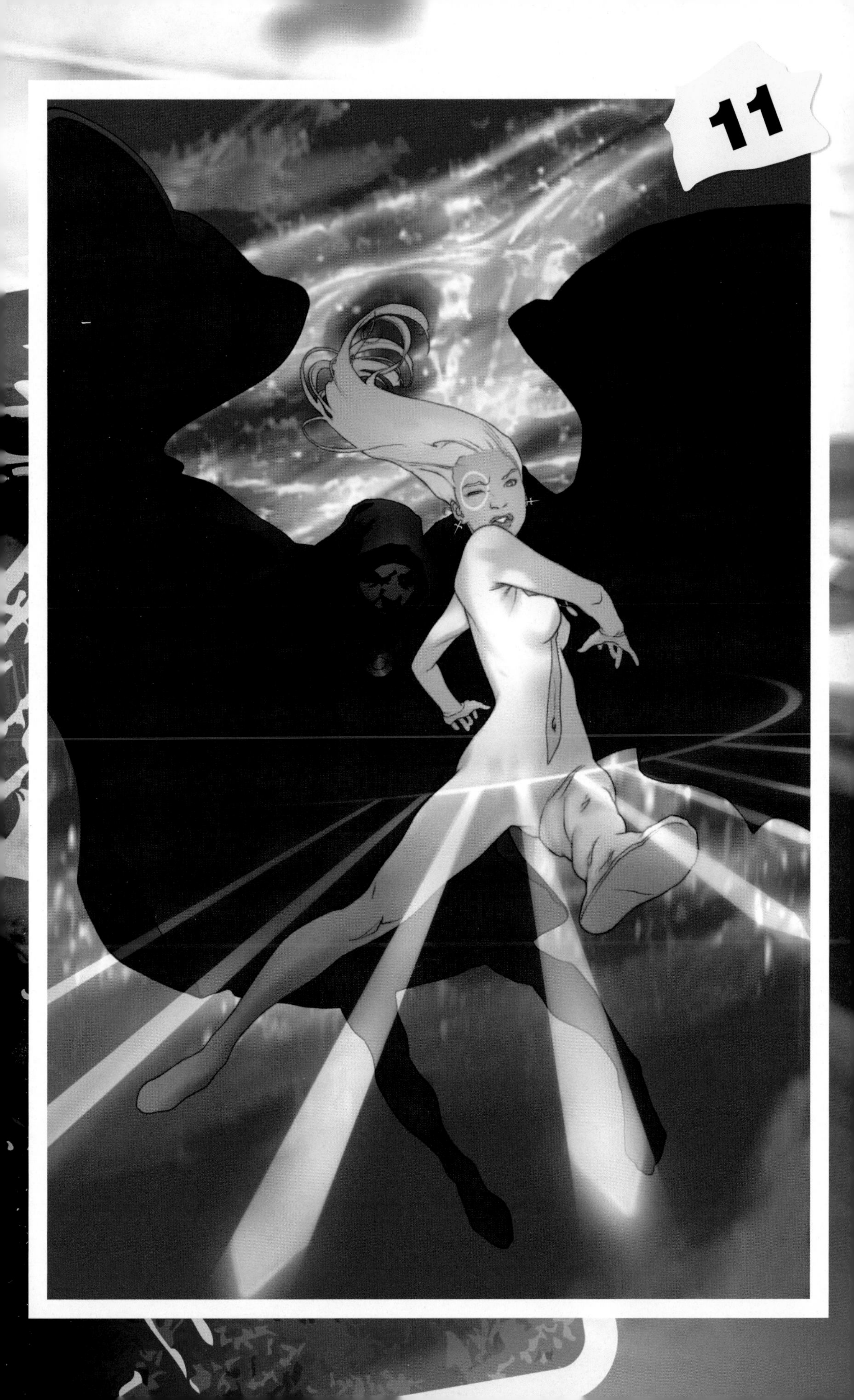
11

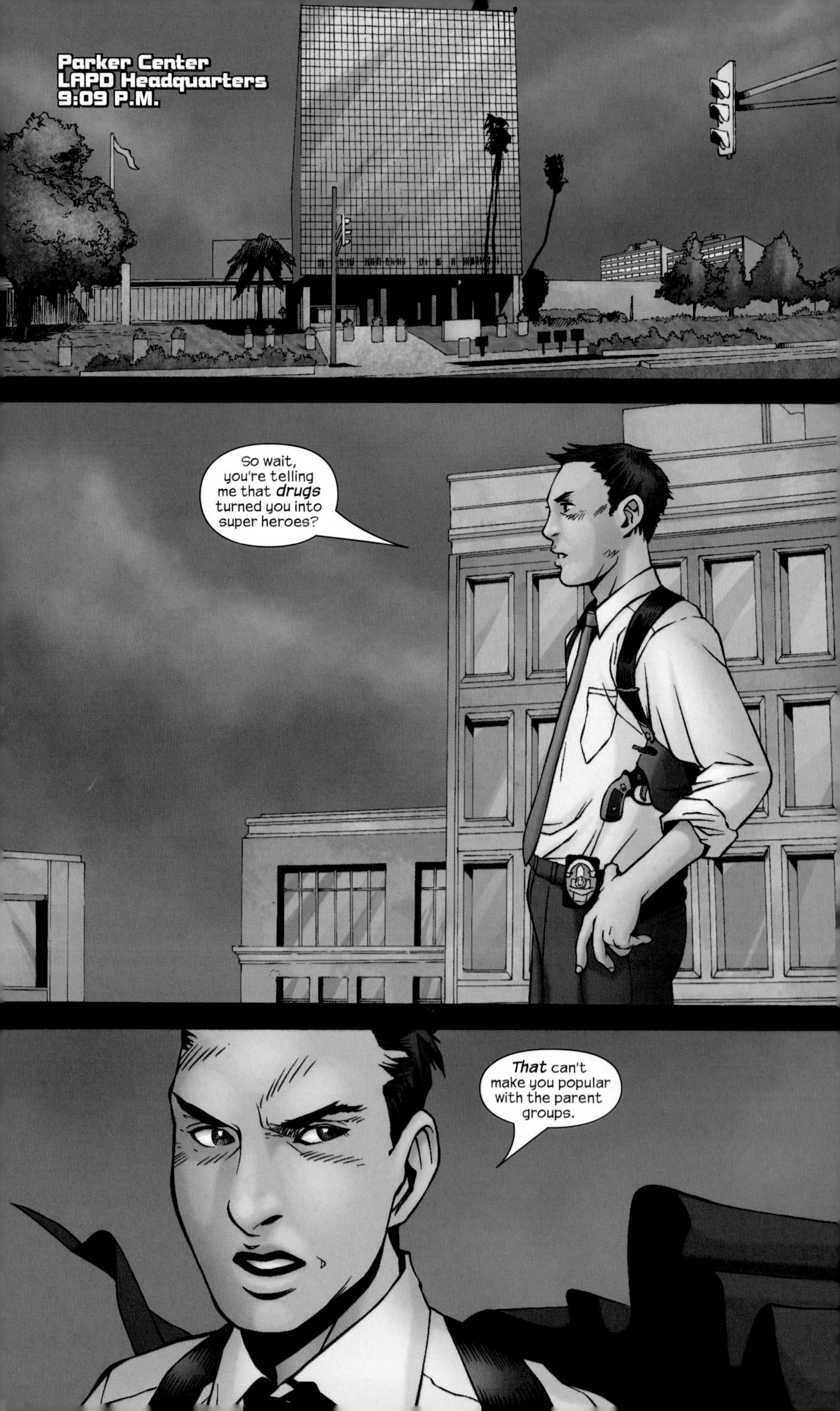
Parker Center
LAPD Headquarters
9:09 P.M.
So wait, you're telling me that *drugs* turned you into super heroes?
That can't make you popular with the parent groups.

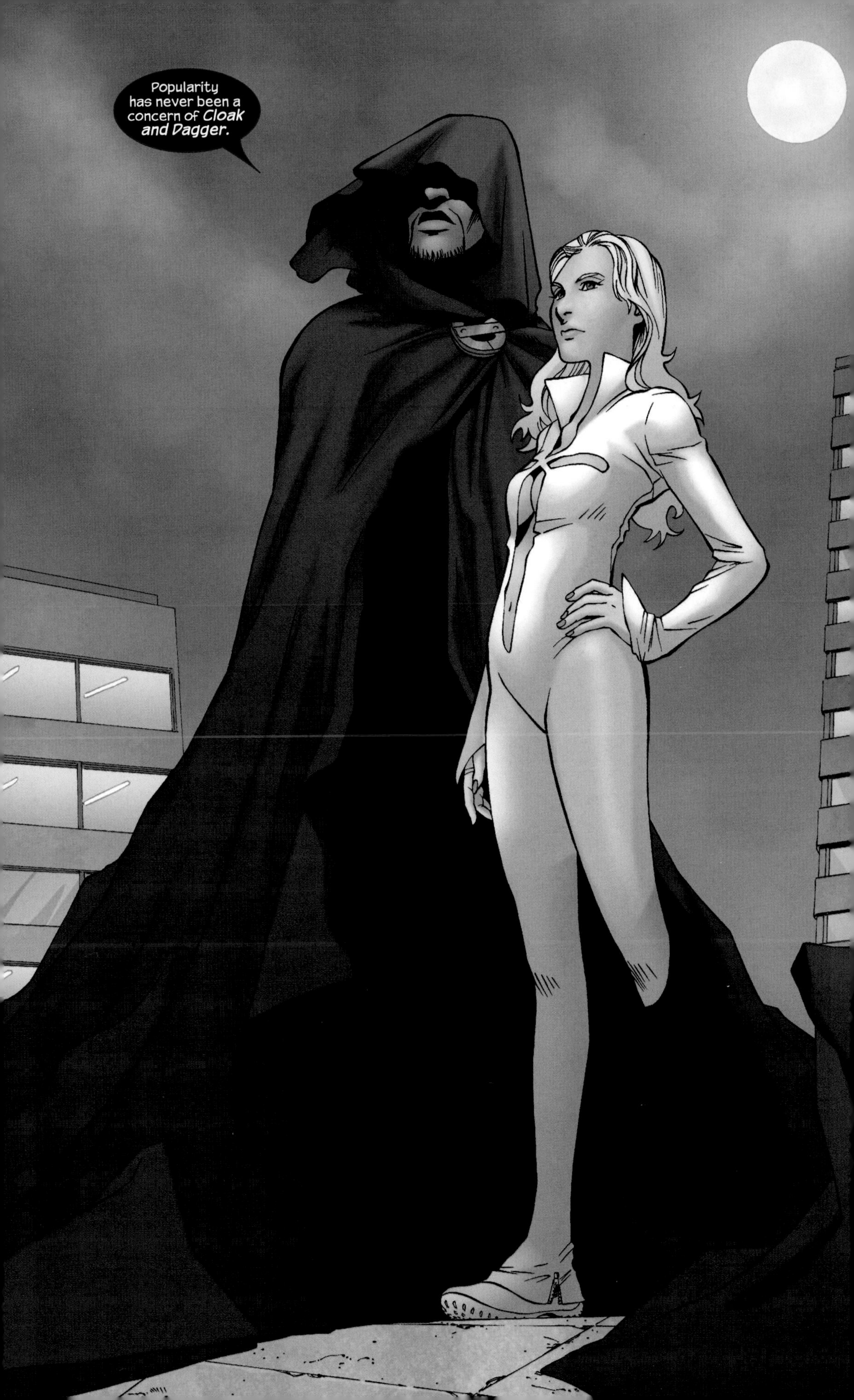
Popularity has never been a concern of *Cloak and Dagger.*

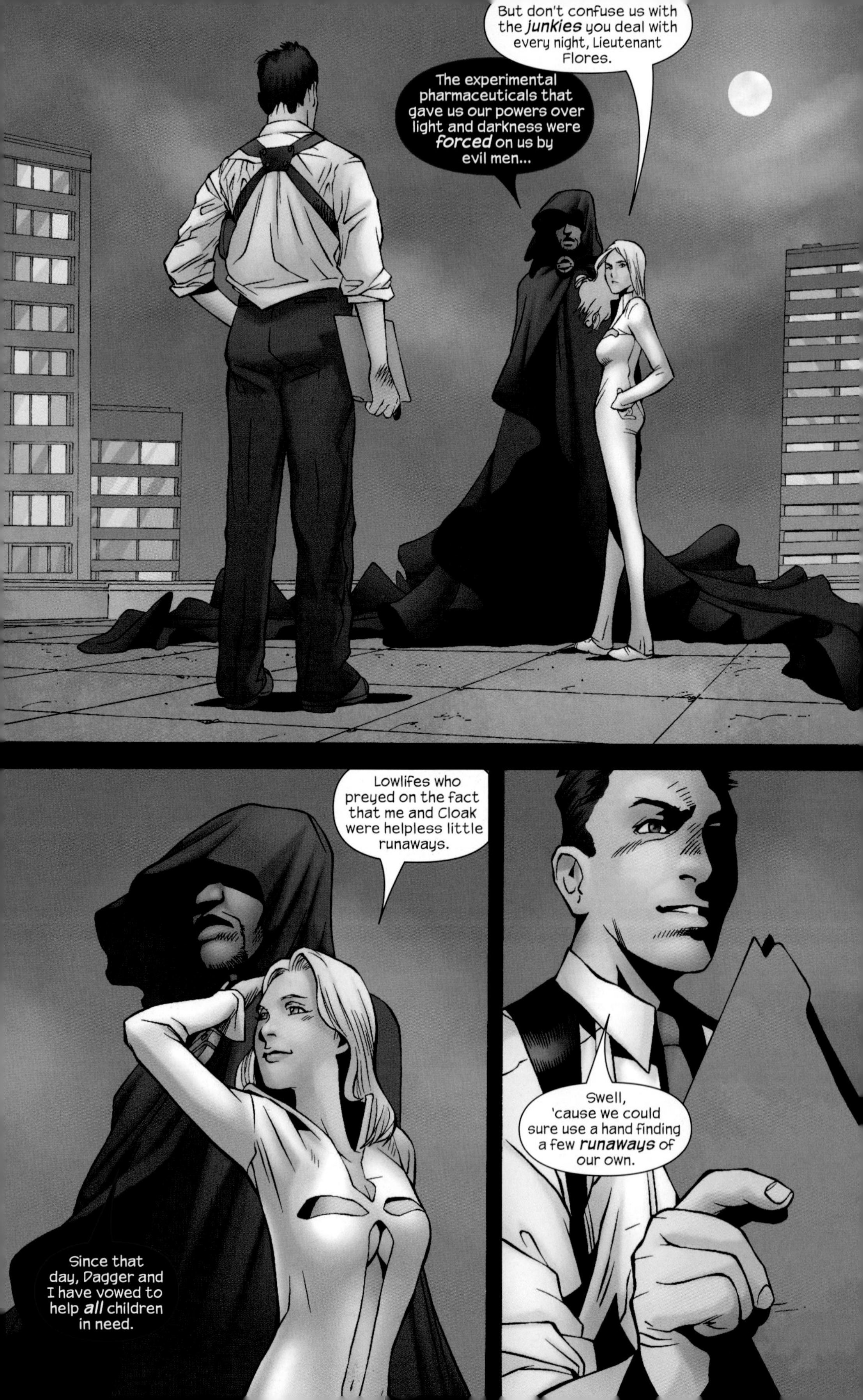
The experimental pharmaceuticals that gave us our powers over light and darkness were forced on us by evil men...
But don't confuse us with the junkies you deal with every night, Lieutenant Flores.
Lowlifes who preyed on the fact that me and Cloak were helpless little runaways.
Since that day, Dagger and I have vowed to help all children in need.
Swell, 'cause we could sure use a hand finding a few runaways of our own.

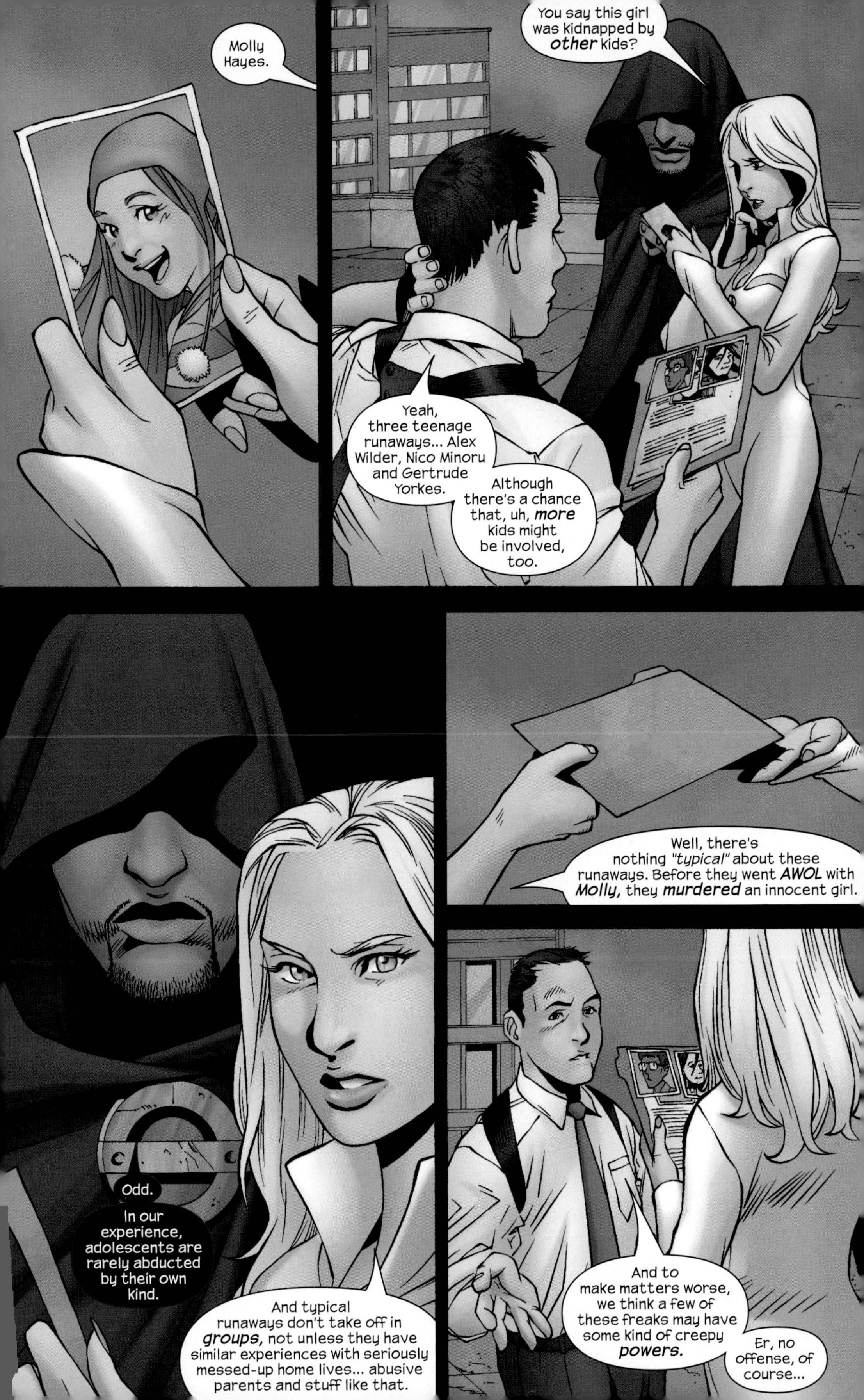
Molly Hayes.
You say this girl was kidnapped by *other* kids?
Yeah, three teenage runaways... Alex Wilder, Nico Minoru and Gertrude Yorkes.
Although there's a chance that, uh, *more* kids might be involved, too.
Odd.
In our experience, adolescents are rarely abducted by their own kind.
And typical runaways don't take off in *groups,* not unless they have similar experiences with seriously messed-up home lives... abusive parents and stuff like that.
Well, there's nothing *"typical"* about these runaways. Before they went *AWOL* with *Molly,* they *murdered* an innocent girl.
And to make matters worse, we think a few of these freaks may have some kind of creepy *powers.*
Er, no offense, of course...

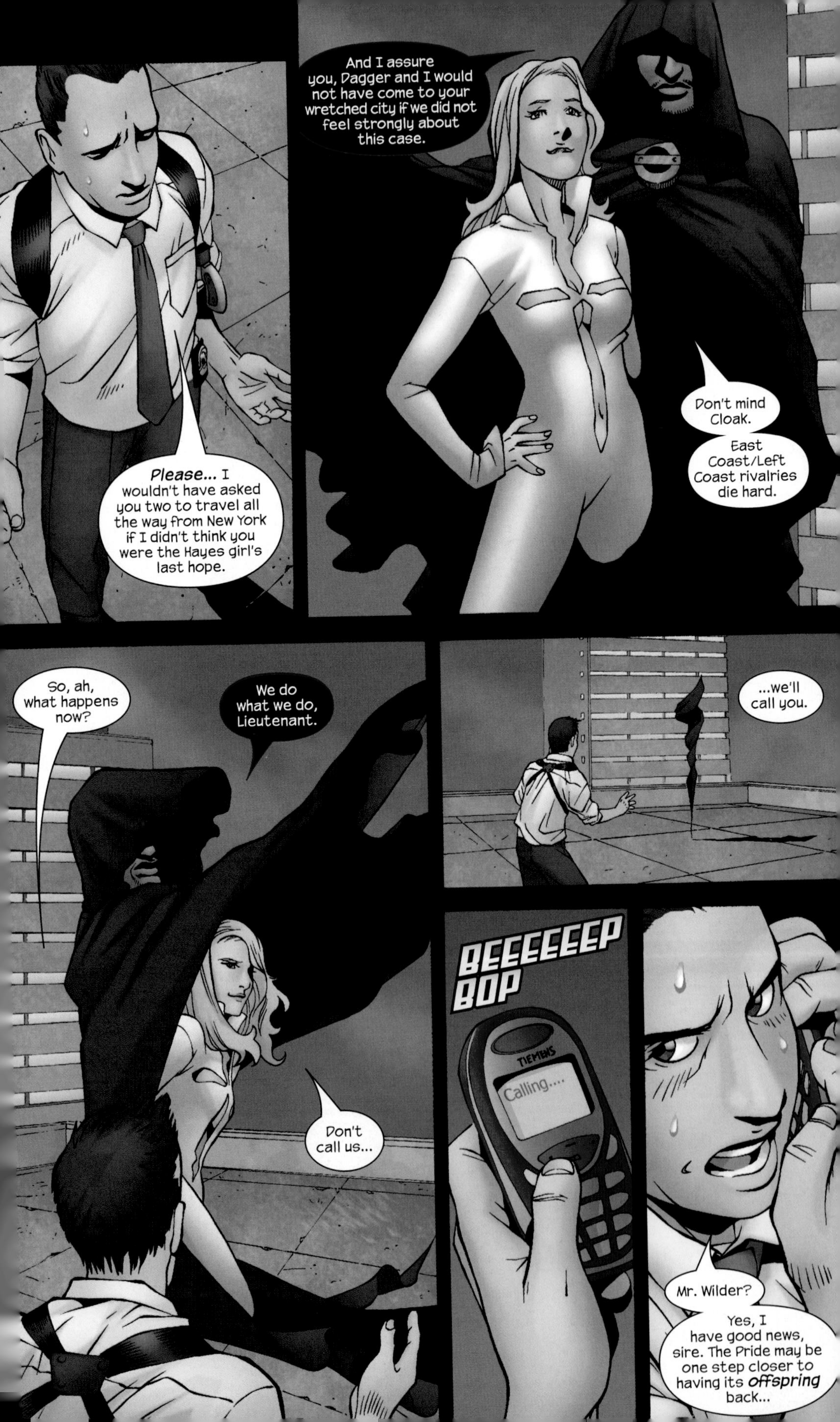
Please... I wouldn't have asked you two to travel all the way from New York if I didn't think you were the Hayes girl's last hope.
And I assure you, Dagger and I would not have come to your wretched city if we did not feel strongly about this case.
Don't mind Cloak.
East Coast/Left Coast rivalries die hard.
So, ah, what happens now?
We do what we do, Lieutenant.
Don't call us...
...we'll call you.
BEEEEEEP BOP
TIEMENS
Calling....
Mr. Wilder?
Yes, I have good news, sire. The Pride may be one step closer to having its offspring back...

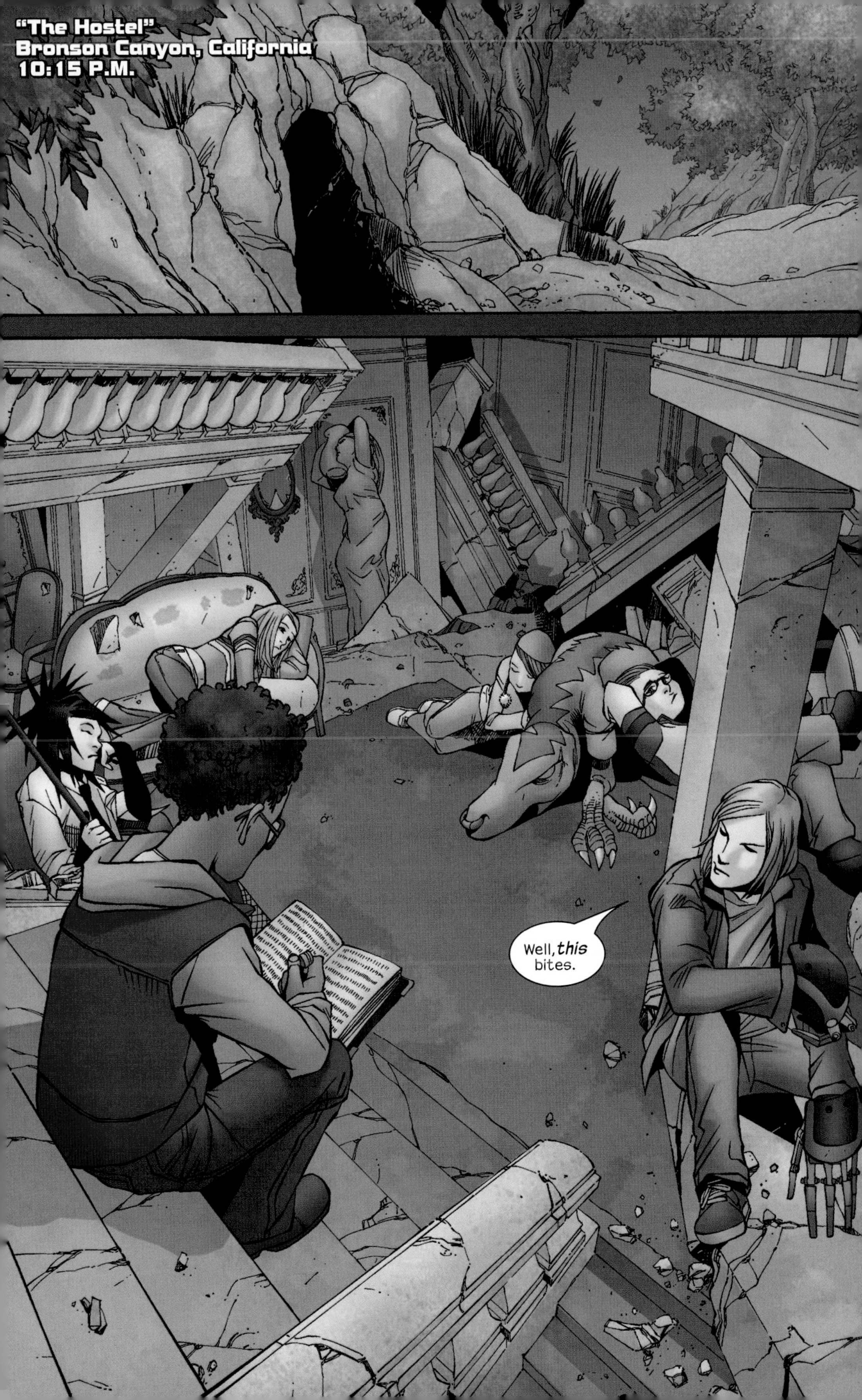
"The Hostel"
Bronson Canyon, California
10:15 P.M.
Well, *this* bites.

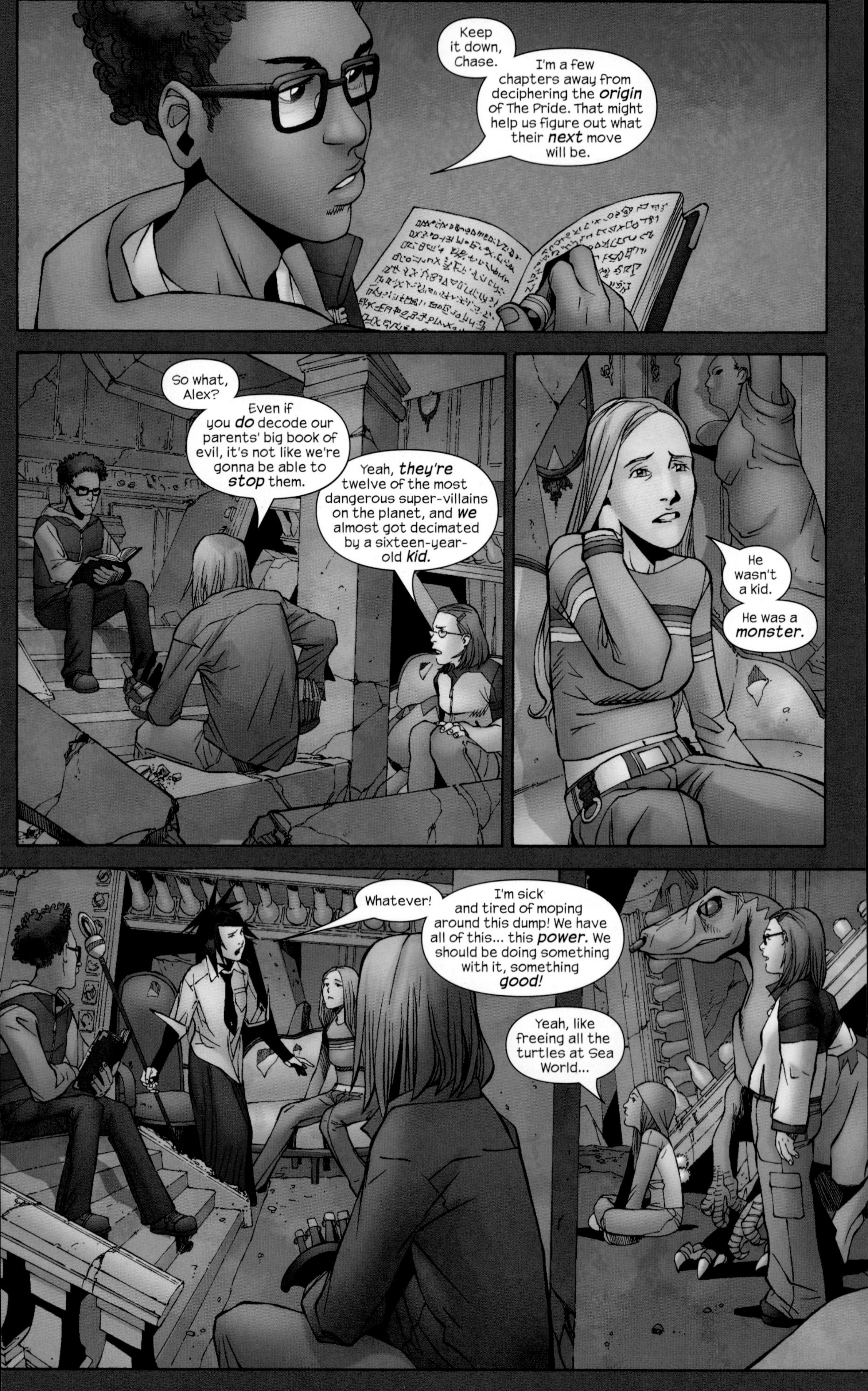
Keep it down, Chase.
I'm a few chapters away from deciphering the origin of The Pride. That might help us figure out what their next move will be.
So what, Alex?
Even if you do decode our parents' big book of evil, it's not like we're gonna be able to stop them.
Yeah, they're twelve of the most dangerous super-villains on the planet, and we almost got decimated by a sixteen-year-old kid.
He wasn't a kid.
He was a monster.
Whatever!
I'm sick and tired of moping around this dump! We have all of this... this power. We should be doing something with it, something good!
Yeah, like freeing all the turtles at Sea World...

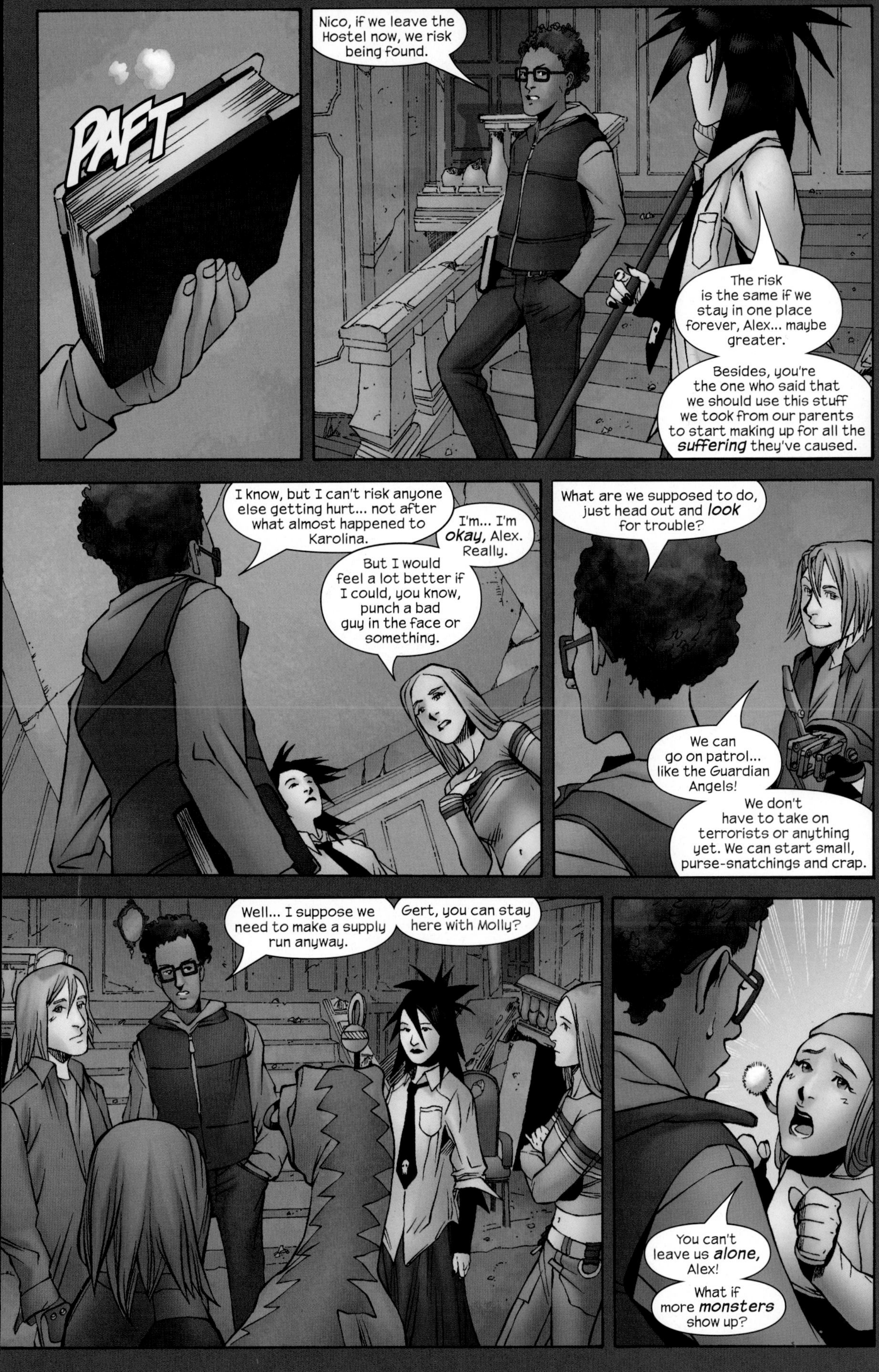

PAFT
Nico, if we leave the Hostel now, we risk being found.
The risk is the same if we stay in one place forever, Alex... maybe greater.
Besides, you're the one who said that we should use this stuff we took from our parents to start making up for all the *suffering* they've caused.
I know, but I can't risk anyone else getting hurt... not after what almost happened to Karolina.
I'm... I'm *okay,* Alex. Really.
But I would feel a lot better if I could, you know, punch a bad guy in the face or something.
What are we supposed to do, just head out and *look* for trouble?
We can go on patrol... like the Guardian Angels!
We don't have to take on terrorists or anything yet. We can start small, purse-snatchings and crap.
Well... I suppose we need to make a supply run anyway.
Gert, you can stay here with Molly?
You can't leave us *alone,* Alex!
What if more *monsters* show up?

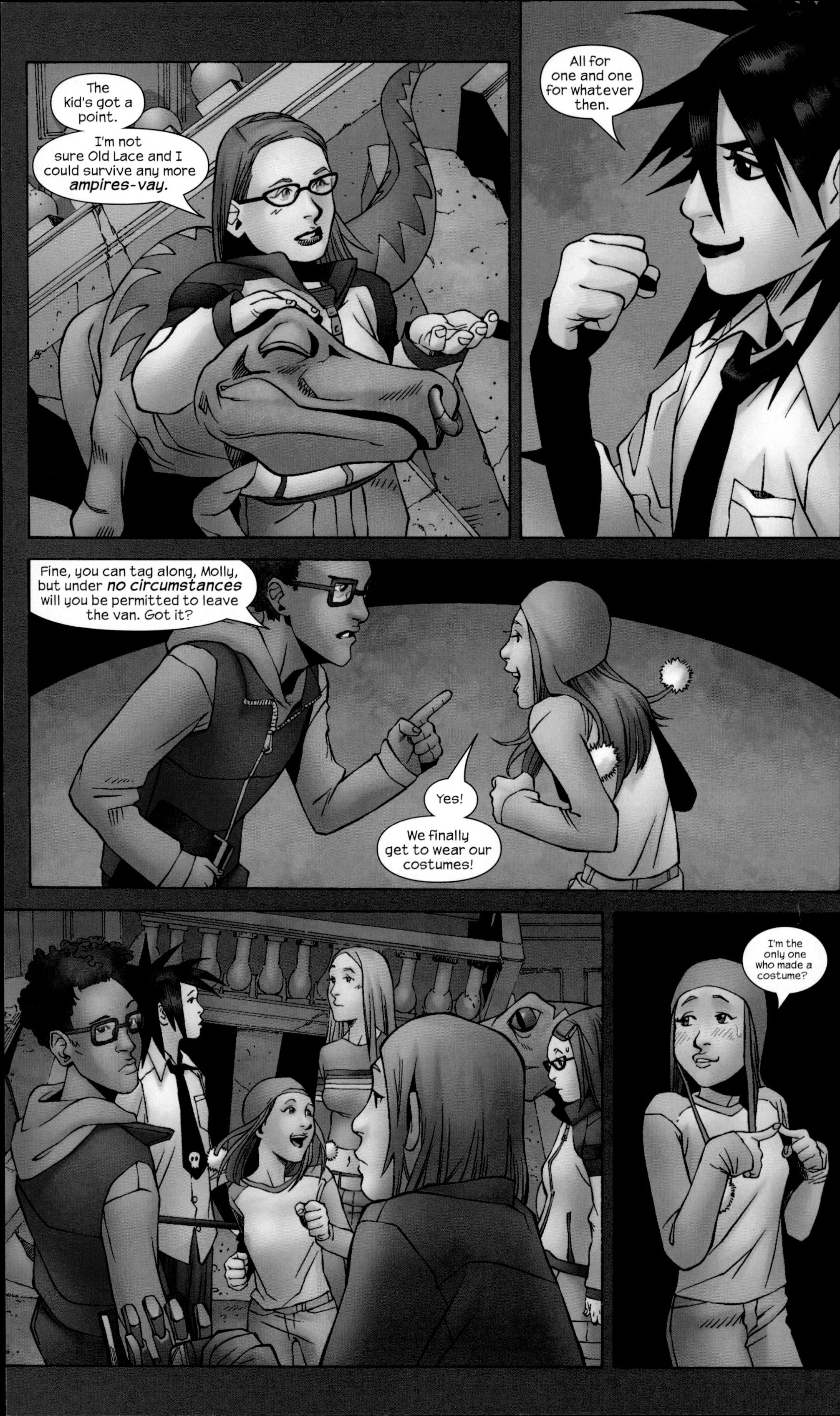
The kid's got a point.
I'm not sure Old Lace and I could survive any more *ampires-vay.*
All for one and one for whatever then.
Fine, you can tag along, Molly, but under *no circumstances* will you be permitted to leave the van. Got it?
Yes!
We finally get to wear our costumes!
I'm the only one who made a costume?

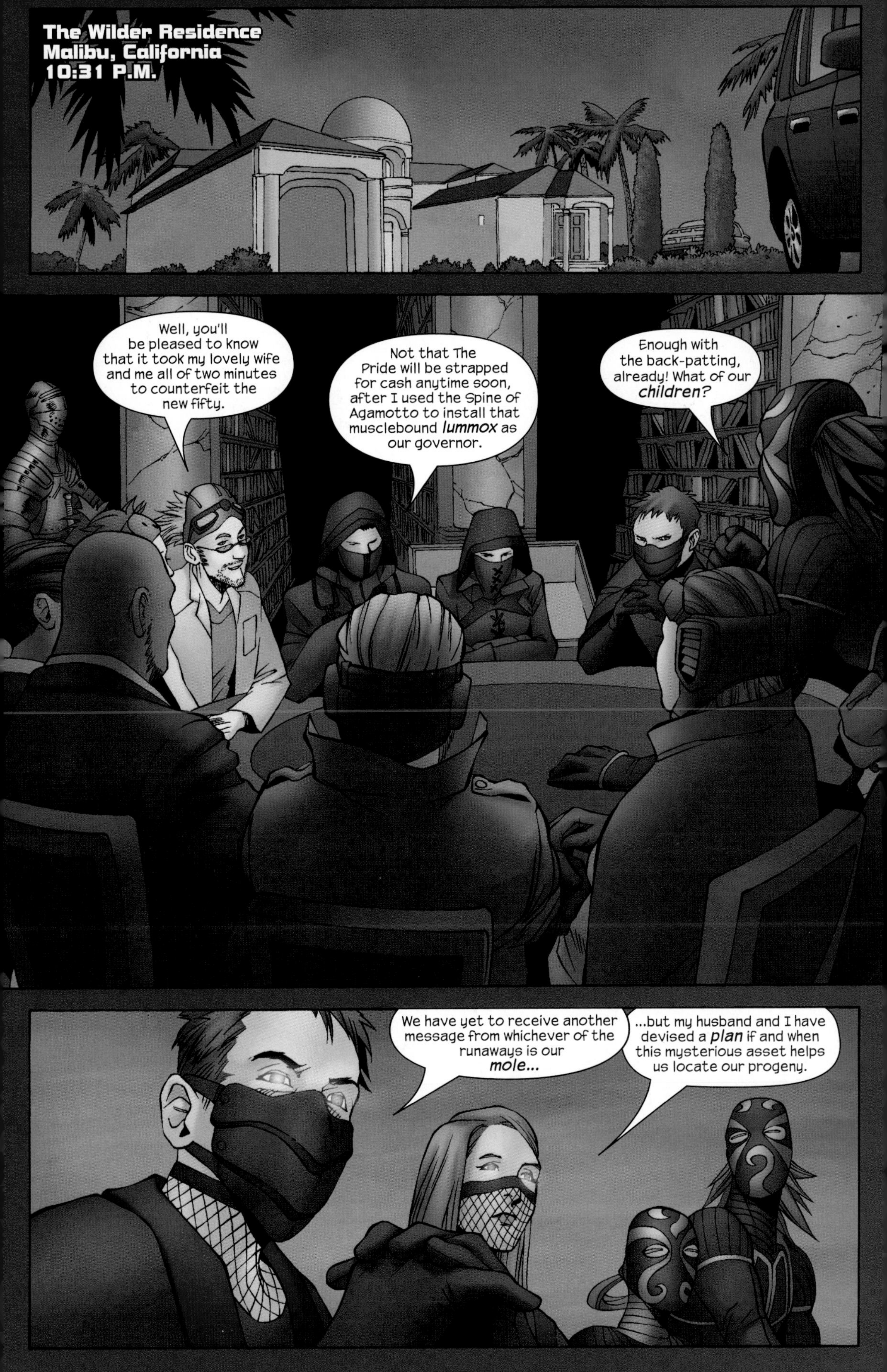
The Wilder Residence
Malibu, California
10:31 P.M.
Well, you'll be pleased to know that it took my lovely wife and me all of two minutes to counterfeit the new fifty.
Not that The Pride will be strapped for cash anytime soon, after I used the Spine of Agamotto to install that musclebound *lummox* as our governor.
Enough with the back-patting, already! What of our *children*?
We have yet to receive another message from whichever of the runaways is our *mole*...
...but my husband and I have devised a *plan* if and when this mysterious asset helps us locate our progeny.

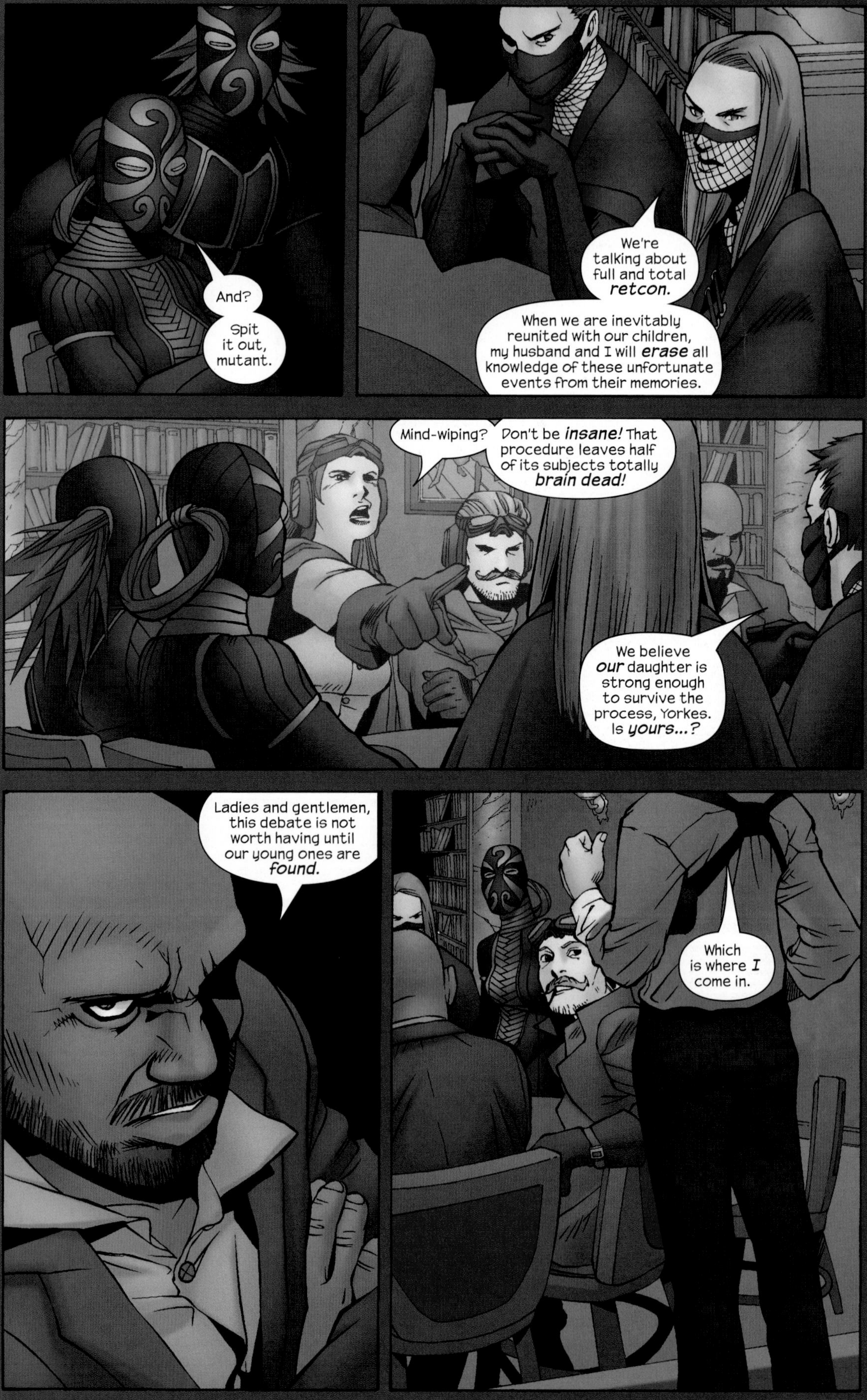
And?
Spit it out, mutant.
We're talking about full and total retcon.
When we are inevitably reunited with our children, my husband and I will erase all knowledge of these unfortunate events from their memories.
Mind-wiping?
Don't be insane! That procedure leaves half of its subjects totally brain dead!
We believe our daughter is strong enough to survive the process, Yorkes. Is yours...?
Ladies and gentlemen, this debate is not worth having until our young ones are found.
Which is where I come in.

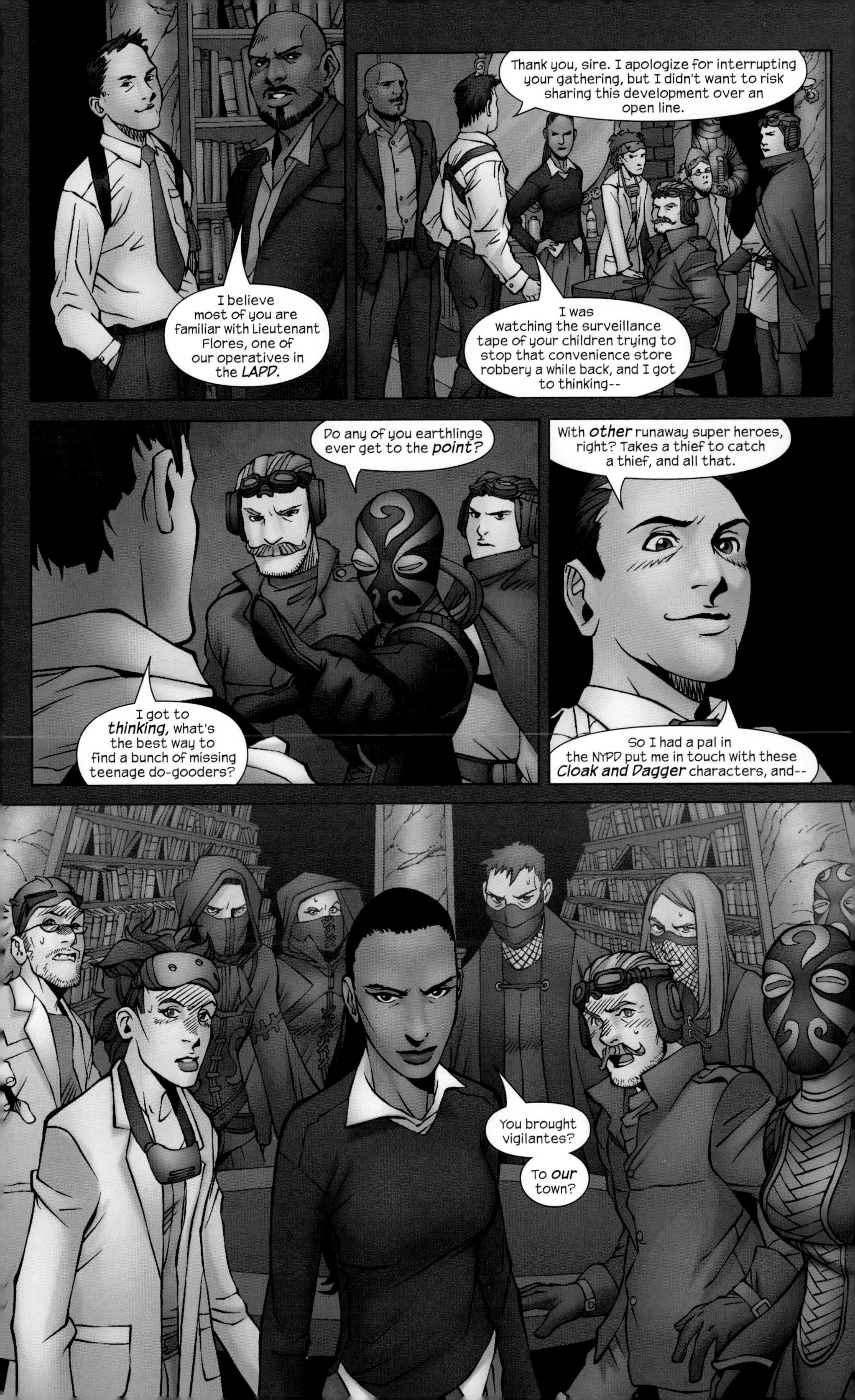
I believe most of you are familiar with Lieutenant Flores, one of our operatives in the *LAPD.*
Thank you, sire. I apologize for interrupting your gathering, but I didn't want to risk sharing this development over an open line.
I was watching the surveillance tape of your children trying to stop that convenience store robbery a while back, and I got to thinking--
I got to *thinking,* what's the best way to find a bunch of missing teenage do-gooders?
Do any of you earthlings ever get to the *point?*
With *other* runaway super heroes, right? Takes a thief to catch a thief, and all that.
So I had a pal in the NYPD put me in touch with these *Cloak and Dagger* characters, and--
You brought vigilantes?
To *our* town?

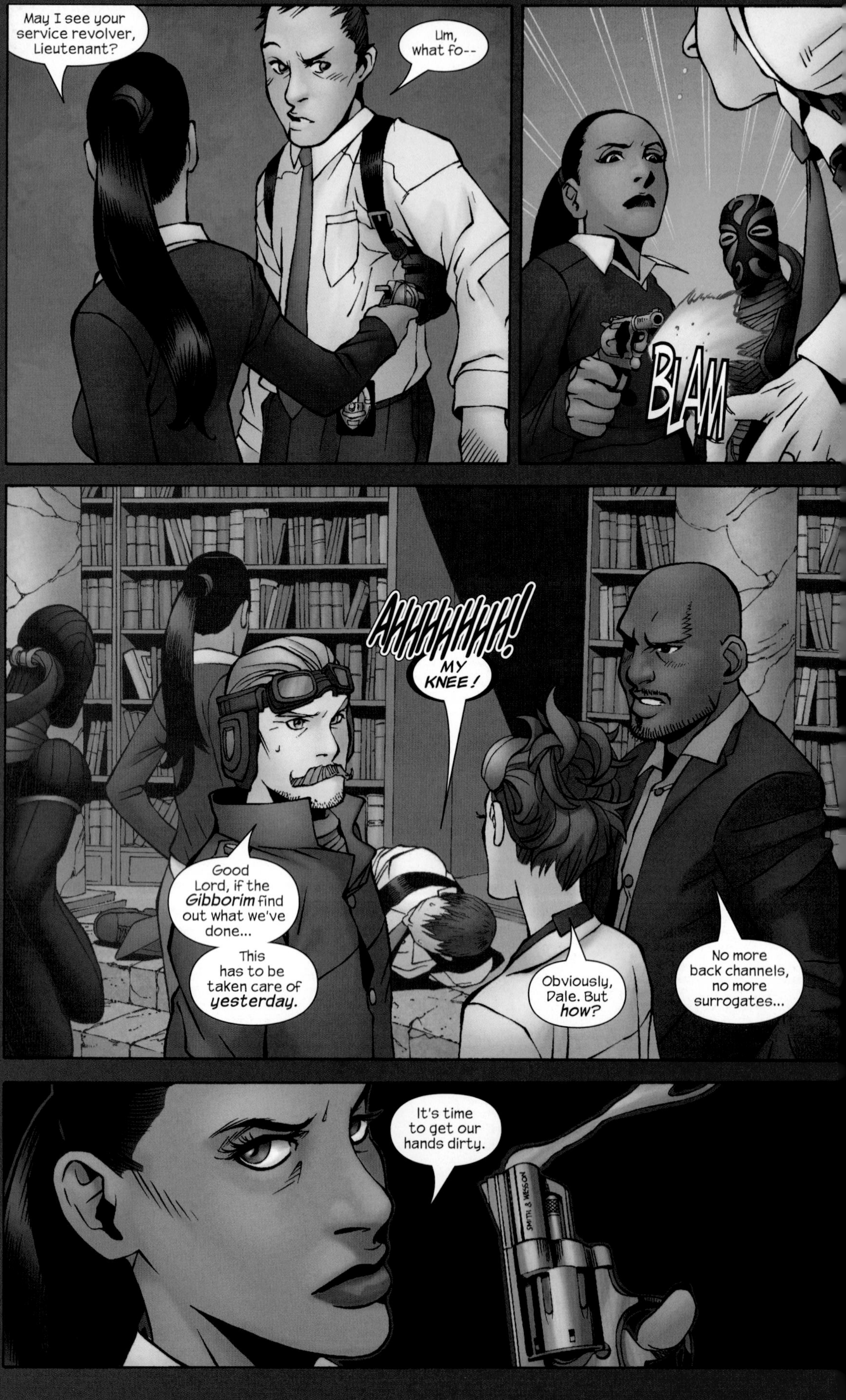

May I see your service revolver, Lieutenant?
Um, what fo--
BLAM
AHHHHHHH! MY KNEE!
Good Lord, if the *Gibborim* find out what we've done...
This has to be taken care of *yesterday*.
Obviously, Dale. But *how*?
No more back channels, no more surrogates...
It's time to get our hands dirty.
SMITH & WESSON

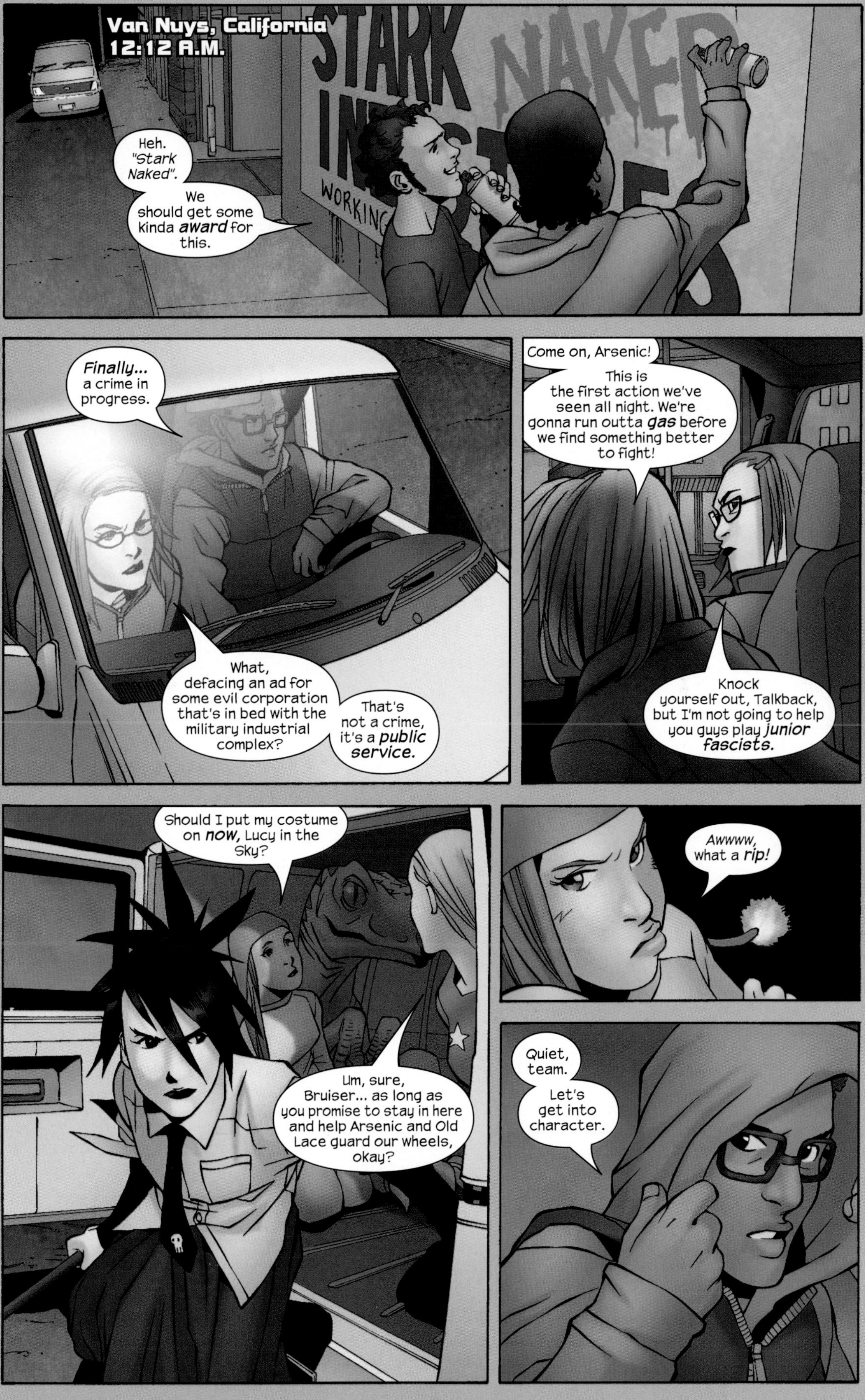
Van Nuys, California
12:12 A.M.
STARK NAKED
WORKING
Heh. "Stark Naked".
We should get some kinda *award* for this.
Finally... a crime in progress.
What, defacing an ad for some evil corporation that's in bed with the military industrial complex?
That's not a crime, it's a *public service.*
Come on, Arsenic!
This is the first action we've seen all night. We're gonna run outta *gas* before we find something better to fight!
Knock yourself out, Talkback, but I'm not going to help you guys play *junior fascists.*
Should I put my costume on *now,* Lucy in the Sky?
Um, sure, Bruiser... as long as you promise to stay in here and help Arsenic and Old Lace guard our wheels, okay?
Awwww, what a rip!
Quiet, team.
Let's get into character.

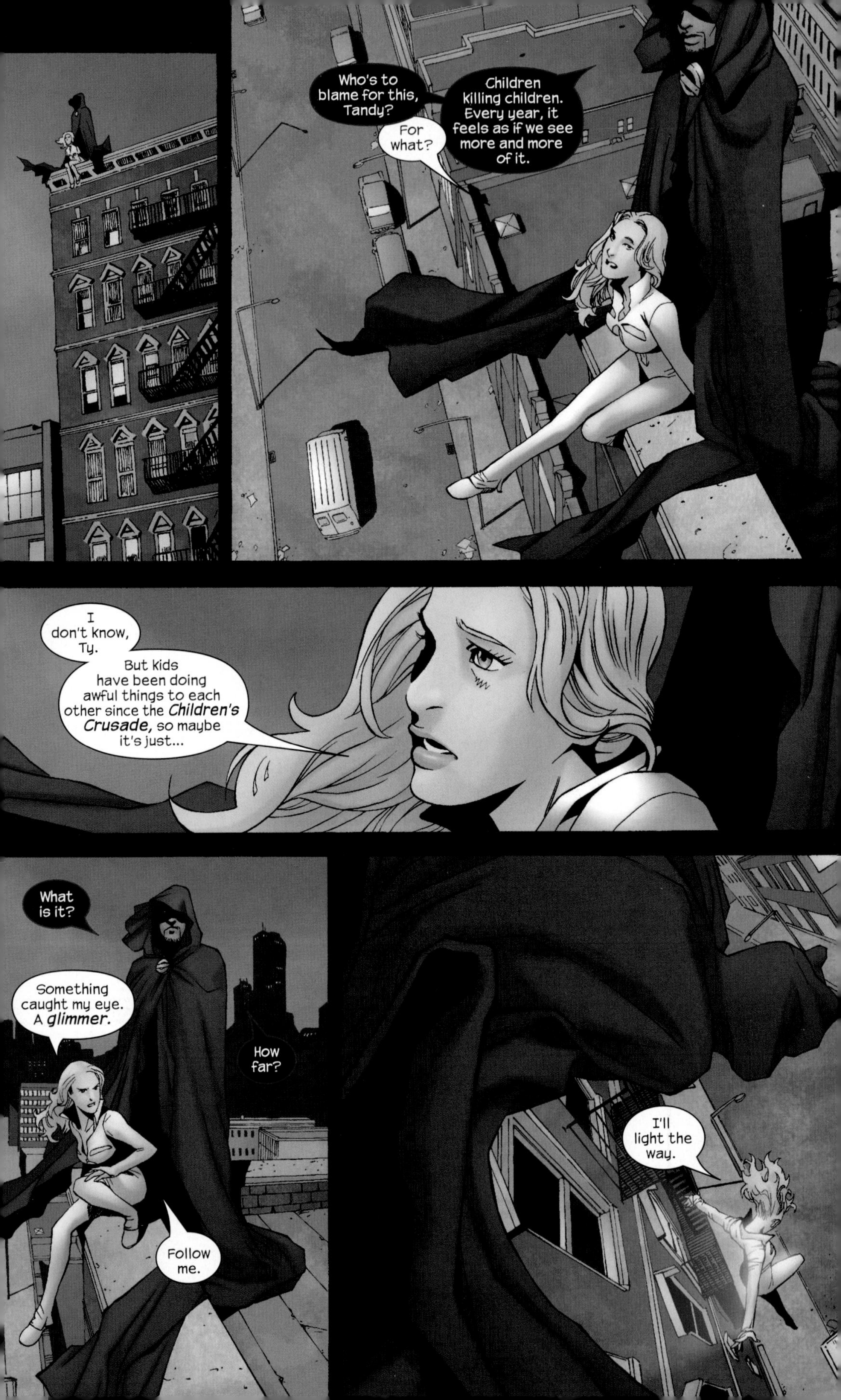
Who's to blame for this, Tandy?
For what?
Children killing children. Every year, it feels as if we see more and more of it.
I don't know, Ty.
But kids have been doing awful things to each other since the *Children's Crusade*, so maybe it's just...
What is it?
Something caught my eye. A *glimmer*.
How far?
Follow me.
I'll light the way.

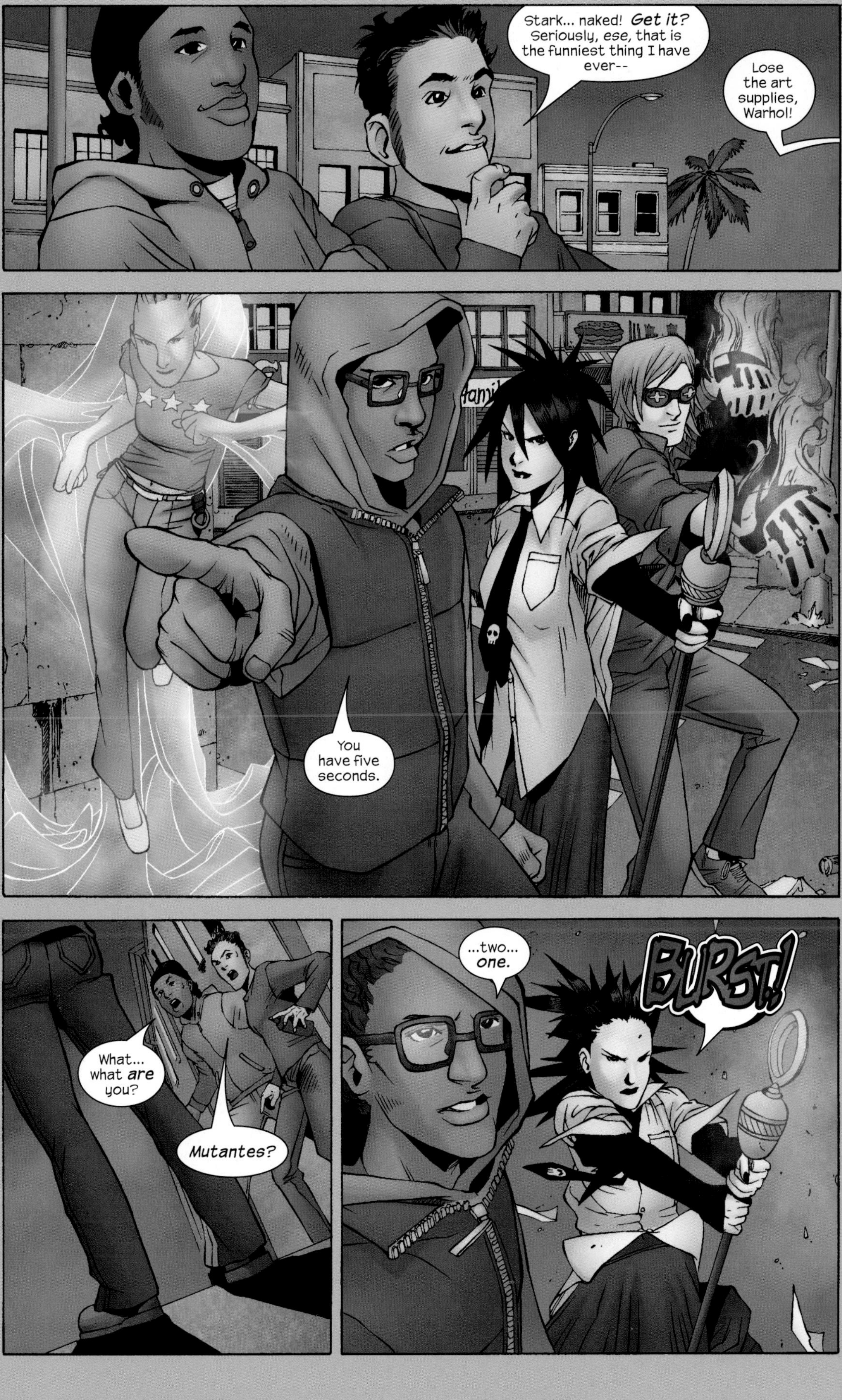
Stark... naked! Get it? Seriously, ese, that is the funniest thing I have ever--
Lose the art supplies, Warhol!
You have five seconds.
What... what are you?
Mutantes?
...two... one.
BURST!

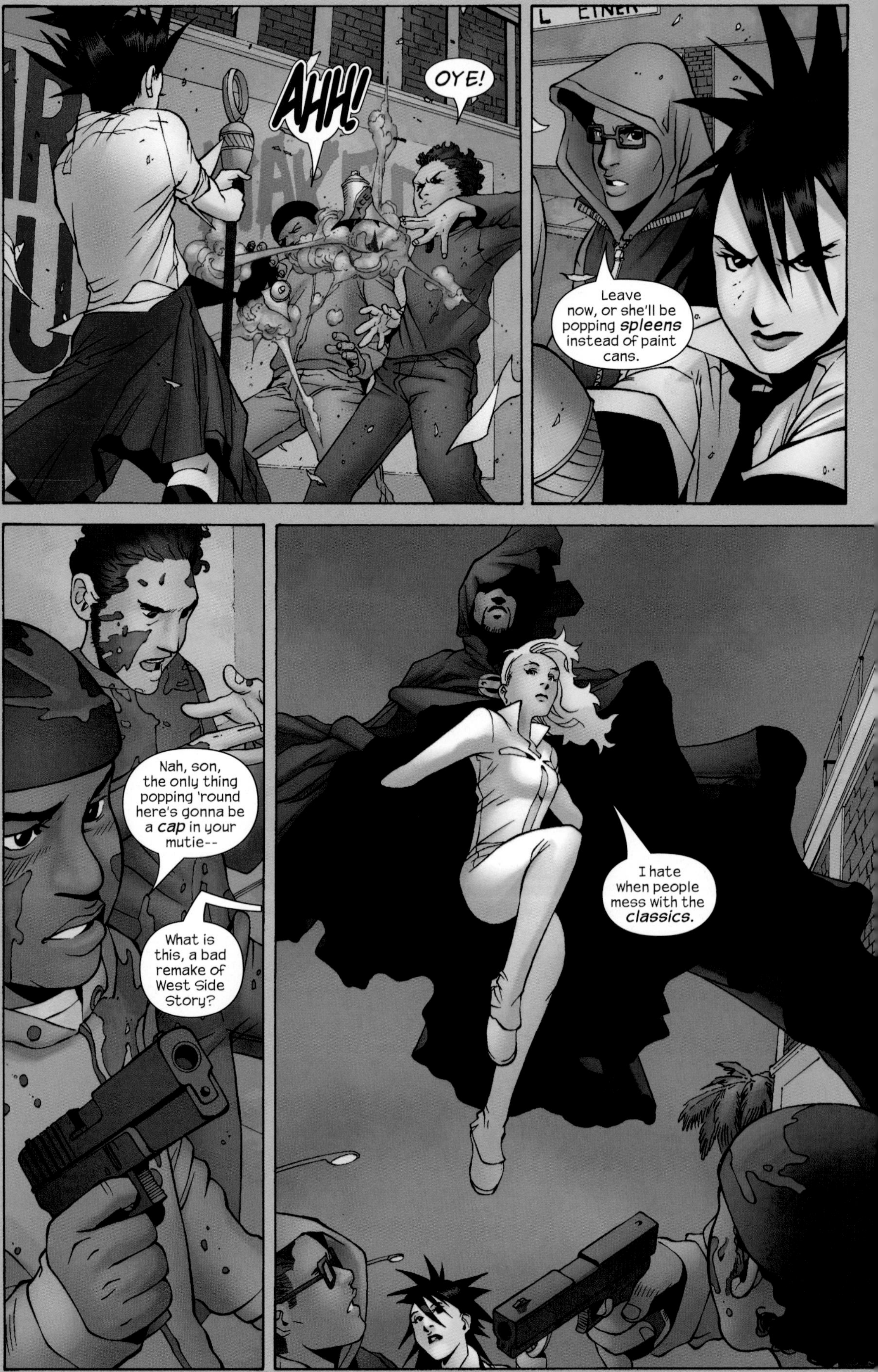
AHH!
OYE!
Leave now, or she'll be popping *spleens* instead of paint cans.
Nah, son, the only thing popping 'round here's gonna be a *cap* in your mutie--
What is this, a bad remake of West Side Story?
I hate when people mess with the *classics.*

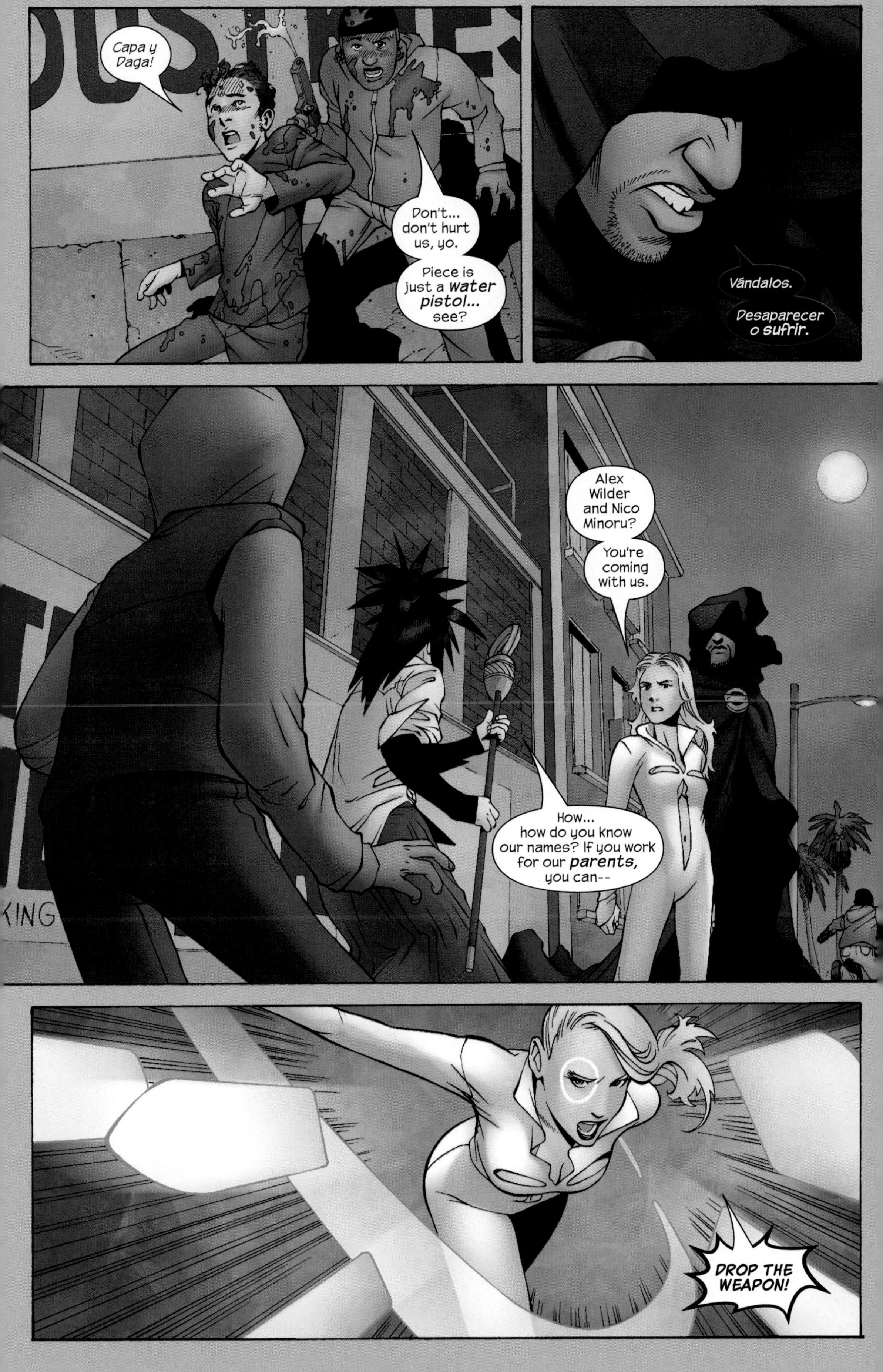
Capa y Daga!
Don't... don't hurt us, yo.
Piece is just a *water pistol...* see?
Vándalos.
Desaparecer o *sufrir.*
KING
Alex Wilder and Nico Minoru?
You're coming with us.
How... how do you know our names? If you work for our *parents,* you can--
DROP THE WEAPON!

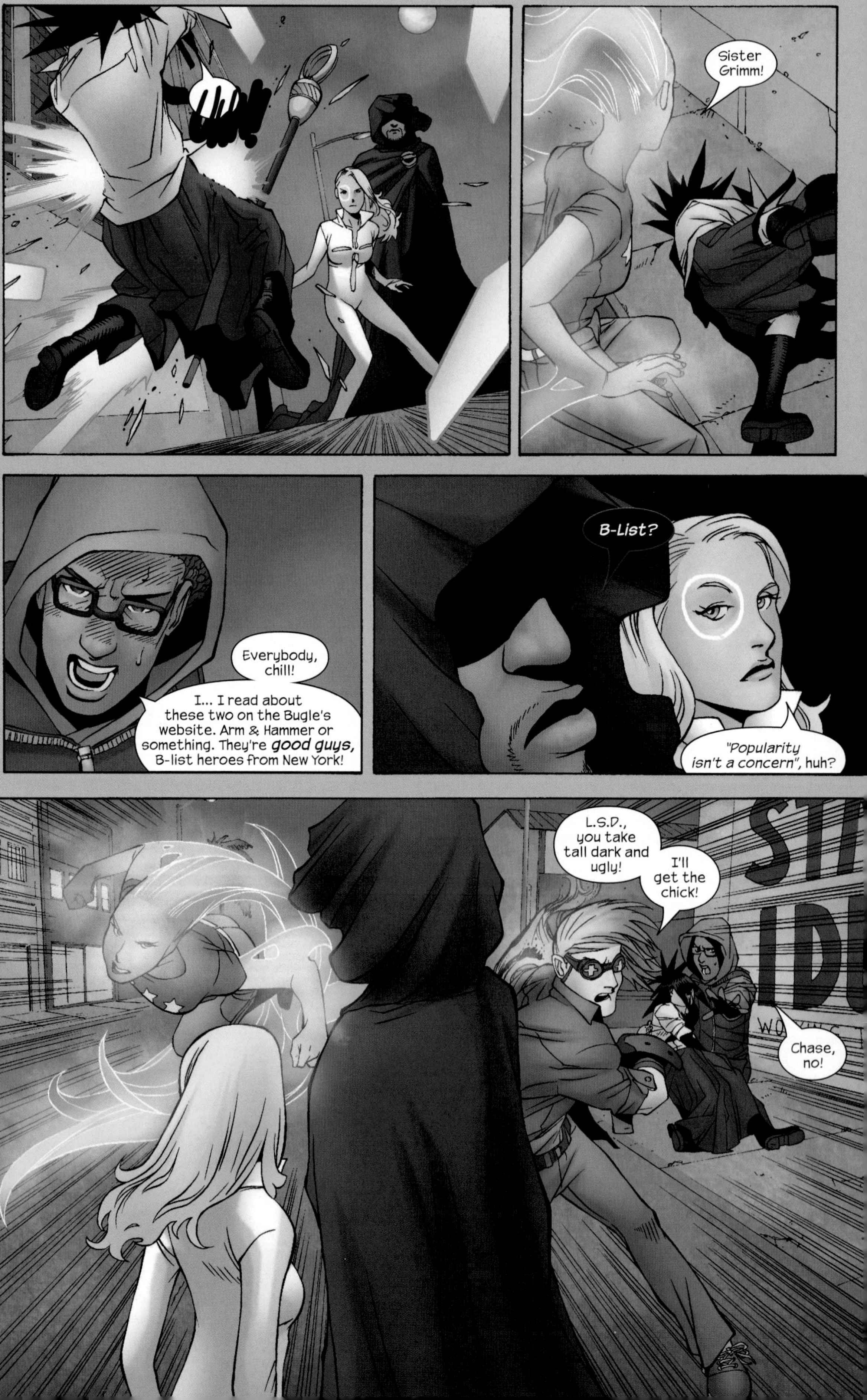

UHH!
Sister Grimm!
Everybody, chill!
I... I read about these two on the Bugle's website. Arm & Hammer or something. They're *good guys,* B-list heroes from New York!
B-List?
"Popularity isn't a concern", huh?
L.S.D., you take tall dark and ugly!
I'll get the chick!
Chase, no!

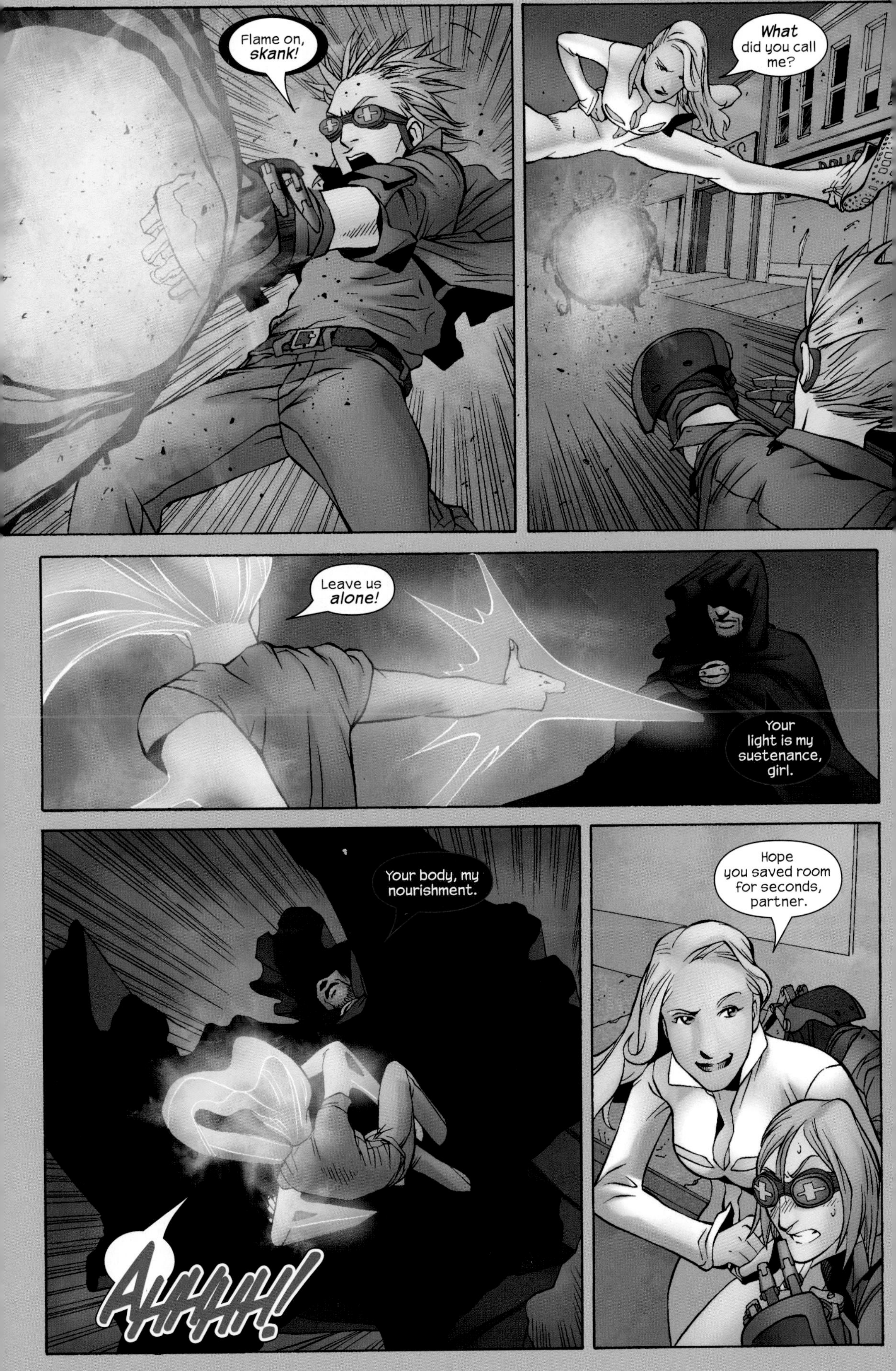
Flame on, skank!
What did you call me?
Leave us alone!
Your light is my sustenance, girl.
Your body, my nourishment.
AHHHH!
Hope you saved room for seconds, partner.

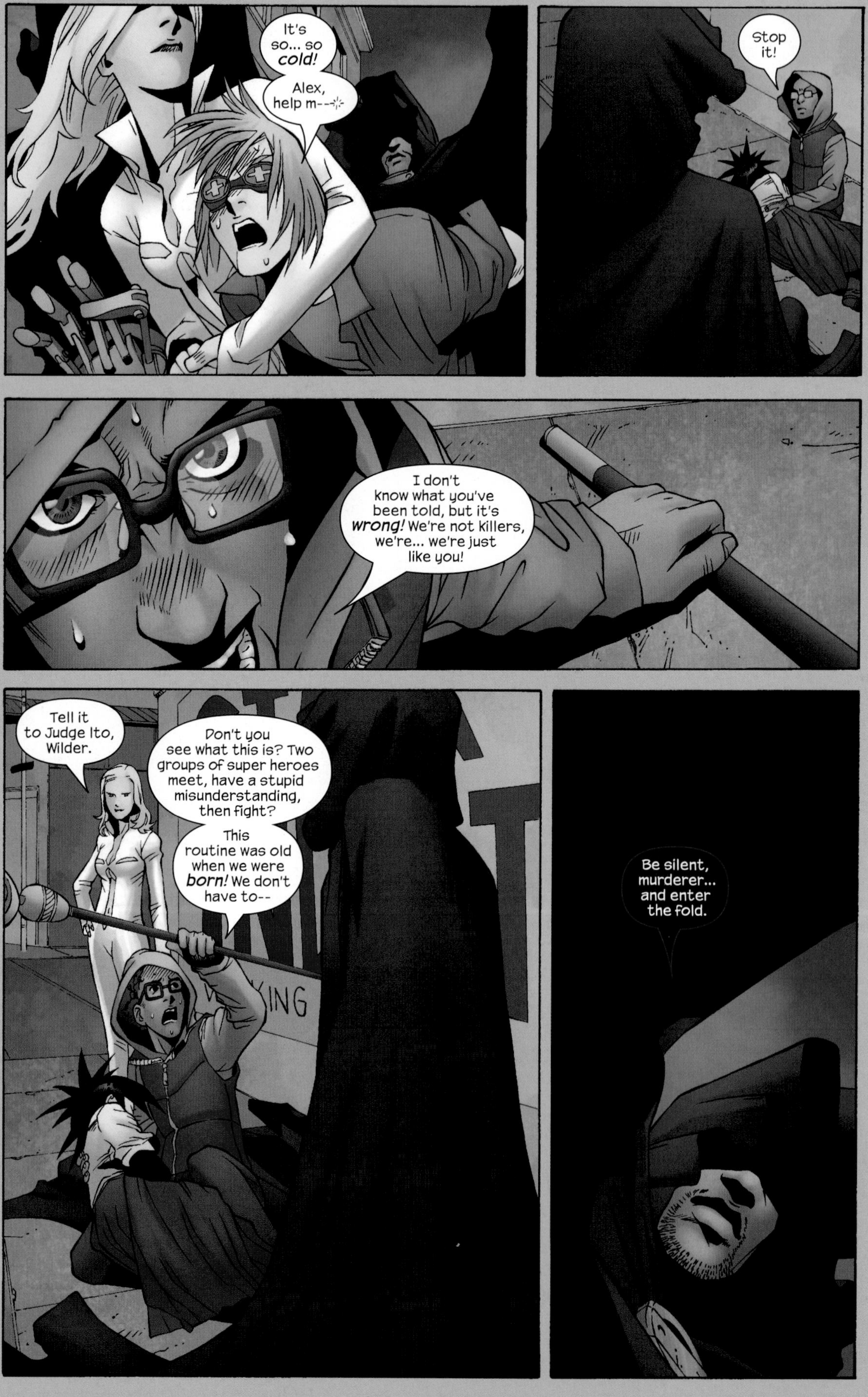
It's so... so *cold!*
Alex, help m--
Stop it!
I don't know what you've been told, but it's *wrong!* We're not killers, we're... we're just like you!
Tell it to Judge Ito, Wilder.
Don't you see what this is? Two groups of super heroes meet, have a stupid misunderstanding, then fight?
This routine was old when we were *born!* We don't have to--
Be silent, murderer... and enter the fold.

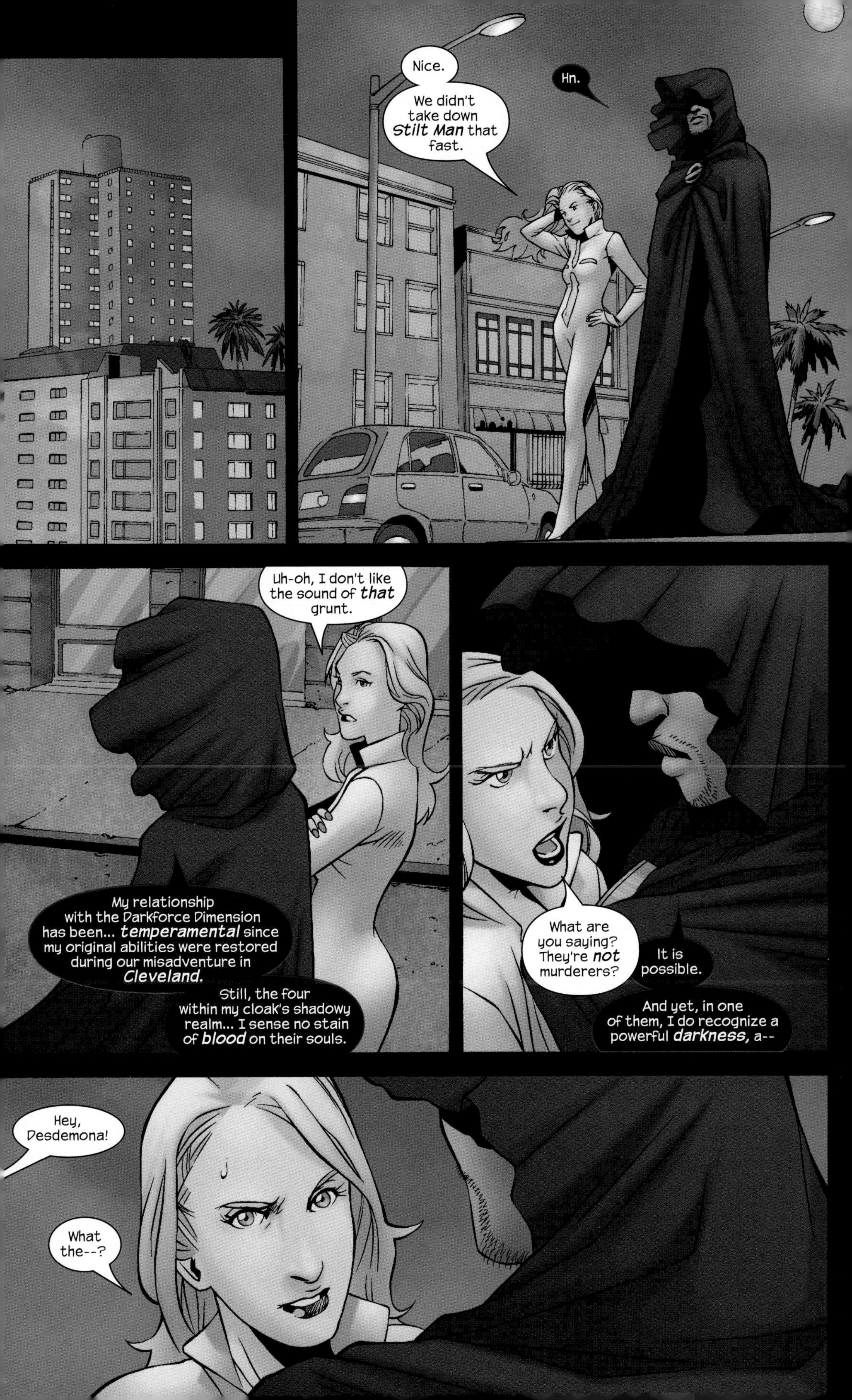
Nice.
We didn't take down Stilt Man that fast.
Hn.
Uh-oh, I don't like the sound of that grunt.
My relationship with the Darkforce Dimension has been... temperamental since my original abilities were restored during our misadventure in Cleveland.
Still, the four within my cloak's shadowy realm... I sense no stain of blood on their souls.
What are you saying? They're not murderers?
It is possible.
And yet, in one of them, I do recognize a powerful darkness, a--
Hey, Desdemona!
What the--?

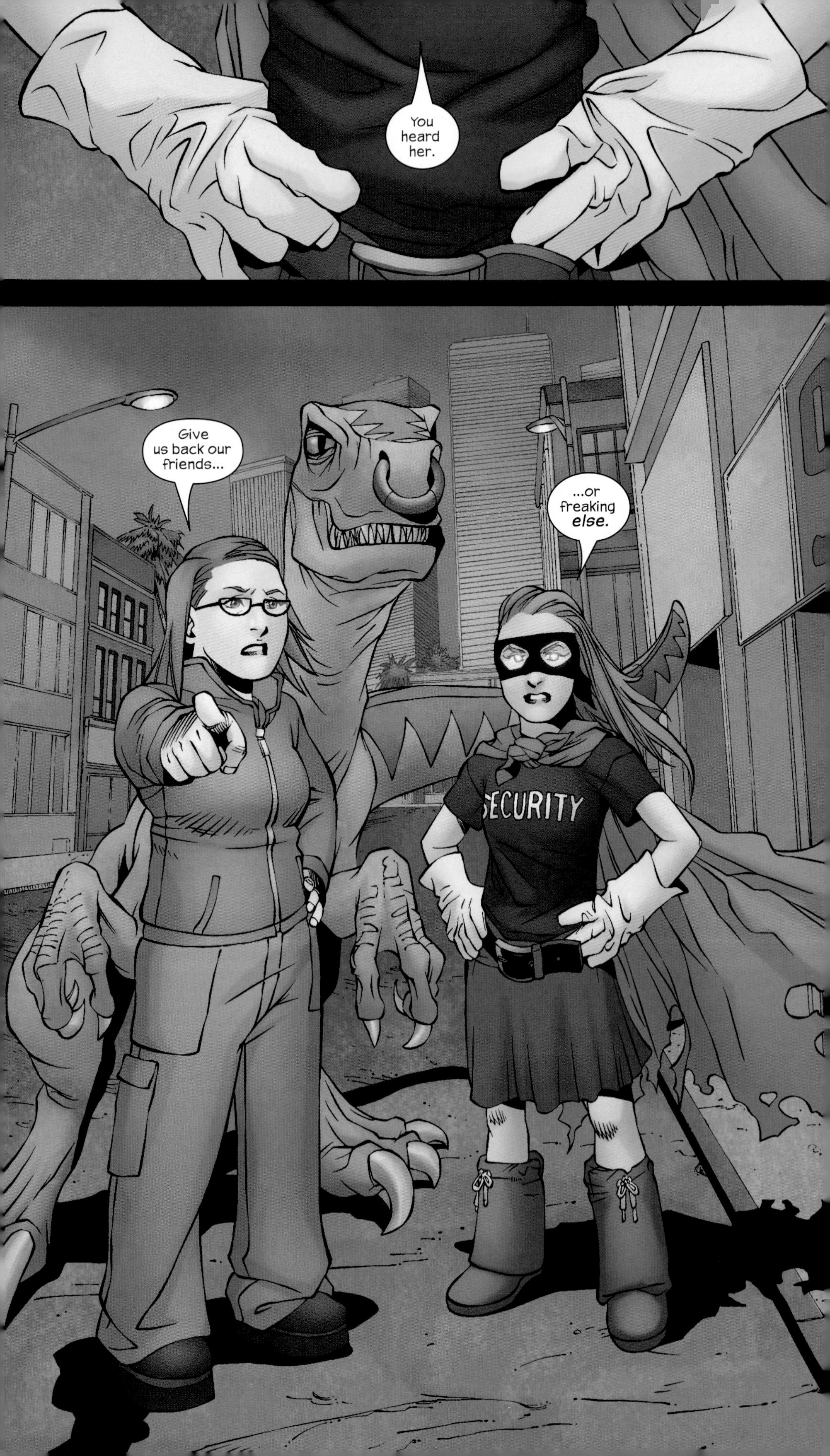
You heard her.
Give us back our friends...
...or freaking *else.*
SECURITY

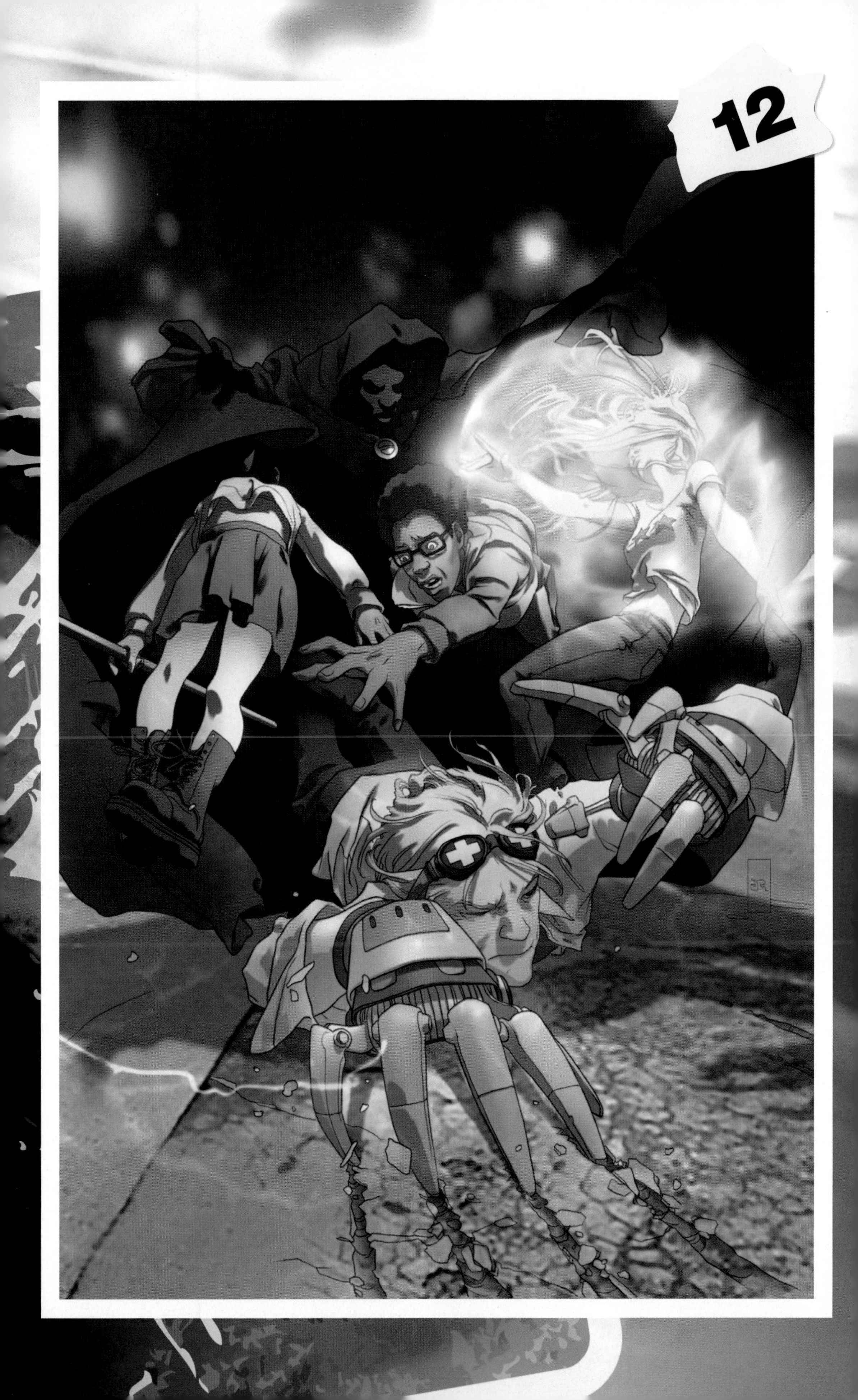
12

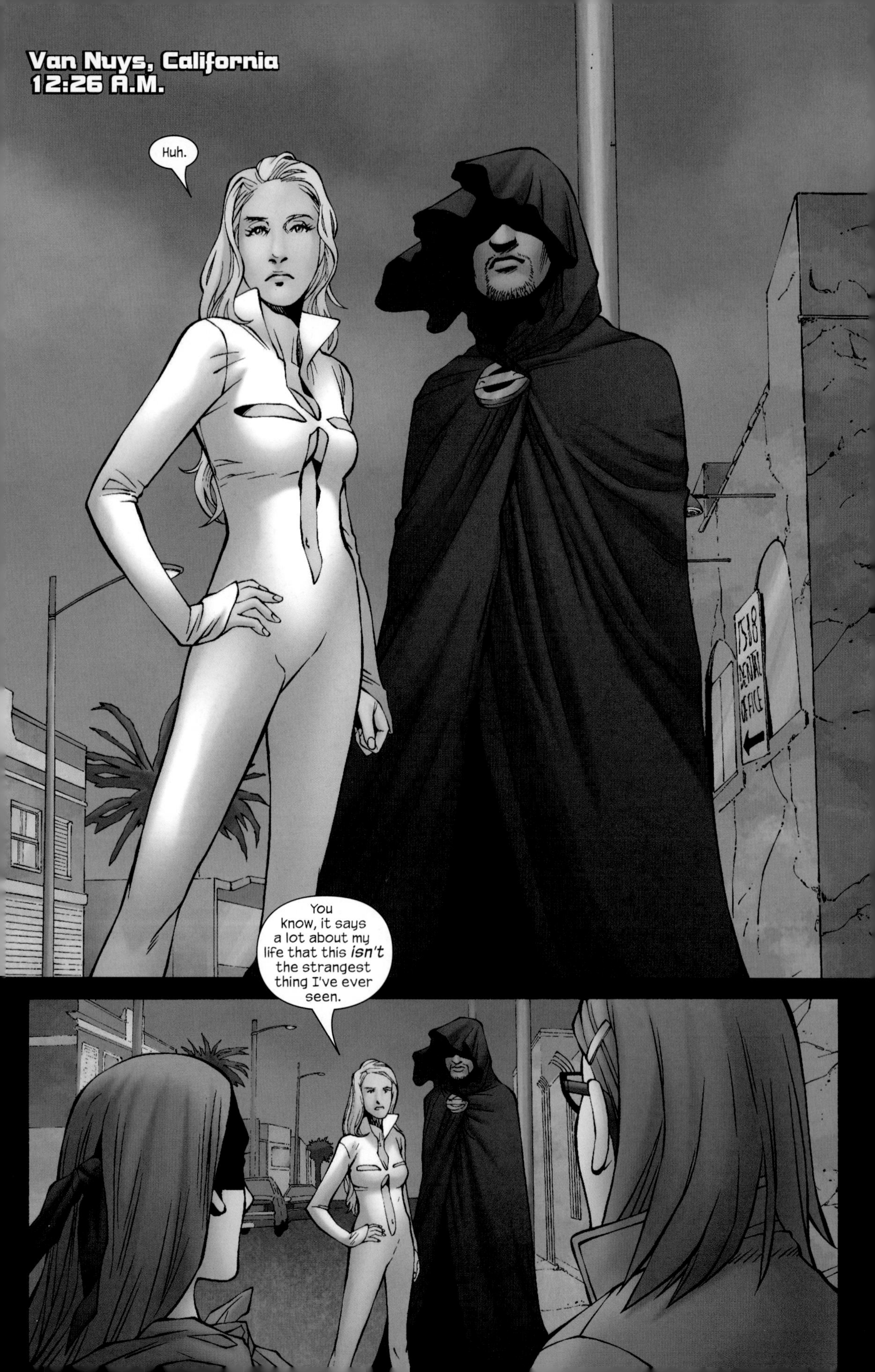
Van Nuys, California
12:26 A.M.
Huh.
You know, it says a lot about my life that this *isn't* the strangest thing I've ever seen.

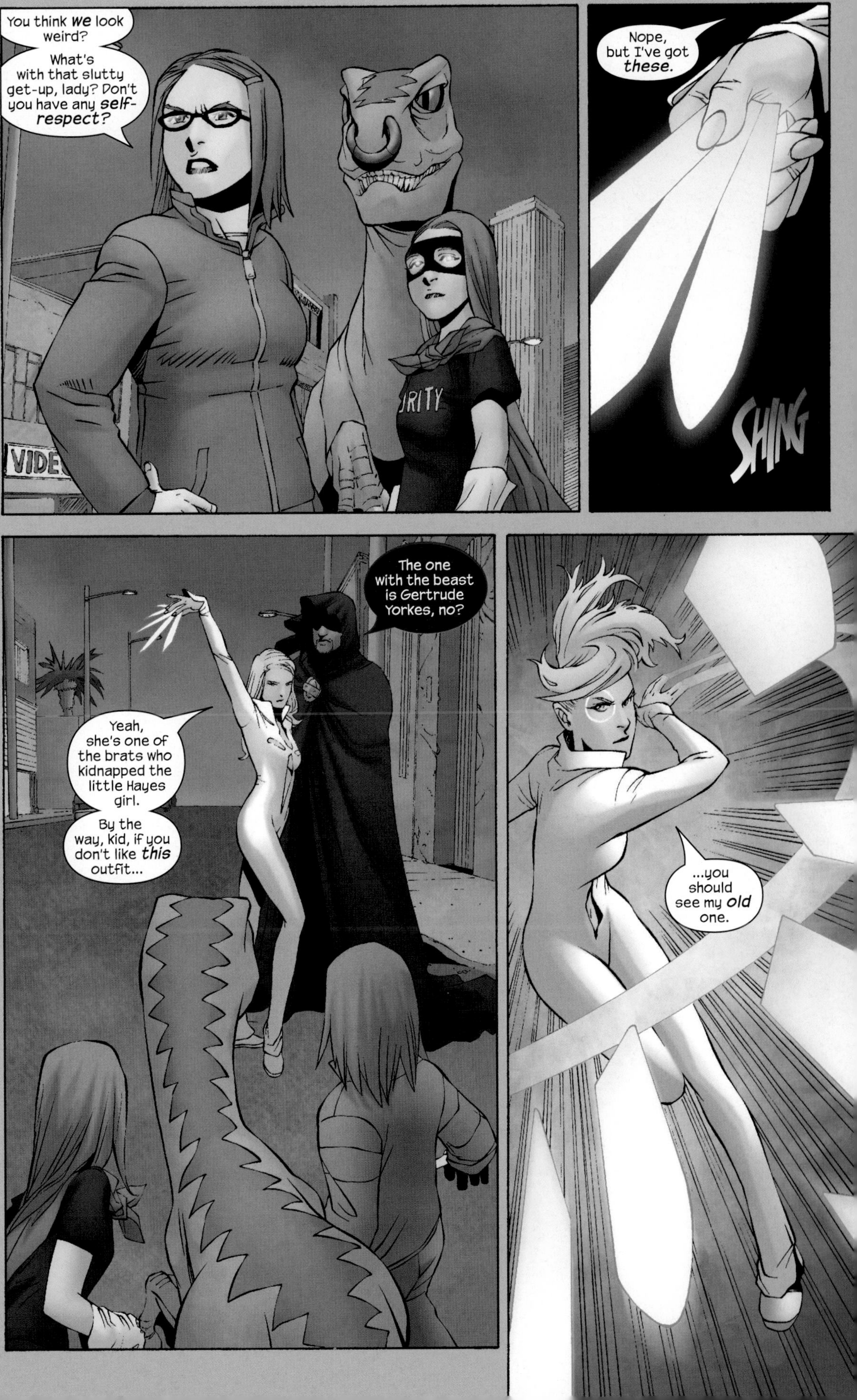

You think *we* look weird?
What's with that slutty get-up, lady? Don't you have any *self-respect*?
VIDE
RITY
Nope, but I've got *these*.
SHING
The one with the beast is Gertrude Yorkes, no?
Yeah, she's one of the brats who kidnapped the little Hayes girl.
By the way, kid, if you don't like *this* outfit...
...you should see my *old* one.

Old Lace, *now!*

RAAARR

Thanks for the cover, O.L.

Is... is she *okay?*

Yeah, just *hungry.*

Um, *problem.*

My powers, they don't have any effect on animals or--

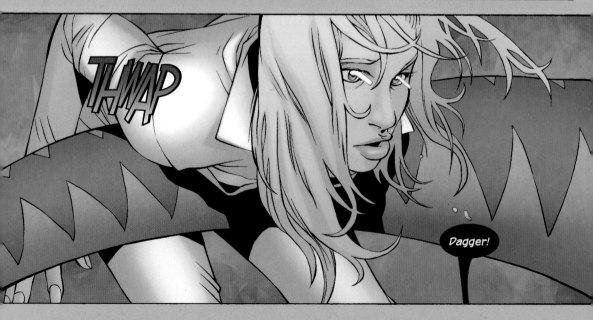

THWAP

Dagger!

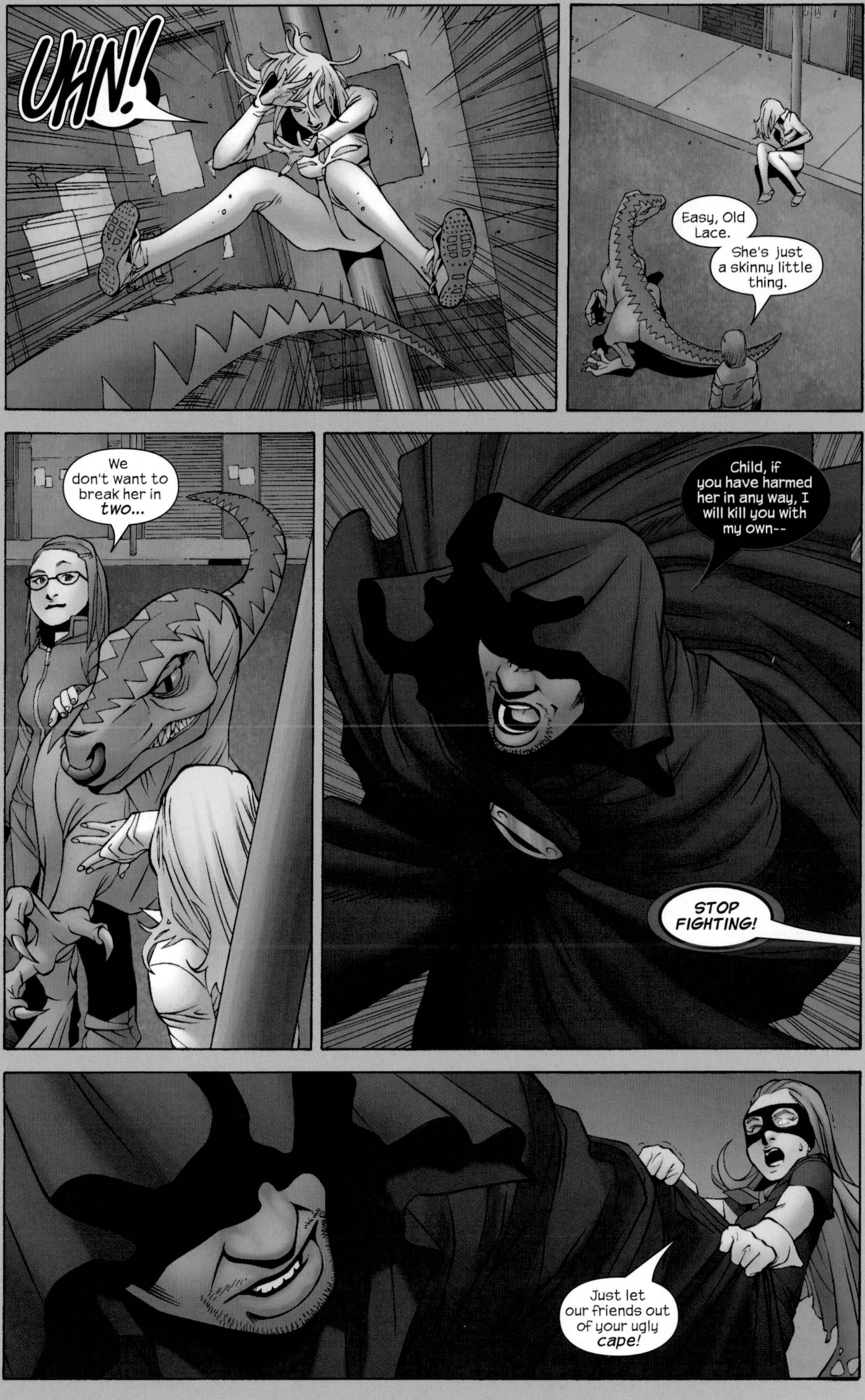
UHN!
Easy, Old Lace.
She's just a skinny little thing.
We don't want to break her in two...
Child, if you have harmed her in any way, I will kill you with my own--
STOP FIGHTING!
Just let our friends out of your ugly cape!

Come on, I don't wanna have to rip up your bed sheets!

This is not a "sheet", girl. It is a *cloak*, a gateway to another realm permanently bonded to my very being.

Not even a *god* has the strength to rend it from my--

UMPH!

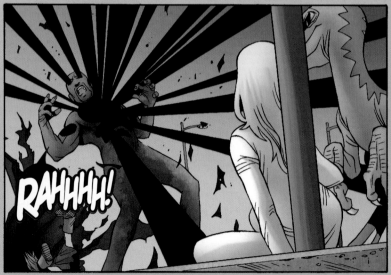

RAHHHH!

TY!

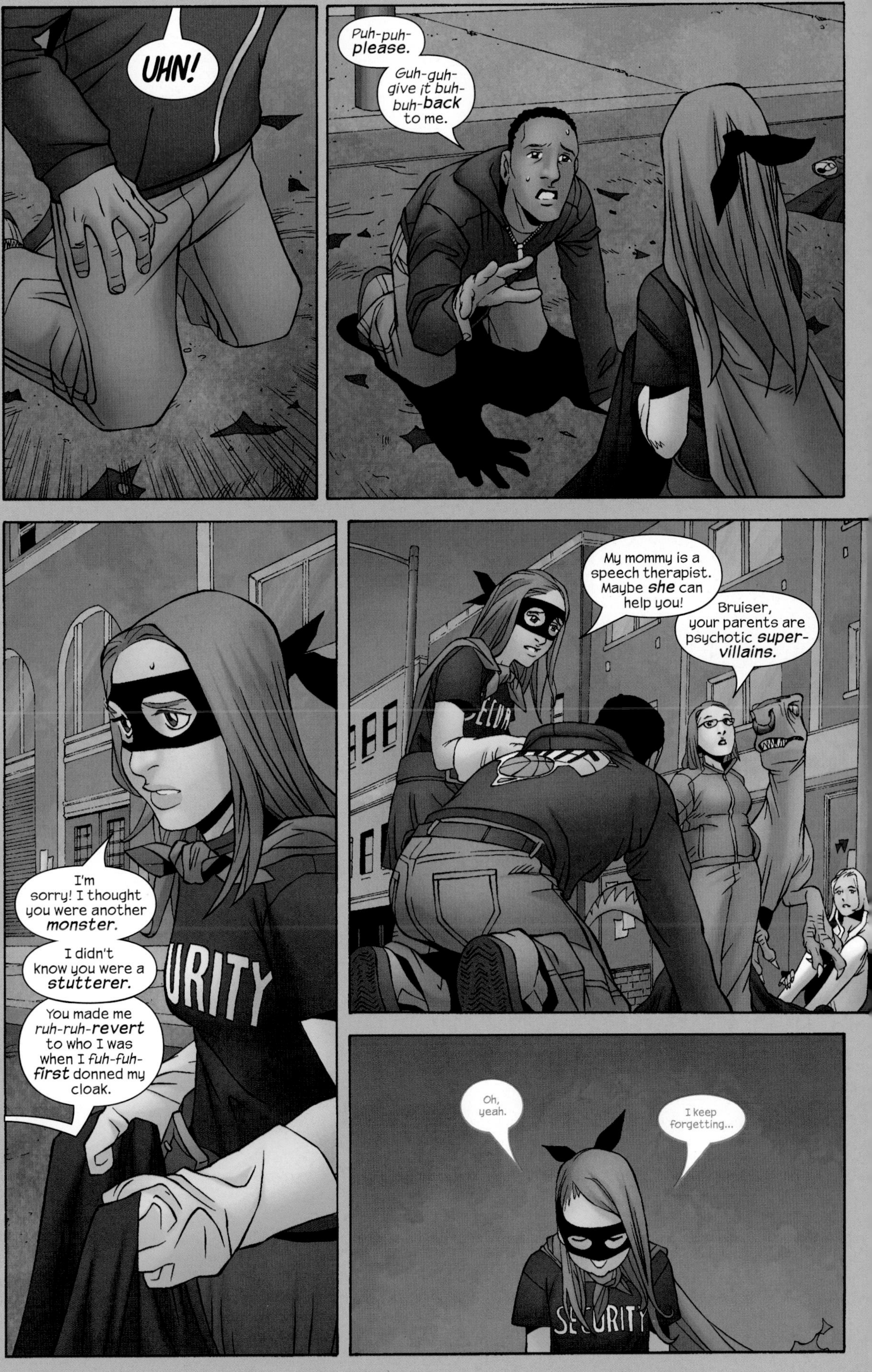
UHN!
Puh-puh-please.
Guh-guh-give it buh-buh-back to me.
I'm sorry! I thought you were another monster.
I didn't know you were a stutterer.
You made me ruh-ruh-revert to who I was when I fuh-fuh-first donned my cloak.
My mommy is a speech therapist. Maybe she can help you!
Bruiser, your parents are psychotic super-villains.
Oh, yeah.
I keep forgetting...

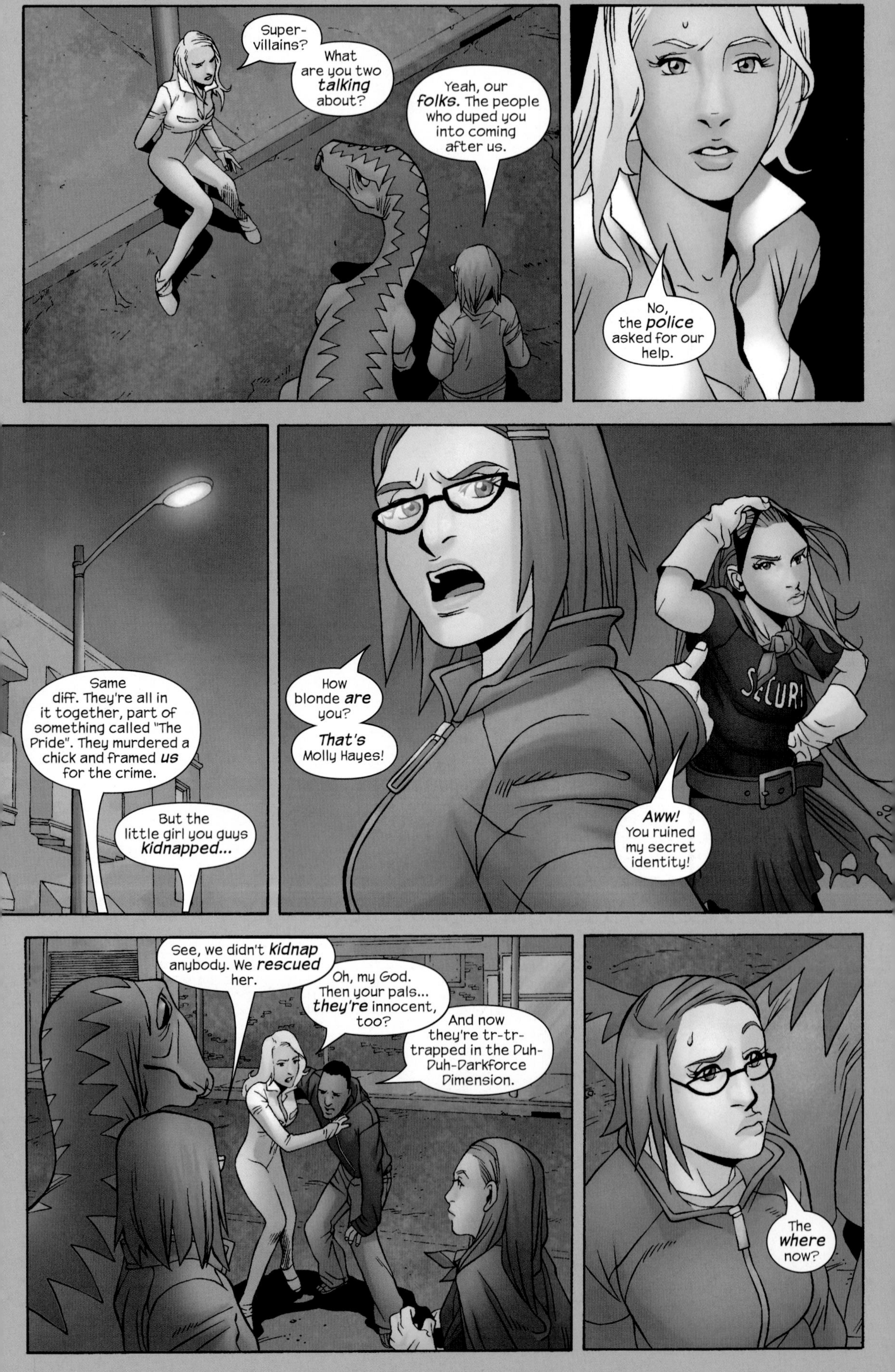
Super-villains?
What are you two talking about?
Yeah, our folks. The people who duped you into coming after us.
No, the police asked for our help.
Same diff. They're all in it together, part of something called "The Pride". They murdered a chick and framed us for the crime.
But the little girl you guys kidnapped...
How blonde are you?
That's Molly Hayes!
Aww! You ruined my secret identity!
See, we didn't kidnap anybody. We rescued her.
Oh, my God. Then your pals... they're innocent, too?
And now they're tr-tr-trapped in the Duh-Duh-Darkforce Dimension.
The where now?

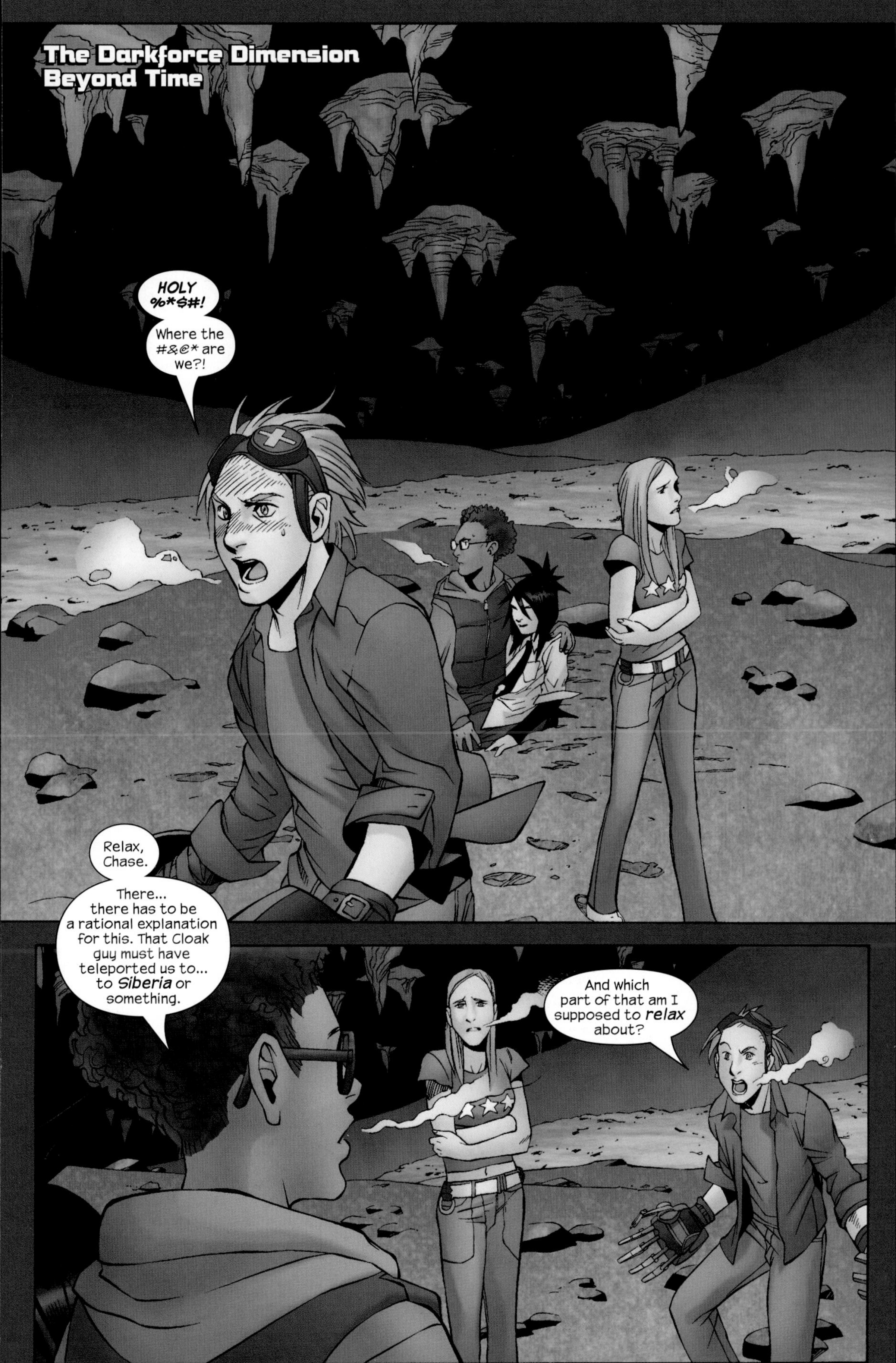
The Darkforce Dimension Beyond Time
HOLY %*$#!
Where the #&@* are we?!
Relax, Chase.
There... there has to be a rational explanation for this. That Cloak guy must have teleported us to... to *Siberia* or something.
And which part of that am I supposed to *relax* about?

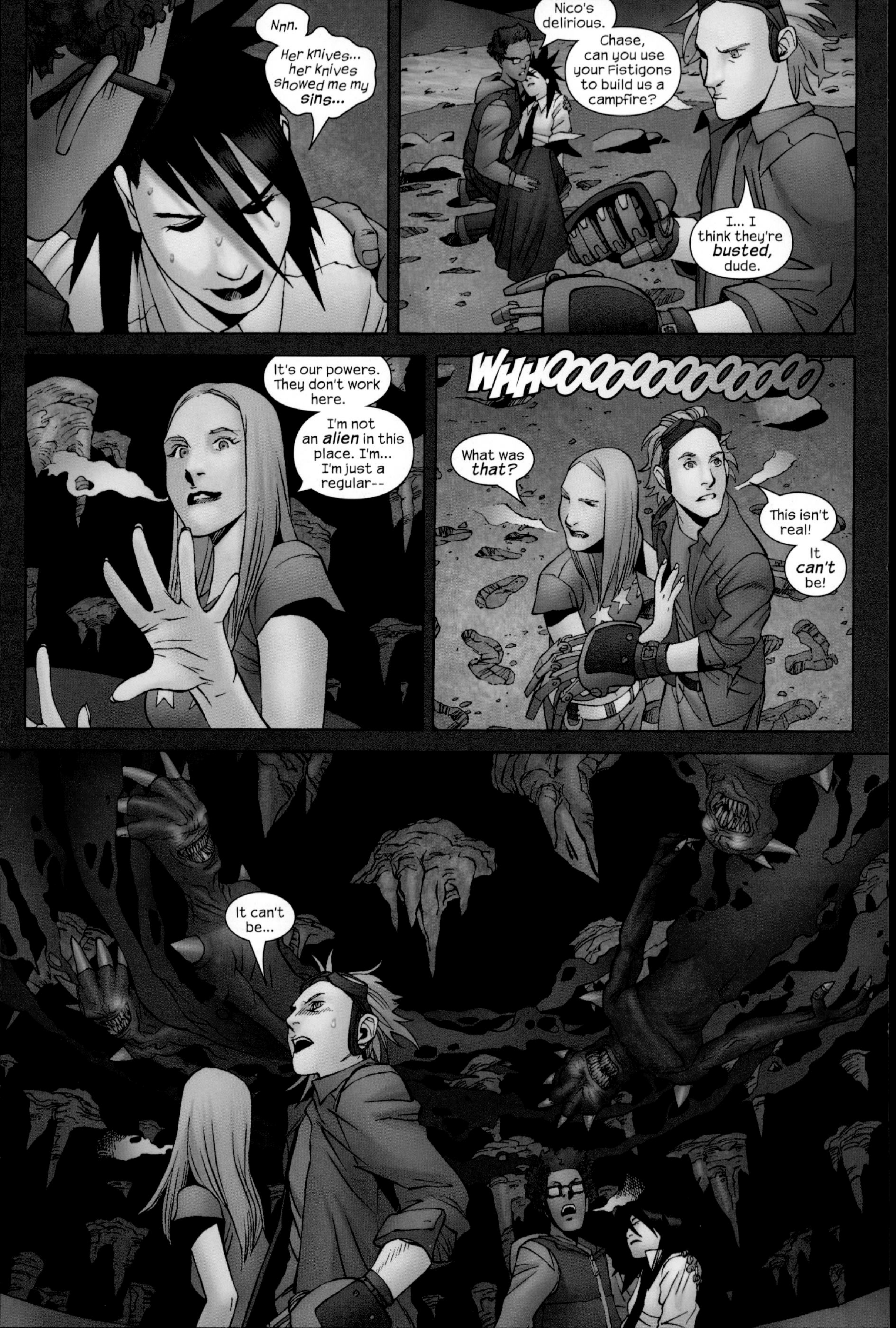
Nnn.
Her knives... her knives showed me my sins...
Nico's delirious.
Chase, can you use your Fistigons to build us a campfire?
I... I think they're busted, dude.
It's our powers. They don't work here.
I'm not an alien in this place. I'm... I'm just a regular--
WHHOOOOOOOOOOOOOO
What was that?
This isn't real!
It can't be!
It can't be...

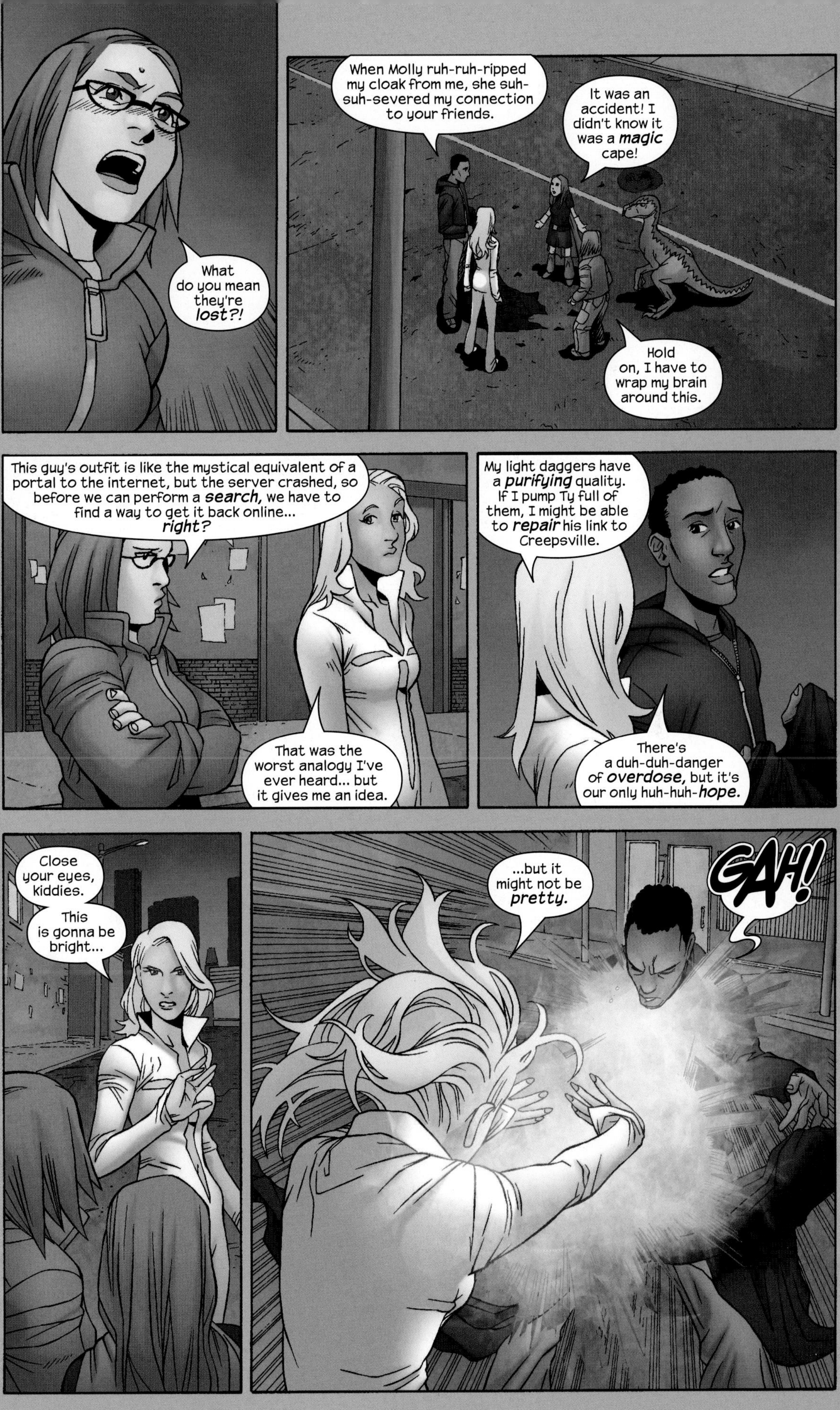
What do you mean they're *lost?!*
When Molly ruh-ruh-ripped my cloak from me, she suh-suh-severed my connection to your friends.
It was an accident! I didn't know it was a *magic* cape!
Hold on, I have to wrap my brain around this.
This guy's outfit is like the mystical equivalent of a portal to the internet, but the server crashed, so before we can perform a *search,* we have to find a way to get it back online... *right?*
That was the worst analogy I've ever heard... but it gives me an idea.
My light daggers have a *purifying* quality. If I pump Ty full of them, I might be able to *repair* his link to Creepsville.
There's a duh-duh-danger of *overdose,* but it's our only huh-huh-*hope.*
Close your eyes, kiddies.
This is gonna be bright...
...but it might not be *pretty.*
GAH!

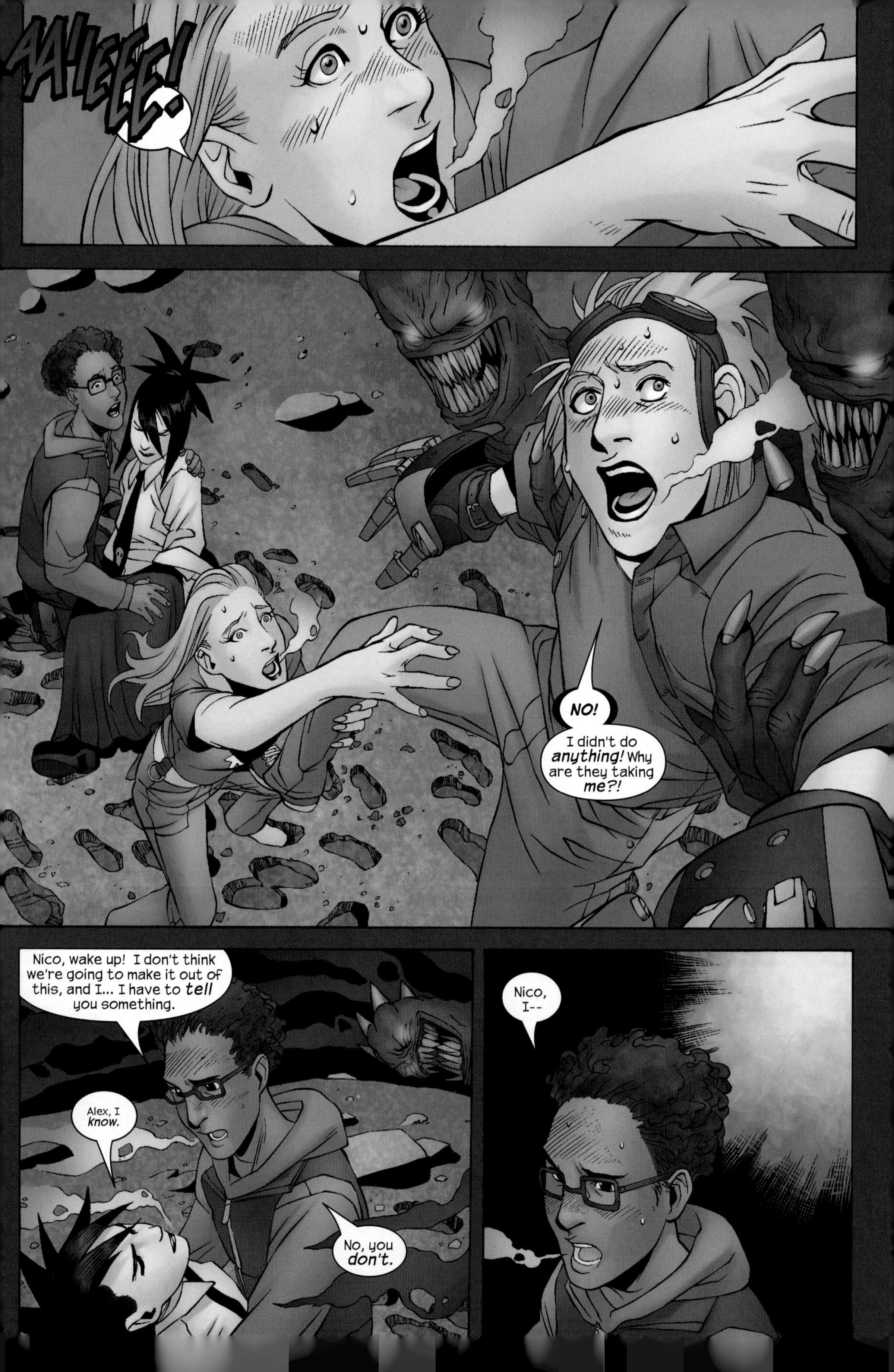
AAHEEEE!
NO!
I didn't do anything! Why are they taking me?!
Nico, wake up! I don't think we're going to make it out of this, and I... I have to tell you something.
Alex, I know.
No, you don't.
Nico, I--

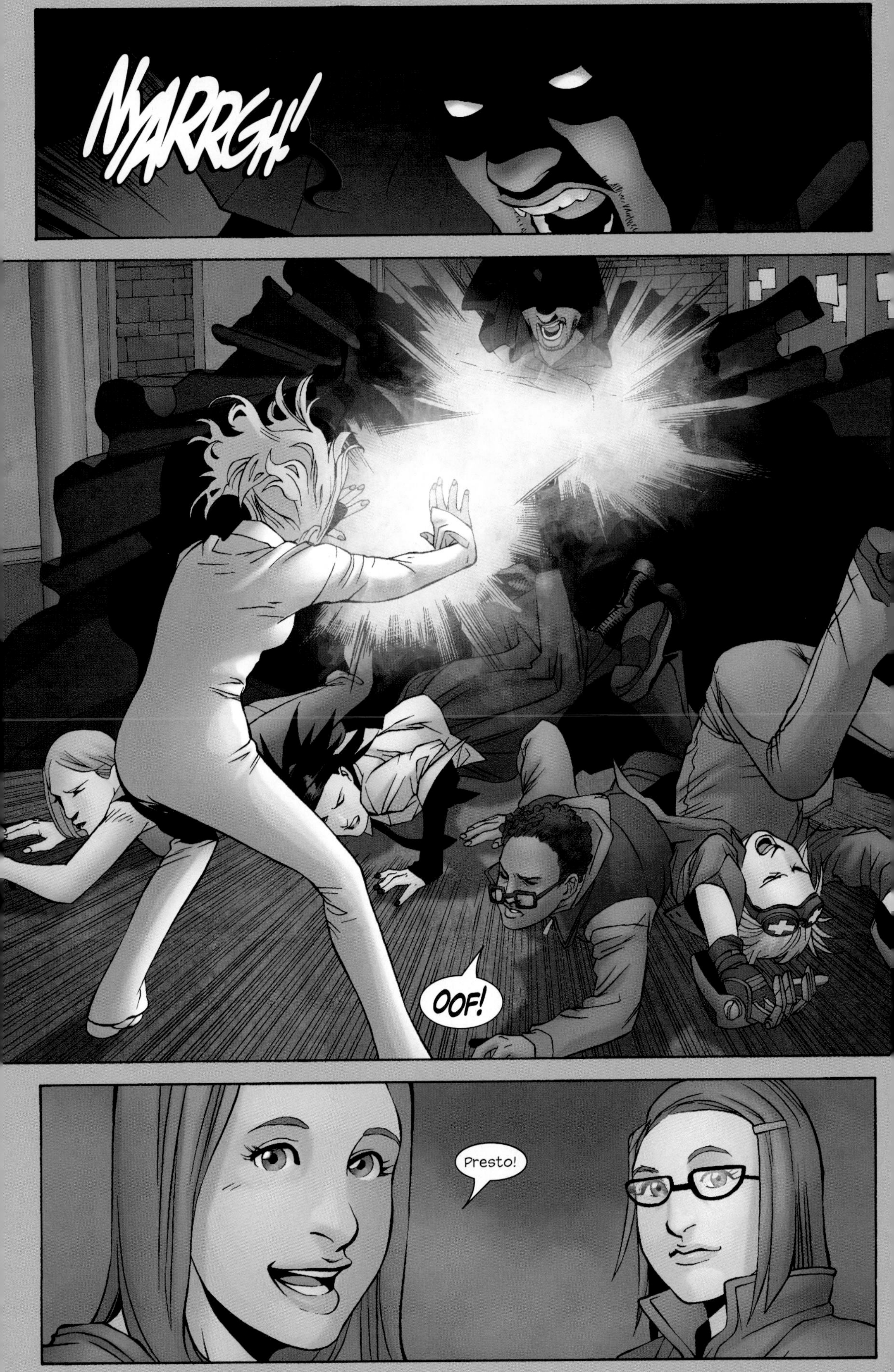
NYARRGH!
OOF!
Presto!

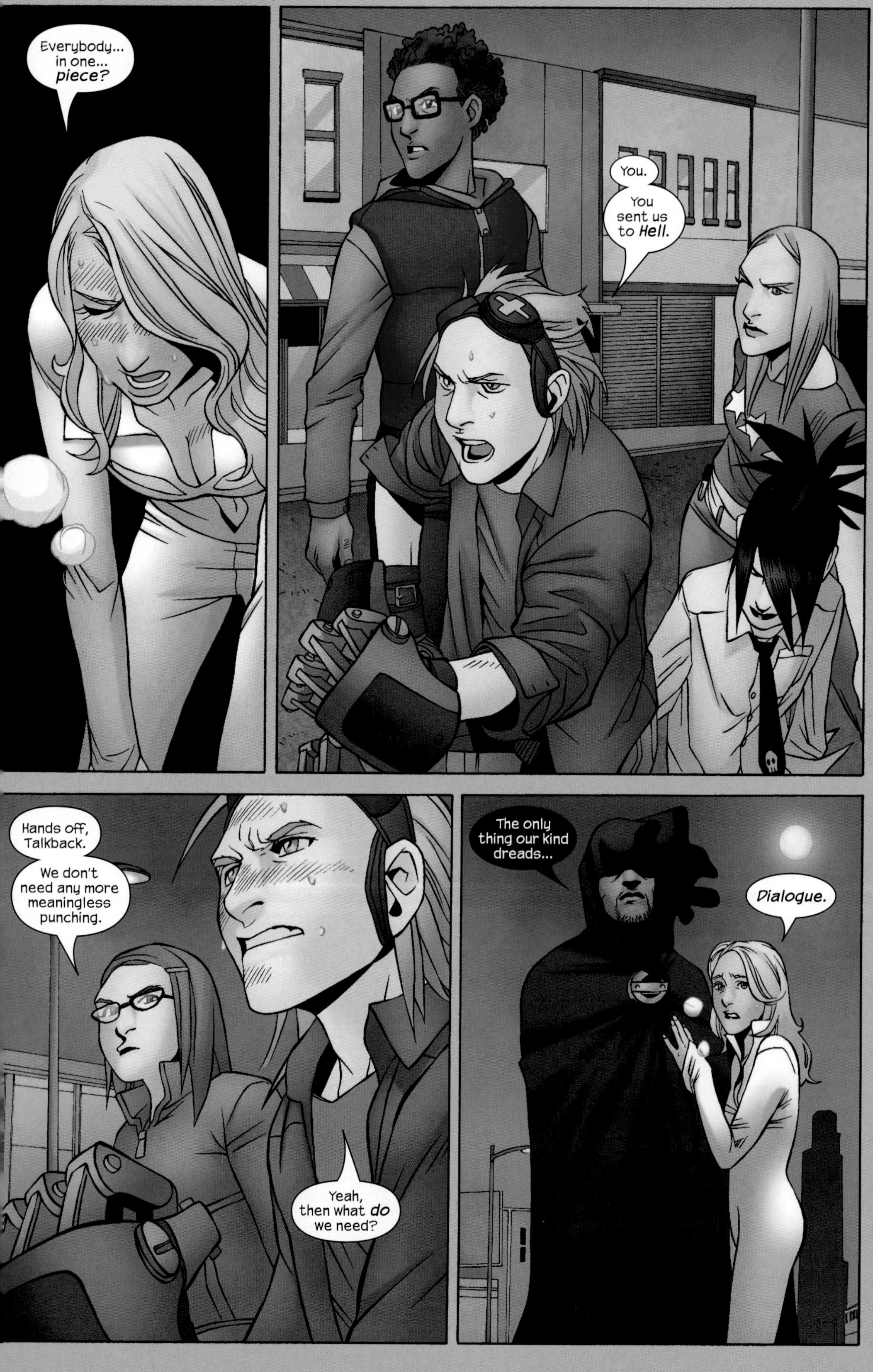

Everybody... in one... *piece?*
You.
You sent us to *Hell.*
Hands off, Talkback.
We don't need any more meaningless punching.
Yeah, then what *do* we need?
The only thing our kind dreads...
Dialogue.

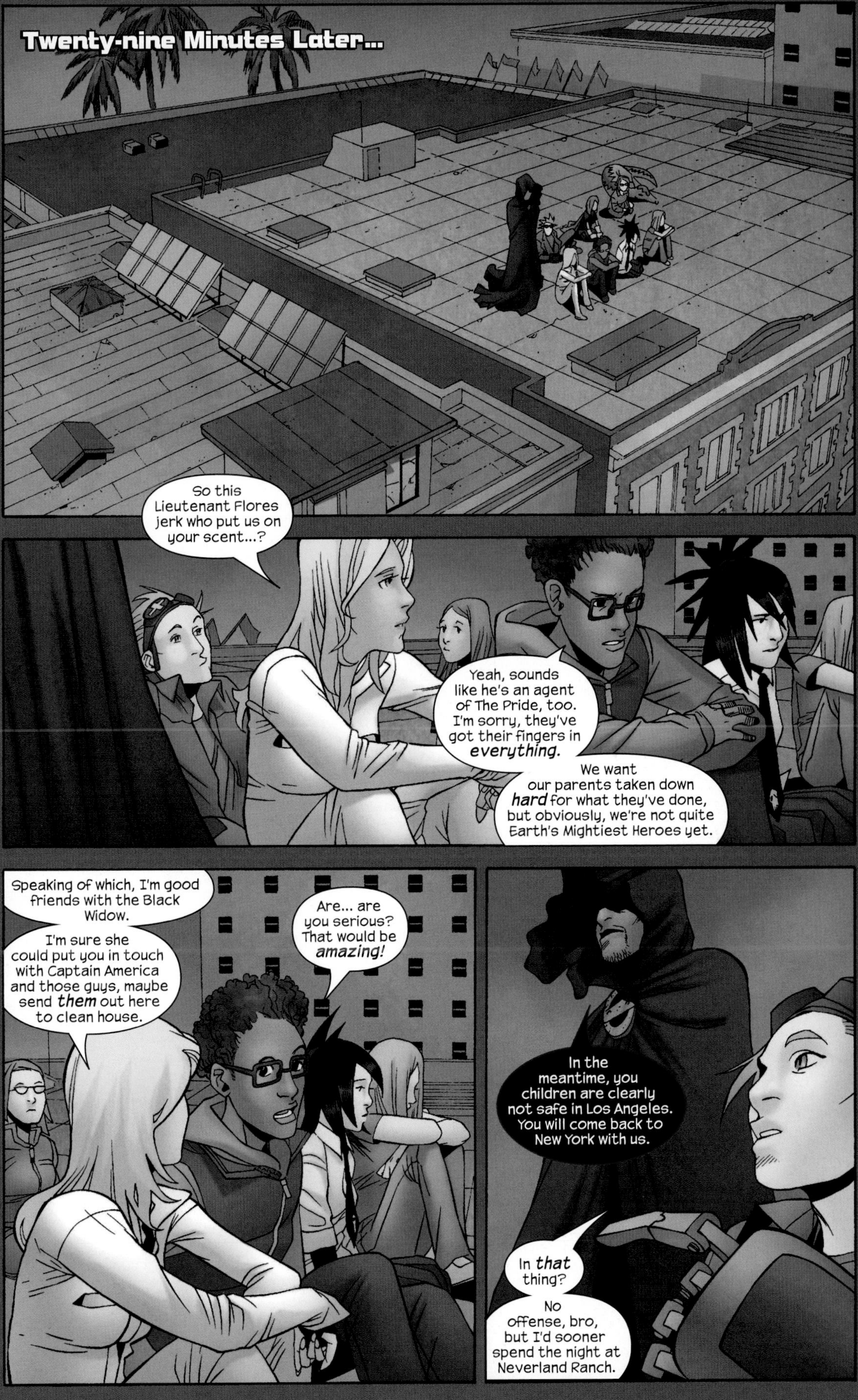
Twenty-nine Minutes Later...
So this Lieutenant Flores jerk who put us on your scent...?
Yeah, sounds like he's an agent of The Pride, too. I'm sorry, they've got their fingers in *everything.*
We want our parents taken down *hard* for what they've done, but obviously, we're not quite Earth's Mightiest Heroes yet.
Speaking of which, I'm good friends with the Black Widow.
I'm sure she could put you in touch with Captain America and those guys, maybe send *them* out here to clean house.
Are... are you serious? That would be *amazing!*
In the meantime, you children are clearly not safe in Los Angeles. You will come back to New York with us.
In *that* thing?
No offense, bro, but I'd sooner spend the night at Neverland Ranch.

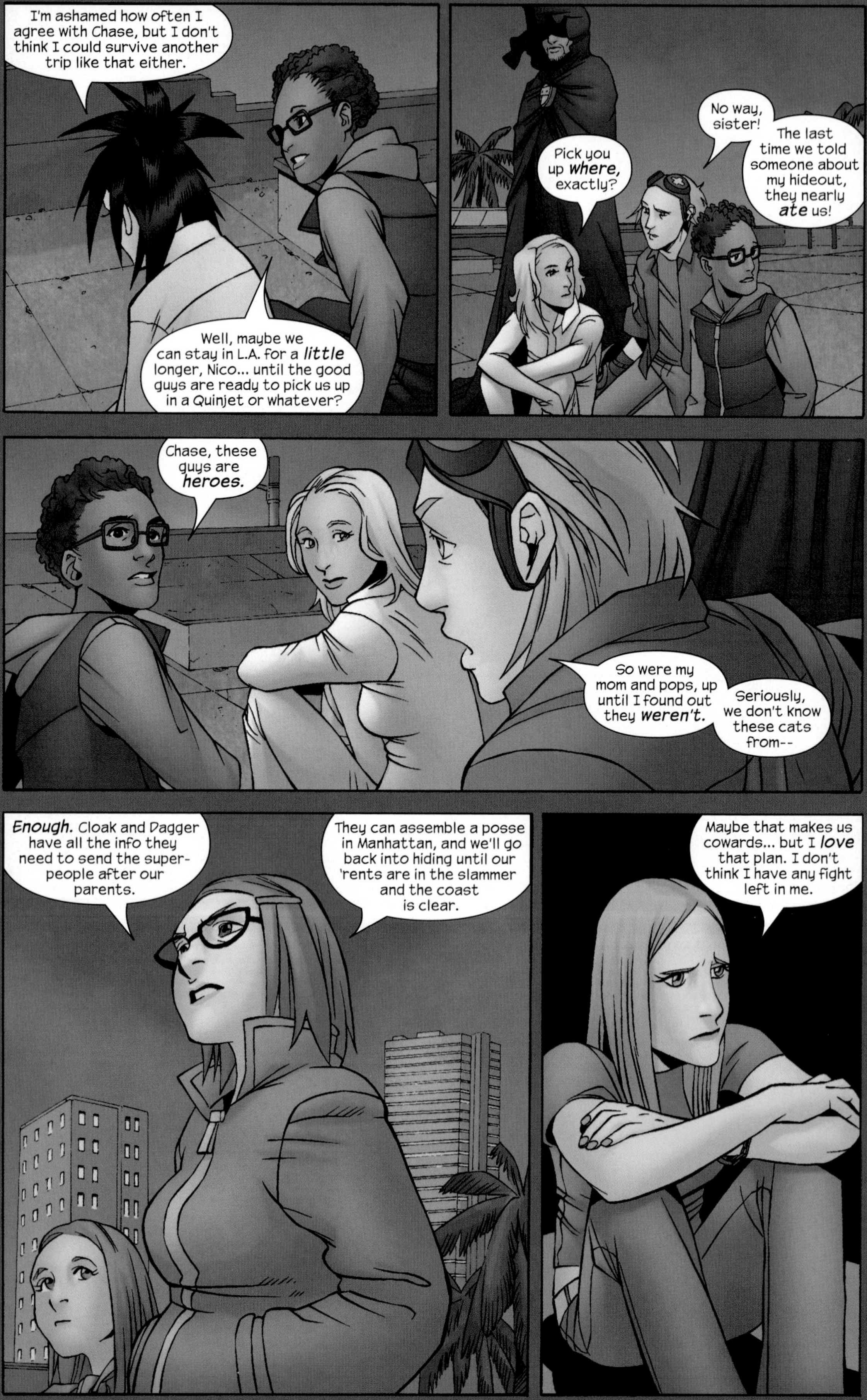
I'm ashamed how often I agree with Chase, but I don't think I could survive another trip like that either.
Well, maybe we can stay in L.A. for a *little* longer, Nico... until the good guys are ready to pick us up in a Quinjet or whatever?
Pick you up *where,* exactly?
No way, sister!
The last time we told someone about my hideout, they nearly *ate* us!
Chase, these guys are *heroes.*
So were my mom and pops, up until I found out they *weren't.*
Seriously, we don't know these cats from--
Enough. Cloak and Dagger have all the info they need to send the super-people after our parents.
They can assemble a posse in Manhattan, and we'll go back into hiding until our 'rents are in the slammer and the coast is clear.
Maybe that makes us cowards... but I *love* that plan. I don't think I have any fight left in me.

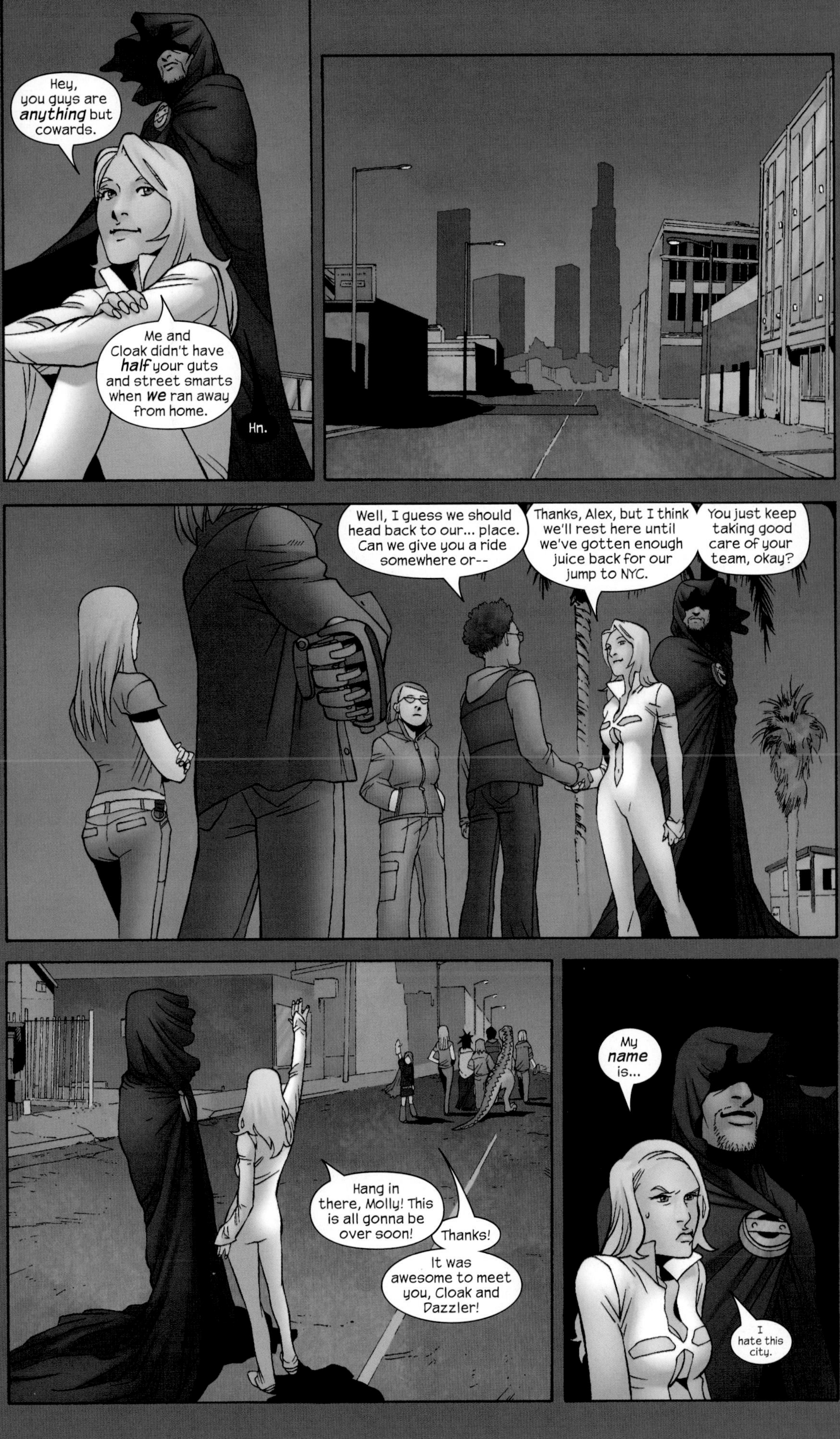
Hey, you guys are *anything* but cowards.
Me and Cloak didn't have *half* your guts and street smarts when *we* ran away from home.
Hn.
Well, I guess we should head back to our... place. Can we give you a ride somewhere or--
Thanks, Alex, but I think we'll rest here until we've gotten enough juice back for our jump to NYC.
You just keep taking good care of your team, okay?
Hang in there, Molly! This is all gonna be over soon!
Thanks!
It was awesome to meet you, Cloak and Dazzler!
My *name* is...
I hate this city.

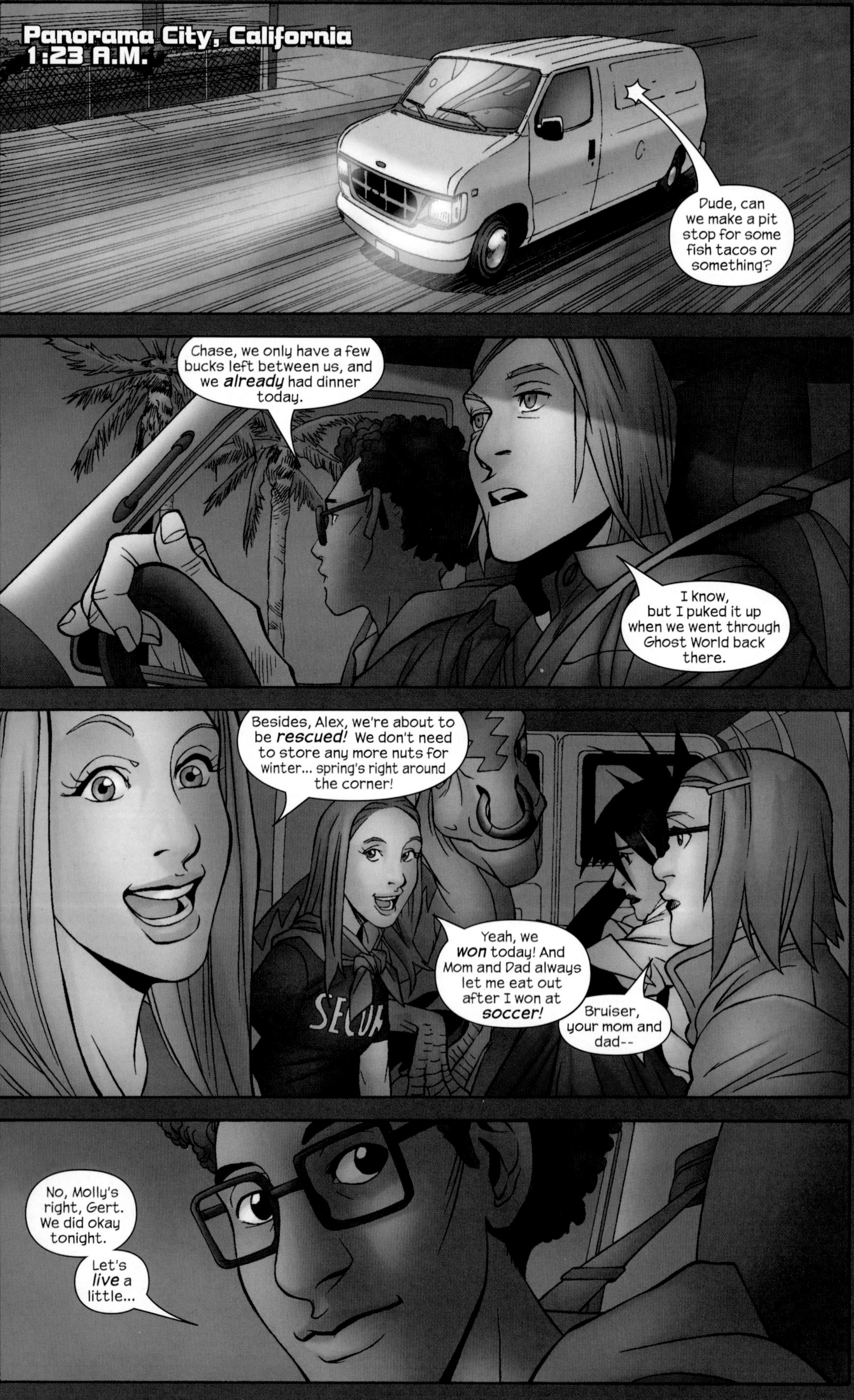

Panorama City, California
1:23 A.M.
Dude, can we make a pit stop for some fish tacos or something?
Chase, we only have a few bucks left between us, and we *already* had dinner today.
I know, but I puked it up when we went through Ghost World back there.
Besides, Alex, we're about to be *rescued!* We don't need to store any more nuts for winter... spring's right around the corner!
Yeah, we *won* today! And Mom and Dad always let me eat out after I won at *soccer!*
Bruiser, your mom and dad--
No, Molly's right, Gert. We did okay tonight.
Let's *live* a little...

UCLA Medical Center
1:34 A.M.

BZZBZZBZZ

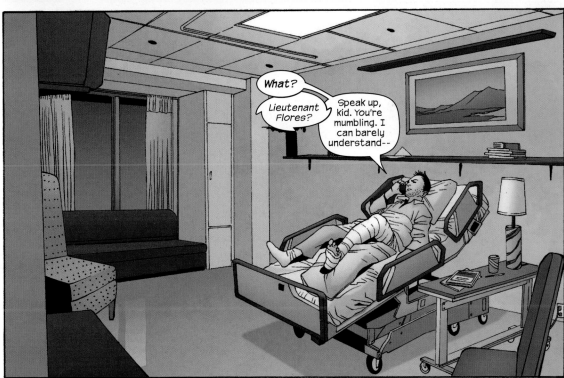

What?

Lieutenant Flores?

Speak up, kid. You're mumbling. I can barely understand--

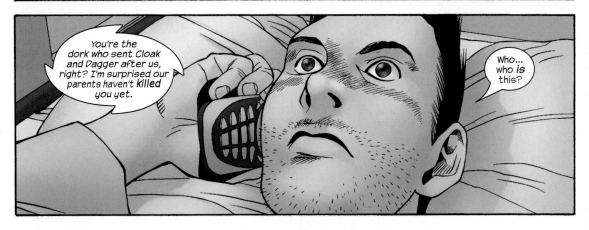

You're the dork who sent Cloak and Dagger after us, right? I'm surprised our parents haven't *killed* you yet.

Who... who *is* this?

Right now, I'm the only friend you've got.

You're one of their *children*, aren't you?

The Pride told me they might have a *mole* in your gang, but I didn't believe--

Quiet. I don't have long. I'm at a payphone outside some taco shack, and the others think I'm in the bathroom.

What do you--

Listen, Cloak and Dagger are on a rooftop in Van Nuys, but I'm not sure how much longer they'll be there.

Lieutenant, they *know* about The Pride.

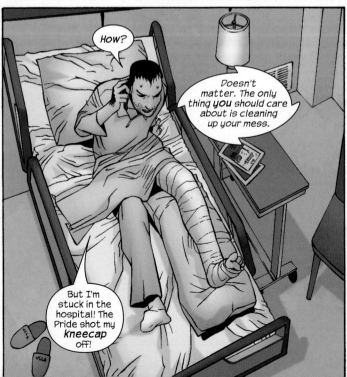

How?

Doesn't matter. The only thing *you* should care about is cleaning up your mess.

But I'm stuck in the hospital! The Pride shot my *kneecap* off!

Do *something*... or the next bullet will probably be to your *brain*.

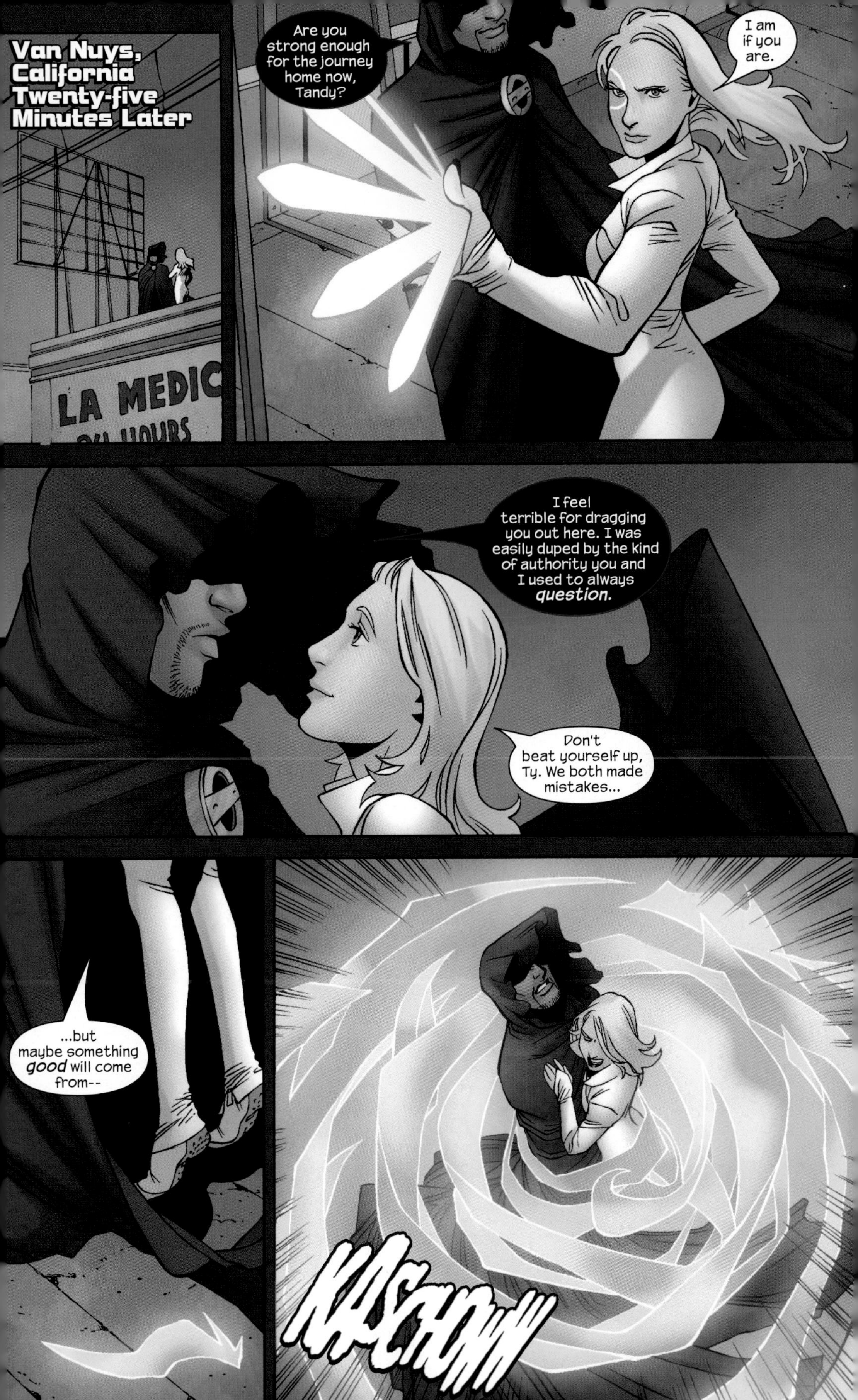
Van Nuys, California Twenty-five Minutes Later
LA MEDIC
Are you strong enough for the journey home now, Tandy?
I am if you are.
I feel terrible for dragging you out here. I was easily duped by the kind of authority you and I used to always question.
Don't beat yourself up, Ty. We both made mistakes...
...but maybe something good will come from--
KASCHOWW

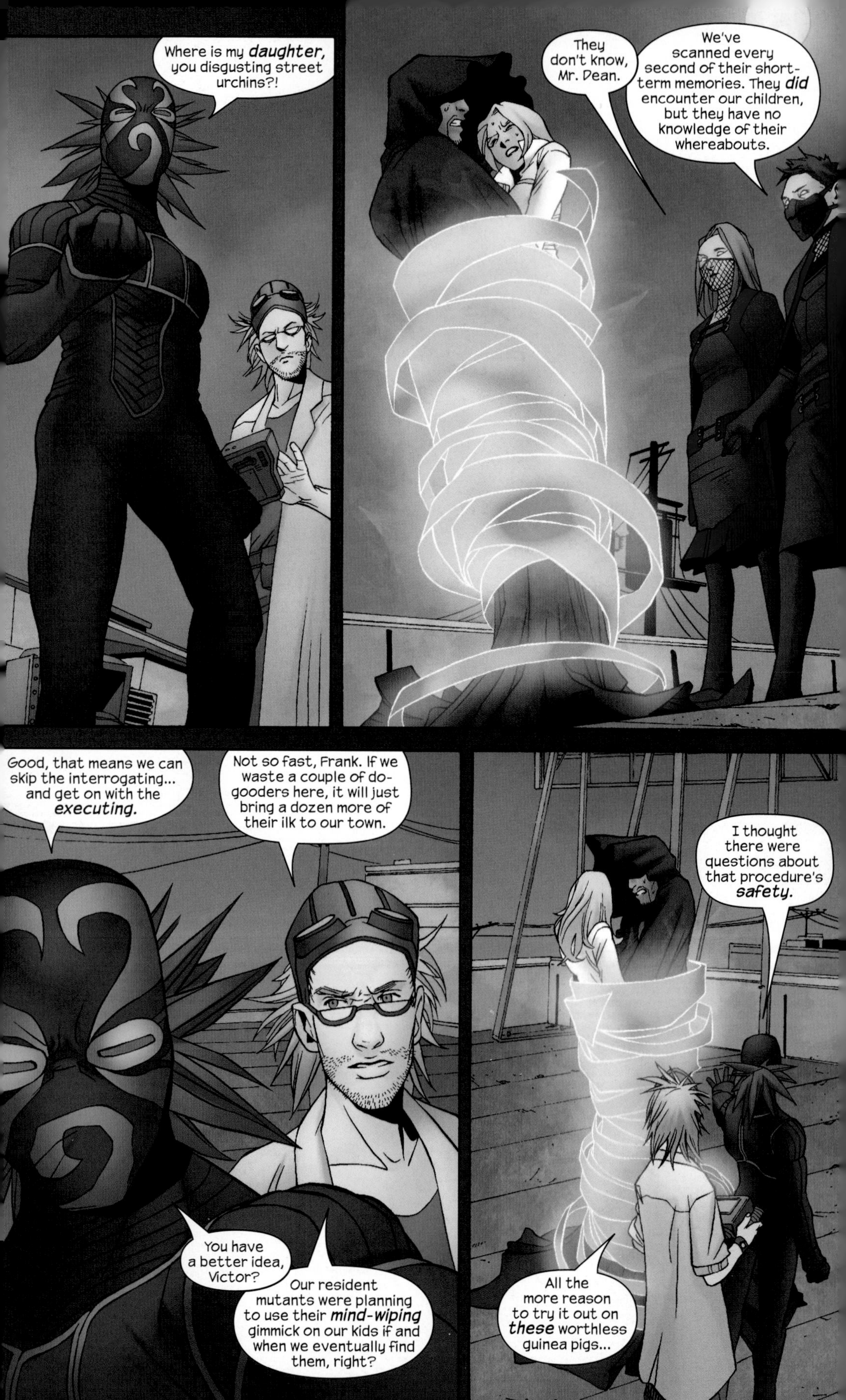
Where is my *daughter,* you disgusting street urchins?!
They don't know, Mr. Dean.
We've scanned every second of their short-term memories. They *did* encounter our children, but they have no knowledge of their whereabouts.
Good, that means we can skip the interrogating... and get on with the *executing.*
Not so fast, Frank. If we waste a couple of do-gooders here, it will just bring a dozen more of their ilk to our town.
You have a better idea, Victor?
Our resident mutants were planning to use their *mind-wiping* gimmick on our kids if and when we eventually find them, right?
I thought there were questions about that procedure's *safety.*
All the more reason to try it out on *these* worthless guinea pigs...

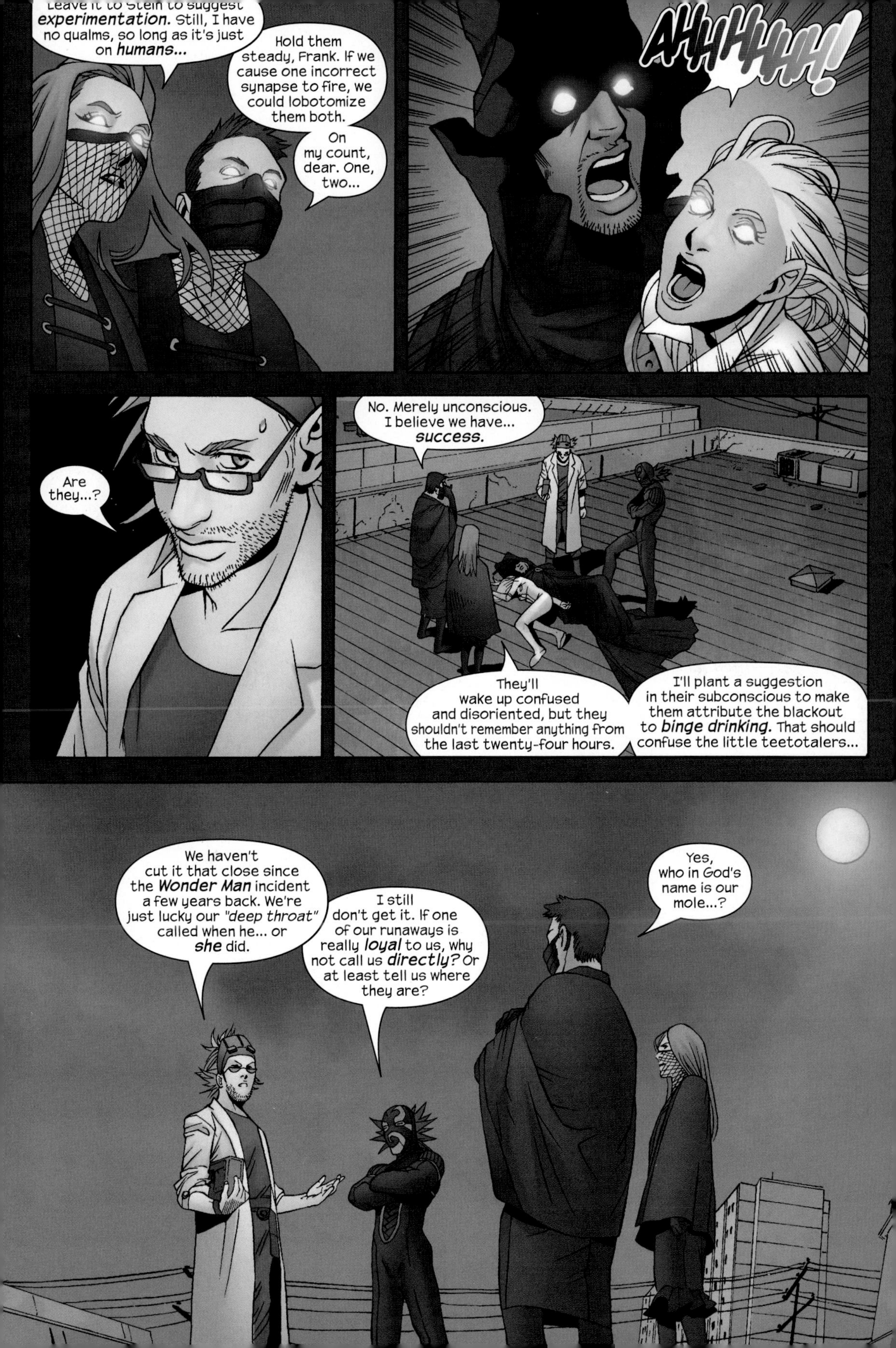
Leave it to Stein to suggest experimentation. Still, I have no qualms, so long as it's just on humans...
Hold them steady, Frank. If we cause one incorrect synapse to fire, we could lobotomize them both.
On my count, dear. One, two...
AHHHHHH!
Are they...?
No. Merely unconscious. I believe we have... success.
They'll wake up confused and disoriented, but they shouldn't remember anything from the last twenty-four hours.
I'll plant a suggestion in their subconscious to make them attribute the blackout to binge drinking. That should confuse the little teetotalers...
We haven't cut it that close since the Wonder Man incident a few years back. We're just lucky our "deep throat" called when he... or she did.
I still don't get it. If one of our runaways is really loyal to us, why not call us directly? Or at least tell us where they are?
Yes, who in God's name is our mole...?

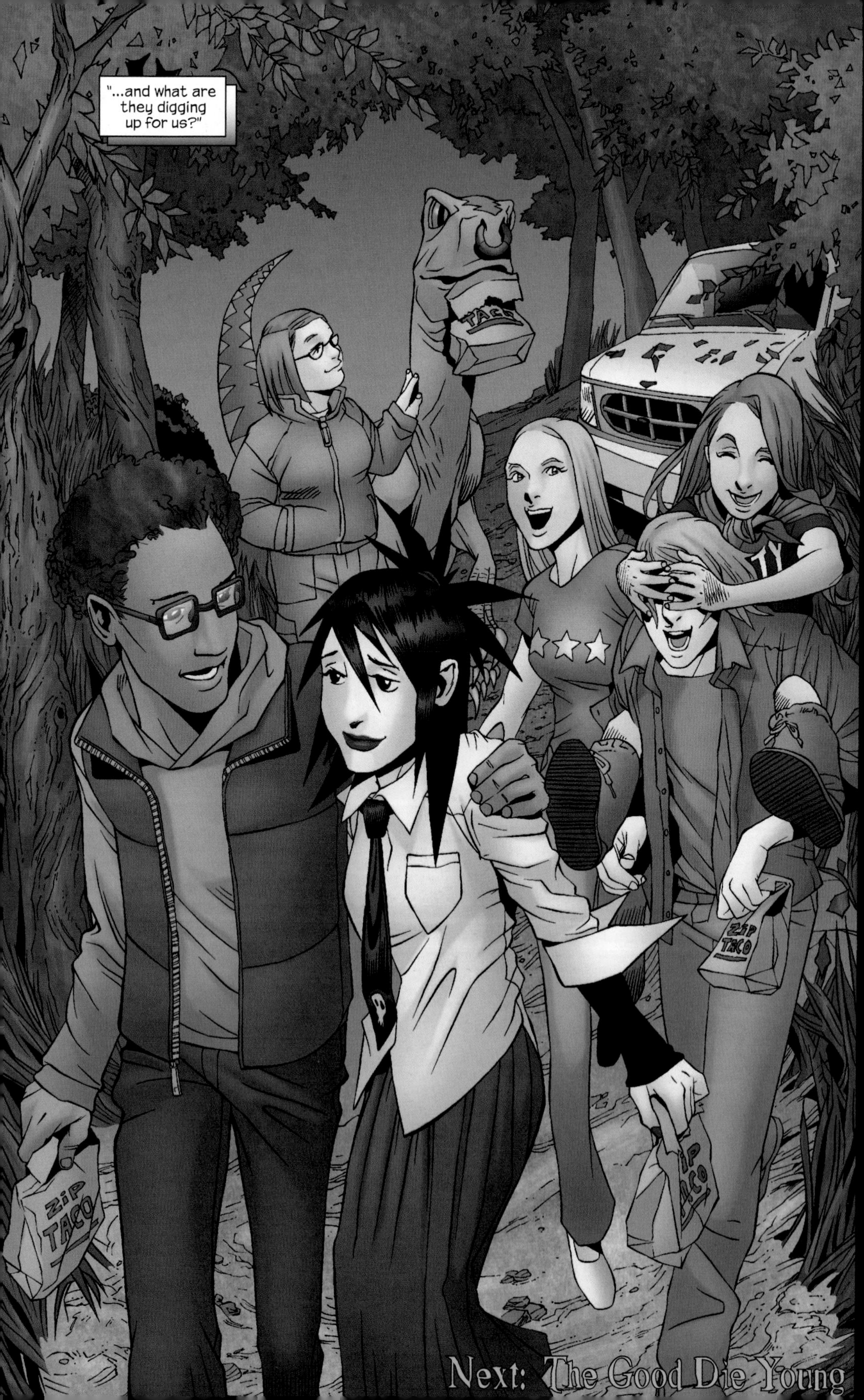
"...and what are they digging up for us?"
TACO
ZIP TACO
ZIP TACO
ZIP TACO
Next: The Good Die Young